Standing Our Ground

Ohio University Press

Series in Race, Ethnicity, and Gender in Appalachia
Series Editor:
Marie Tedesco

Memphis Tennessee Garrison:
The Remarkable Story of a Black Appalachian Woman,
edited by Ancella R. Bickley and Lynda Ann Ewen

The Tangled Roots of Feminism, Environmentalism,
and Appalachian Literature,
by Elizabeth S. D. Engelhardt

Red, White, Black, and Blue:
A Dual Memoir of Race and Class in Appalachia,
by William R. Drennen Jr. and Kojo (William T.) Jones Jr.,
edited by Dolores M. Johnson

Beyond Hill and Hollow:
Original Readings in Appalachian Women's Studies,
edited by Elizabeth S. D. Engelhardt

Loving Mountains, Loving Men,
by Jeff Mann

Power in the Blood: A Family Narrative,
by Linda Tate

Out of the Mountains: Appalachian Stories,
by Meredith Sue Willis

Negotiating a Perilous Empowerment:
Appalachian Women's Literacies,
by Erica Abrams Locklear

Standing Our Ground: Women, Environmental Justice,
and the Fight to End Mountaintop Removal,
by Joyce M. Barry

STANDING OUR GROUND

Women, Environmental Justice, and the
Fight to End Mountaintop Removal

Joyce M. Barry

OHIO UNIVERSITY PRESS ◆ ATHENS

Ohio University Press, Athens, Ohio 45701
ohioswallow.com
© 2012 by Ohio University Press

To obtain permission to quote, reprint, or otherwise reproduce or distribute material
from Ohio University Press publications, please contact our rights and permissions
department at (740) 593-1154 or (740) 593-4536 (fax).

Printed in the United States of America
Ohio University Press books are printed on acid-free paper ∞ ™

21 20 19 18 17 16 15 14 13 12   5 4 3 2 1

Library of Congress Cataloging-in-Publication Data

Barry, Joyce M.
    Standing our ground : women, environmental justice, and the fight to
end mountaintop removal / Joyce M. Barry.
        p. cm. — (Ohio University Press series in race, ethnicity, and
gender in Appalachia)
    Includes bibliographical references and index.
    ISBN 978-0-8214-1997-7 (hc : alk. paper) —
    ISBN 978-0-8214-4410-8 (electronic)
    1. Environmental justice—Appalachian Region. 2. Women—Political
activity—Appalachian Region. 3. Mountaintop removal mining—
Social aspects—Appalachian Region. 4. Landscape protection—
Appalachian Region—Citizen participation. 5. Coal mines and
mining—Environmental aspects—Appalachian Region. 6. Community
activists—Appalachian Region. I. Title.
GE235.A13B37 2012
622'.334—dc23
                                                2012027267

For Julia "Judy" Bonds

You have stolen our land, and used despicable stereotypes of mountain people to justify yourselves to national media. You consigned hundreds of thousands of men and boys to horrible working conditions with great loss of life and limb. You took away freedom and dignity and trampled on civil liberties. You brought violence to bear against people who stood up for their rights. You evicted the widow and orphans from their homes. You polluted our rivers first, then our groundwater. You polluted and corrupted and cheapened the political process in this state, and made a mockery of government by the people. You abandoned our communities without sewage and water systems and left our school systems in poverty. You shifted your tax burden onto the people of this state. You condemned miners to the living death of black lung while denying them just compensation. You destroyed our roads with overloaded coal trucks and bragged publicly about breaking the law. You condemned those counties most dependent on coal to the greatest and most intractable poverty in this state. You filled our rivers with silt and increased the dangers of flooding. You tore families apart. You destroyed the habitat of our native animals. You deny workers the right to organize. You discourage the development of alternative energy sources. You lay off WV deep miners to employ out-of-state strip miners. 27 years ago today, you killed 125 men, women and children on Buffalo Creek and dared to blame it on God. You are flattening our mountains and filling in our hollows, and this is the last evil you will do.

—Denise Giardina, Coalfield Justice Rally, February 1999

CONTENTS

ACKNOWLEDGMENTS

I WISH TO ACKNOWLEDGE MANY PEOPLE FOR THEIR
interest and assistance in the production of this book. Thanks for the support of everyone at Ohio University Press, particularly Gillian Berchowitz. I also want to thank Lynda Ann Ewen, whom I met at the annual Appalachian Studies Conference in 2009, and who expressed interest in this topic. Of course, I am deeply appreciative of those working to end mountaintop removal coal mining (MTR) in Appalachia, and especially grateful to all of the activists who shared their time and experiences with me when requested. Over the years so many have inspired, angered, and motivated me with their life stories and passion to secure justice in the Appalachian coalfields. In particular I wish to thank Vivian Stockman, Ohio Valley Environmental Coalition Project Coordinator, my first contact in the coalfields, who graciously put me in touch with many women fighting Big Coal in West Virginia. Thanks also to Freda Williams, who first made me aware of what life in the coalfields is like in this era of MTR; and to Maria Gunnoe, Sarah Haltom, Lorelei Scarbro, Pauline Canterbury, Mary Miller, and Patty Sebok.

I am immeasurably grateful to Julia "Judy" Bonds, who died of cancer on January 3, 2011, and to whom this book is dedicated. Many people consider Judy to be the godmother of the anti-MTR movement, an indefatigable woman who made the fight against MTR the local, national, and international environmental justice issue it is today. Judy, who was very generous with her time and knowledge, impressed me with the great sense of urgency she consistently demonstrated while fighting Big Coal in Appalachia. I enjoyed our conversations over the years, and this book could not have been written without her assistance. To me, Judy was one of those people you meet in life who change you just by knowing them. While her loss is deeply felt by many working to end MTR, her life's work will continue to inspire and challenge all of us.

I would like to thank my supportive colleagues at Hamilton College: Vivyan Adair, Vige Barrie, Donald Carter, Katheryn Doran, Peter Cannavo,

Amy Gowans, Barbara Gold, Margaret Gentry, Jenny Irons, Chaise LaDousa, Heather Merrill, Onno Oerlemans, Bill Pfitch, Carl Rubino, Katherine Terrell, Julio Videras, Robin Vanderwall, and Steve Yao. I also want to thank my amazing students at Hamilton College, who consistently challenge me with their passion for learning and intellectual curiosity. Thanks also to everyone at the Hamilton College Library (particularly the interlibrary loan department) for your help with this research. I was fortunate to receive a National Endowment of the Humanities summer grant in 2006 entitled "Regional Studies and the Liberal Arts: An Appalachian Exemplar," and I would like to thank the facilitators of this program at Ferrum College, Ferrum, Virginia, for their support of this project. In particular I wish to thank Peter Crow, Tina Hanlon, Susan Mead, George Loveland, Daniel Woods, and my fellow participant Gloria Goodwin Raheja. And I am deeply indebted to Phillip G. Terrie, who was there when I first became interested in environmental justice and the impact of MTR in Appalachia, as a PhD student in the American Culture Studies Department at Bowling Green State University in Bowling Green, Ohio.

Finally, I wish to thank my mother, Viola Kathryn Barry, and my father, the late John Joseph Barry, for their love and support, and to other family members in West Virginia who, despite the controversial nature of this topic, had the courage to support this research. I could not have written this book without the emotional and intellectual assistance of my partner, Anne E. Lacsamana, who patiently read every word of the manuscript and served as my toughest editor. I am grateful for your love and commitment to this project and to me.

INTRODUCTION

I BECAME AWARE OF THE PROCESS OF MOUNTAINTOP removal coal mining (MTR) in late 1997 during a visit home to West Virginia. While visiting family, I read local newspaper reports on this controversial form of coal extraction. Many people were becoming more cognizant of changes in the coal industry that ushered in this highly mechanized form of coal mining, and some were horrified by its damage to the lush Appalachian Mountains, and the displacement of small communities in the coalfields. Other citizens defended the coal industry and its place in the state's history and economy. Indeed, mountaintop removal coal mining has been controversial since its beginnings, and continues to polarize citizens in the "Mountain State." When I returned to Ohio after my trip home, the *New York Times*, *Washington Post*, and other national publications were beginning to report this emerging story from the coalfields of central Appalachia.

In early 1998 I visited Larry Gibson's camp on Kayford Mountain in West Virginia and saw an MTR site for the first time. Like many people who view the massive environmental alteration known as mountaintop removal, I was shockingly disturbed that MTR was legal and occurring in my home state. Four generations of my family have lived in the coalfields of West Virginia. My father worked as a coal miner, and my mother was a stay-at-home mom who raised six children in Eccles, West Virginia. Growing up in the Appalachian Mountains, I have a deep affinity for this landscape, as do many people from this region of the United States. Coming of age in West Virginia, the beautiful mountains that surrounded us were inextricably linked to our history, culture, and sense of place in the world. To learn they are now razed for coal extraction, left in ruins by heavy machinery and the technicians who operate them, is simply unacceptable, and far too much to bear for many Appalachians.

When I first began researching this topic, I quickly learned that many West Virginia women and their families were being impacted by MTR operations,

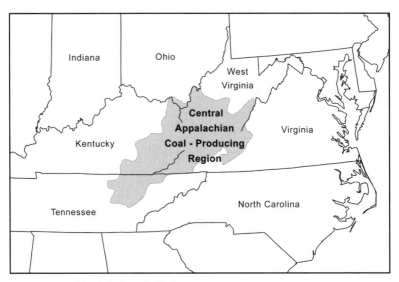

Central Appalachian Coal-Producing Region

and were forming or joining organizations designed to raise awareness about MTR and galvanize support in the fight to end it. In the late 1990s and early 2000s, coalfield women such as Freda Williams, Janice Nease, Pauline Canterbury, Mary Miller, Judy Bonds, and others began to speak out against MTR and its effects on humans and the natural environment of coalfield communities. These early participants helped put the issue on the political and environmental map. Women began monitoring MTR sites, attending state permit hearings, lobbying the state and federal legislatures, and engaging media to educate the public on coal-related issues. For example, many of these women frequently wrote letters to the editor in state newspapers; organized and participated in road shows such as Appalachian Treasures; and spoke at colleges, universities, and community groups throughout the country. Some women worked with scientists and members of the state EPA to collect air quality samples that demonstrated Big Coal's impact on the quality of life in mountain communities. In short, women grassroots activists in this movement have taken a multipronged approach in their fight against MTR and Big Coal in Appalachia. Their presence in this movement has been vigorous and consistent, and women, in large numbers, still serve these vital roles today as the movement changes and progresses.

I have spent more than a decade researching mountaintop removal through an environmental justice lens and conducting fieldwork in central Appalachia, primarily in the coalfields of southern West Virginia. Over the years I have toured MTR sites, visited vanishing coal towns, met with ex–coal miners and families whose homes are at ground zero for MTR operations, drank coffee with professional environmentalists, talked with lawyers and policymakers, and of course met many grassroots activists working to end MTR and mitigate the deleterious effects of Big Coal in Appalachian mountain communities. Until the middle part of the 2000s, this topic was very difficult to write about. Academic resources were limited, and I frequently had to rely on journalistic accounts to support the research I was gathering on the ground in West Virginia.

Despite those early reports in the 1990s, and Ken Ward Jr.'s groundbreaking series "Mining the Mountains" in the *Charleston Gazette*, the issue of MTR was slow to grab national mainstream attention. National environmental groups had little to say about mountaintop removal, and academic analyses were rare. I published the first scholarly article on this topic, "Mountaineers Are Always Free: An Examination of the Effects of Mountaintop Removal in West Virginia," in *Women's Studies Quarterly* in 2001. At the time of this writing, there is only one other academic book on this subject: Shirley Stewart Burns's *Bringing Down the Mountains*, but additional academic treatment of this multifaceted topic is certainly warranted. I am happy to report that thanks to the sustained and vigorous grassroots activism in Appalachia, mountaintop removal coal mining is now a national and international issue. Mainstream environmental groups have taken notice, and additional academic work is being published on what many consider one of the greatest human and environmental tragedies of our time.

This book situates MTR and the environmental justice (EJ) activism against it within a particular time period, 1998 to 2012. Surface mining has existed, in some form or fashion, for decades in Appalachia.[1] However, MTR operations increased in the 1990s, the mainstream press began covering this story in that decade, and organized environmental responses to mountaintop removal became more vigorous and focused during this decade.[2] For example, one of the most prominent West Virginia groups, the Coal River Mountain Watch (CRMW), began in 1998 as a direct response to the incursions of MTR on small communities in Boone County, West Virginia.[3] The Ohio Valley Environmental Coalition (OVEC), based in Huntington, West Virginia, was formed in 1987 and has focused much of its energy on MTR and other coal industry abuses since the late 1990s.[4] Regional organizations such as Appalachian Voices, based in Boone, North Carolina, began offering financial support to the budding anti-MTR movement in the latter part of this decade as well.

I should also make clear that the anti-MTR movement does not focus exclusively on MTR, but serves as a general watchdog for Big Coal, monitoring its assaults on both the human and the nonhuman environments. For example, activists raise awareness about many industry practices deemed harmful as well as the impact of coal on human health, publicize information on coal containment issues, and counter the coal lobby in Washington. Judy Bonds frequently referred to mountaintop removal coal mining as a "poster child" for the detrimental effects of coal production and consumption and the need for the development of alternative energy sources.[5] Sadly, Bonds, codirector of the CRMW, died of cancer in January 2011. This book is dedicated to her memory.

In addition, this manuscript refers to the coal industry as Big Coal, rather than King Coal, because the former denotes one of the most powerful global industries, while King Coal suggests a company operating solely in the Appalachian region as in the older days of coal. In short, Big Coal is more encompassing and reflective of the current political-economic hegemony in relation to the production and consumption of coal. As Coal River Mountain Watch member Sarah Haltom says, the greatest challenge to those fighting MTR is that "we at the grassroots level are dealing with one of the biggest industries in the world that has so much money and power."[6] Despite the enormity of Big Coal's influence, activists continue to work for environmental justice and sustainable coalfield communities.

Mountaintop Removal Coal Mining and Big Coal in West Virginia

Let's consider the well-established facts of this coal extraction process bluntly designated "mountaintop removal." This mechanized form of surface coal mining has existed for decades but became more prevalent in the 1990s because of an increased demand for electricity. MTR removes central Appalachian mountains away from coal seams through large-scale blasting and the use of heavy machinery that scoops up the coal, moving the waste into nearby containment sites called "valley fills."[7] Mountaintop removal differs from previous incarnations of surface mining, not only in that it concentrates on removing mountaintops, but also, and most notably, by the sheer scale of these operations. "The greatest earth-moving activity in the United States" is an apt description, considering the data assessing the scope of MTR: An average MTR site removes 600–800 feet of mountain, stripping roughly 10 miles, dumping the waste from this process into 12 valley fills that can be as large as 1,000 feet wide and a mile long.[8] Figures from 2009 estimate that in Appalachia, 6,000 valley fills impacting 75,000 acres of streams have been approved.[9] "Earth-moving," indeed.

According to scientists, MTR is causing irreparable damage to the central Appalachian landscape. On average, twenty-five hundred tons of explosives are used by

West Virgina Coal Counties

technicians daily in Appalachian communities to blast the mountaintops, covering nearby streams with waste, throwing ecosystems out of balance, and causing increased flooding and the loss of biodiversity in the mountains.[10] Area water supplies are contaminated by the use of valley fills, and also by the containment of toxic wastes from processing coal into nearby earthen dams called slurry ponds.[11] The impacts on human health are considerable. Scientists note an increase in respiratory and heart problems by citizens living in mining zones, including chronic pulmonary disorders and lung cancer.[12] Mortality rates are also elevated in areas surrounding surface mining locations.[13] A most recent scientific study indicates that higher birth defect rates occur in mountaintop removal mining areas in Appalachia.[14]

Mountaintop removal coal mining was made possible by federal attempts to regulate strip-mining in the United States through the 1977 Surface Mining Control and Reclamation Act (SMCRA).[15] The legislation permitted surface-mining as long as coal companies were able to reclaim and return mined areas to their "approximate original contour" (AOC) to repurpose the affected land into sites for commercial or residential use.[16] However, a variance to the AOC rule was permissible if mountaintops were being removed. Because MTR mines cannot return mountains to their approximate original contour, coal companies receive an AOC variance as long as they demonstrate that the mined land will be used in a way "equal to or better than the way it was used" before mining operations began.[17] The realities of reclaiming the land postmining are predictable: coal companies spend less than 1 percent of revenue on land reclamation, spraying hydroseed and coating rocks with a mix of "fertilizer, cellulose mulch, and seeds of nonnative grasses," before moving on to the next operation.[18] Economic development takes place on less than 5 percent of flattened areas that were once mountains.[19] In addition to SMCRA, mountaintop removal coal mining is also supported by federal appeals courts, which have overturned two notable cases that sought to make MTR illegal, or more specifically, valley fills, which compromise Clean Water Act mandates.

The first case, *Bragg vs. Robertson*, filed in 1998 by attorney Joe Lovett, charged the Army Corps of Engineers and the Department of Environmental Protection (DEP) with violating the Clean Water Act by issuing permits for valley fills at MTR operations.[20] The plaintiffs were local residents impacted by MTR, including Patricia Bragg, a housewife from Pie, West Virginia.[21] In 1999, Federal District Judge John Haden ruled in favor of the plaintiffs, agreeing that valley fills violated the Clean Water Act. This decision sent shock waves into the coalfields of West Virginia, prompting state senators Robert Byrd and Jay Rockefeller to draft a rider to an appropriations bill nullifying portions of the ruling.[22] Ultimately, *Bragg vs. Robertson* was appealed by coal companies, and in 2001the Fourth Circuit Court of Appeals overturned Haden's decision by arguing that the case should be tried in state court, and citizens did not have the right to sue state regulators over a failure to enforce the Surface Mining Control and Reclamation Act.[23]

Similar litigation was pursued again by Joe Lovett in 2005 when a suit against the Army Corps of Engineers was filed on behalf of three state environmental groups: the Ohio Valley Environmental Coalition, the Coal River Mountain Watch, and the West Virginia Highlands Conservancy. This case charged the Army Corps of Engineers with improper permitting processes of MTR operations. In 2007, US District Court Judge Robert Chambers ruled in favor of the plaintiffs and cited the Corps with failure to meet the standards of the Clean Water Act and the National Environmental Policy Act.[24] This ruling required more-stringent environmental reviews of MTR, but was overturned in 2009 by the Fourth District Court of Appeals, which claimed that the US Army Corps of Engineers had the authority to issue Clean Water Act permits for MTR operations without extensive review.[25] In between these two legal actions by citizens and state environmental groups, the Bush administration sought to simplify the regulatory process of mountaintop removal by redefining the concept of waste to "fill" material, rendering the use of valley fills legally permissible in 2002.[26]

Currently, the Obama administration promises tighter enforcement of the Clean Water Act in regard to MTR and greater regulation of the mining permit process, but refuses to place a moratorium on mountaintop removal coal mining. In April 2010 the EPA issued the first comprehensive guidelines to protect communities from the impacts of MTR, "using the best available science and following the law." The newly established "comprehensive guidance" set "clear benchmarks for preventing significant and irreversible damage to Appalachian watersheds at risk from mining activity."[27] When presenting the regulatory framework, EPA director Lisa P. Jackson said, "The people of Appalachia shouldn't have to choose between a clean, healthy environment in which to raise their families and the jobs they need to support them. That's why the EPA is providing even greater clarity on the direction the agency is taking to confront pollution from mountaintop removal."[28] Interestingly, like coal industry officials, the EPA often refers to MTR as "mountaintop mining," omitting the more descriptive and apt word "removal" when referring to the practice.

Despite the rhetoric of tighter enforcement and regulation over this type of coal extraction, in June 2010 the EPA approved its first MTR mine under the new guidelines: Arch Coal's Pine Creek Mine in Logan County, West Virginia, a 760-acre MTR operation containing three proposed valley fills.[29] Environmental groups and activists were displeased with the decision, expecting more from the Obama administration's environmental protection agency. However, in 2011 the Obama EPA did revoke the permit for the Spruce No. 1 Mine in Logan County, the largest proposed MTR operation to date, signifying a major victory for the anti-MTR movement.[30] Despite this regulatory success, Maria Gunnoe, Ohio Valley Environmental Coalition community organizer and 2009 recipient of the Goldman Environmental Prize, objects to the regulation of mountaintop removal coal mining:

> I will never believe that they can regulate, in any way, shape, form, or fashion, doing MTR or filling valley fills. I think it's impossible to regulate doing that. "Regulate," in my opinion, is a way to find excuses for it, and there is no excuse for doing it. . . . They mislead people into thinking that since these words are on paper that this just isn't happening anymore, and that's not the case.[31]

When the regulatory guidelines were initially released, and the Pine Creek Mine was approved under the new rules, Amanda Starbuck, a representative of the international environmental organization Rainforest Action Network, also voiced objections:

This is a devastating first decision under guidelines that had offered so much hope for Appalachian residents who thought the EPA was standing up for their health and water quality in the face of a horrific mining practice. . . . The grand words being spoken by Administrator Jackson in Washington are simply not being reflected in the EPA's actions on-the-ground. This continues the inconsistent and contradictory decisions that have plagued the EPA's process on mountaintop removal coal mining all along.[32]

Environmental groups continue to pressure the administration in hopes that MTR will cease in central Appalachia. Local activists repeatedly invite Lisa Jackson to the coalfields to see an MTR site firsthand. At the time of this writing, she has ignored all requests.

Environmental Justice, Gender, and Anti–Mountaintop Removal Activism

Standing Our Ground: Women, Environmental Justice, and the Fight to End Mountaintop Removal is fundamentally an examination of women's environmental justice activism in the anti–mountaintop removal coal mining movement in West Virginia. The working-class white women and Cherokee women profiled in this book have ties to coalfield communities and have been directly impacted by the rise of MTR in West Virginia. Some have lost their homes and been forced to relocate, while others fight to stay in their homes and communities. While the book trains its analysis on West Virginia women's participation in this movement, and the voices of these coalfield women are contained throughout the manuscript, this is not an ethnographic study. Ultimately, this book is an interdisciplinary cultural studies examination of the environmental justice movement against MTR. Even though I focus attention on those most directly affected by Big Coal, the women contained in these pages are not the only ones working tirelessly for environmental justice in the central Appalachia coalfields. Women such as Vivian Stockman, Diane Bady, and Janet Keating have committed their professional lives to coalfield justice through their work in the Ohio Valley Environmental Coalition. In fact, chances are that if you view a picture of an MTR site contained in books, magazines, or newspaper articles, it was taken by Vivian Stockman.

There are other women, too, such as Sandra Diaz, Steph Pistello, and Mary Ann Hitt, who speak out against MTR and engage in lobbying efforts within the coalfields and in Washington, DC. Also, Teri Blanton, member of Kentuckians for the Commonwealth, has been active against Big Coal for years now. Ann League is fighting MTR in Tennessee as part of the Save Our Cumberland

Mountains organization, Jane Branham and Kathy Selvage organize against Big Coal with the Southern Appalachian Mountain Stewards in Virginia, Elisa Young fights the industry in Ohio as founder of the Meigs Citizens Action Now organization, and Julia Sendor and Debbie Jarrell are members of the Coal River Mountain Watch in West Virginia. And, of course, there are many men work-ing for environmental justice in the coalfields. Men such as Larry Gibson; Bo Webb; Vernon Haltom; Ed Wiley; ex–coal miner Chuck Nelson; Julian Martin, member of the West Virginia Highlands Conservancy; and Bill Price, a West Virginia native who represents the Sierra Club in the coalfields, are all on the ground in West Virginia and very active in anti-MTR campaigns. In fact, Judy Bonds noted that the gender composition of the movement has changed from the late 1990s. She acknowledged that "as the movement has become bigger, and more people have become involved in this, more men have stepped up to the plate. . . . It's very much needed and appreciated that the men are starting to become more involved, and in that way it diversifies the movement."[33]

Indeed, the movement to end mountaintop removal coal mining in cen-tral Appalachia is diverse, and since the late 1990s has grown tremendously. What began as a purely local issue in the coalfields of Appalachia has become a regional, national, and international campaign to end this destructive form of coal extraction. The movement involves people from all walks of life: house-wives, former coal miners, professional environmentalists, high school and col-lege students, musicians, academics, scientists, actors, filmmakers, and many others who are compelled to work for environmental justice in Appalachia. However, this work argues that MTR became an environmental justice issue through the tireless work of primarily women dealing firsthand with the ef-fects of Big Coal in their communities. Coal River Mountain Watch member Sarah Haltom claims that in her experience, women are more vocal and less afraid to speak out than men in the movement, and "tend to see the issue with more urgency than men."[34] OVEC community organizer Maria Gunnoe claims that "women are the ones who began this movement, and I think it's because we recognized what it was doing to our kids."[35] Gunnoe recalls a 2003 meet-ing where twelve women discussed MTR and strategies for fighting Big Coal: "There was a lot of women around that table when we decided, no compromise. . . . It has to be stopped."[36] Women's activism in the coalfields put this issue on the map, so to speak, and my work highlights their participation and centralizes gender in environmental justice theory and praxis.

Discussions of environmental justice, and the ways in which it differs from mainstream environmentalism, are numerous and well-established in the EJ canon.[37] Environmental justice began in the late 1970s and early 1980s in the United States, and was birthed by the civil rights movement.[38] Environmental justice seeks to highlight the ways human injustices based on race, gender, class, nation, and so forth are connected to environmental problems. It differs from mainstream environmentalism in that it defines the environment as where we "live, work, and play," complicating the long-standing conception of the environment as remote wilderness infrequently touched by humans.[39] Conversely, EJ emanates from human communities and concentrates on improving and preserving those communities in the face of industrial incursions. Environmental justice operates from the assumption that poor people occupy poor environments, and it seeks justice for vulnerable human populations and the natural spaces that house them.

In particular, EJ argues that minority communities are disproportionately impacted by environmental pollution and resource depletion, and community members often form or join collectives that fight for political, economic, and environmental remediation.[40] EJ scholar Filomina Chioma Steady argues that environmental justice has "inspired movements that challenge environmental racism all over the world, especially in the African Diaspora and in Africa and has appealed mostly, though not exclusively, to people of color, indigenous people, and poor people in endangered environments."[41] Indeed, environmental justice scholarship has focused primarily on race and class because of its origins in communities of color. This manuscript applies EJ scholarship and actions rooted in communities of color to primarily white, working-class coalfield communities in West Virginia, expanding the elastic purview of EJ. In addition, I centralize gender in environmental justice thought and practice by focusing on women's participation in the anti-MTR movement.

Feminist political ecologists argue that women have a unique connection to environmental issues, not based solely or exclusively in biology, but primarily in the work they perform in their homes and communities. Because women are often responsible for providing and managing life's basic necessities, such as food, clothing, child care and elder care, they view environmental problems in unique ways. Dianne Rocheleau argues that these responsibilities put women "in a position to oppose threats to health, life, and vital subsistence resources, regardless of economic incentives, and to view environmental issues from the perspective of home, as well as that of personal and family health."[42] As examined in parts of this book, some feminists argue that this particular connection to home, community, and environment precipitates women's large numbers in environmental justice groups in the United States and beyond. West Virginia women active in the movement to end MTR are representative of the formidable presence of women in environmental justice groups. Regardless of the community, or the environmental justice issues at hand, women, working-class white women, and women of color form and join EJ groups in large numbers.[43]

Even with women's undeniable presence in environmental justice practice, much of environmental justice scholarship fails to analyze and include gender in its analysis in substantial ways. Nancy C. Unger suggests that "while race and class are regularly addressed in environmental justice studies, scant attention has been paid to gender," but "women's responses to the ever-shifting responsibilities prescribed to their gender, as well as to their particular race and class, have consistently shaped their abilities to affect the environment in positive ways."[44] Women in West Virginia, like many women in EJ groups throughout the world, transform work associated with the private sphere into public, community-based activism. In doing so, they show the importance of women's influence in both the public and the private sectors of society.

Chapter Summaries

Chapter 1 examines the material conditions of West Virginia women in this age of mountaintop removal coal mining, guided by the assumption that in searching for solutions to the political, economic, and environmental problems associated with MTR and Big Coal in the state, the perspectives of poor and working-class women must be considered. This focus is important, given that it is poor, rural women (nationally and internationally) who not only bear the costs of uneven political and economic conditions, but who form or join collectives to fight injustices in their communities. In discussing the material conditions of women in West Virginia, this chapter examines how gender ideologies have been shaped by the coal industry, and how women's participation in the anti-MTR movement simultaneously embraces and defies traditional gendered prescriptions.

Chapter 2 places the anti-MTR movement, and women's participation, within the context of environmental justice activism in the United States. The EJ framework provides a productive way to assess the anti-MTR movement because of its historic focus on the connections between adverse environments and disenfranchised human populations. Environmental justice links social justice—economic, political, and cultural—with the natural world, exposing the root causes of both environmental problems and social inequity. This chapter reviews EJ's historic focus on race and class, but, more important, centralizes gender in this analysis of the movement to end MTR and Big Coal's influence in West Virginia. EJ has done a tremendous job of emphasizing the importance of class, social justice, and vulnerable communities' connections to the environment, but, as indicated above, insufficiently assesses the role of gender in EJ thought and practice. Too often the tireless efforts of women EJ activists are not fully examined by environmental justice scholars, even though working-class white women, and women of color, participate in these movements in large numbers.

Chapter 3 situates West Virginia women's environmental justice activism in the anti-MTR movement within the history and culture of grassroots protest in Appalachia. Historically, women in the region have joined coal industry reform efforts such as labor strikes and unionization campaigns. Women were also active in anti-strip-mining activism of the 1960s and 1970s. Women in the anti-MTR movement, unlike previous instantiations of women's activism, envision a life without coal in central Appalachia, focusing their efforts on creating economically and environmentally sustainable communities. In doing so, they promote a vision of West Virginia that sees the mountains as inextricably tied to the area's culture and history. They highlight this connection, while supporters of Big Coal argue that coal, and not mountains, is the defining marker of West Virginia's cultural history.

Chapter 4 examines racial constructions inherent in the popular anti-MTR slogan "Save the Endangered Hillbilly," positioning this call within white studies scholarship and as a directive to mainstream environmentalism, which has historically separated humans from the nonhuman environment. The culturally derogative term "hillbilly" has a long history in this country, and is a descriptor used both racially and in terms of class in American society. Activists in the anti-MTR movement reclaim this pejorative term and use it to foster a sense of pride in coalfield residents. In their embrace of "hillbilly," they mark themselves by race and class in their efforts to preserve the culture and environment of West Virginia in this age of mountaintop removal coal mining.

Finally, chapter 5 situates mountaintop removal coal mining, and the movement to end it, within the global context of neoliberal economic transformations, global energy, climate change, and environmental justice protest. Appalachian activists realize that the adverse impact of MTR does not remain in the isolated mountainous communities where coal is extracted. Coal provides half of this country's electricity, and is, indeed, the primary source for electricity generation in the world, but emits the largest amount of CO_2 into the earth's atmosphere, contributing greatly to climate change. With this knowledge, grassroots Appalachian activists are concerned with making global environmental justice connections in their efforts to end MTR. These activists work with the realization that while they are all rooted locally, they are socially and environmentally connected to the world at large.

CHAPTER 1

Living in a Sacrifice Zone: Gender, the Political
Economy of Coal, and Anti–Mountaintop
Removal Activism

> We're trying to preserve something, and save this creation.
> . . . We're trying to push the state forward, you know, and
> to stop the destruction and diversify the economy.
>
> —Judy Bonds

Introduction

ON A JANUARY EVENING IN 2003, COAL RIVER MOUNTAIN
Watch codirector Judy "Julia" Bonds was home with her grandson when the
telephone rang, and the caller ID revealed that the incoming call was from
California. Bonds answered, and the man on the other end of the line identified himself as Richard Goldman, phoning to inform her that she was the
2003 North American recipient of the Goldman Environmental Prize for her
work against mountaintop removal coal mining in Appalachia.[1] Bonds, who
knew nothing about the Goldman Foundation or this prestigious prize that
annually gives monetary awards to one environmental justice activist from
each continent, casually responded, "Oh, okay. Well, thanks. I appreciate that."[2]

During their brief conversation, Goldman gave Bonds a web address and
encouraged her to read more about this prize. She explained, "I looked it up
on the computer and then I was in total shock. . . . It took my breath away."[3]
Bonds learned that she was one of seven environmental justice activists in
the world that year to win $125,000 for her work with the Coal River Moun-
tain Watch.[4] She said winning this prize was personally monumental but
also significant for her organization and the anti-MTR movement, as "people
began to realize who CRMW was. They began to realize what MTR is, and

it started a snowball effect" of more people becoming educated about MTR and its impact on Appalachian communities and, as a result, wanting to join the fight to end it.[5]

Five years earlier, in 1998, Judy Bonds went to the CRMW offices looking for help after being forced off her land in Marfork Hollow, near Whitesville, West Virginia, by coal operations that rendered the area unfit for habitation. Bonds, whose family has lived in this area for ten generations, noticed dramatic changes in her environment when Massey coal operations began there in the 1990s. She witnessed color and consistency changes to the water sources in her backyard, and was particularly alarmed when her grandson, playing in a creek behind her home, asked, "What's wrong with these fish?"[6] His innocent question alerted Bonds to fish kills in the water, and she then knew something was horribly wrong. After this, Bonds said, "I started to notice as my neighbors moved out, there was coal trucks running constantly, and it just . . . devalued our property, our quality of life. We were in danger . . . and it was basically the quality of the air and water that made me find out more about what's happening in my own holler, and the coal industry."[7] Feeling under siege from MTR blasting, the persistent presence of coal trucks, and the inability to drink water in her home or visit the family cemetery, she moved nine miles away to Rock Creek, West Virginia. She was the last resident to leave the community of Marfork.

Prior to joining the CRMW, Bonds had no experience in grassroots activist politics, but at an early age she began to develop a deep sensitivity to economic and social injustice. All the men in her family, including her father, grandfather, ex-husband, cousins, and others worked in nearby coal mines. She spent her childhood in Birch Creek, the upper reaches of Marfork Hollow, where her family grew large gardens, foraged for edible plants in the surrounding mountains, kept livestock, and hunted animals for their own subsistence. Bonds lived in Birch Creek until she was seven, when a coal company forced her family off their land. They settled nearby in Marfork Hollow, and her father worked for Bethlehem Coal Company.[8]

She recalled seeing one of her father's paychecks, and the anger she felt upon learning his weekly compensation was a meager $15. She said, "Fifteen dollars for a man risking his life and his health. Fifteen dollars is what he gets for that?"[9] Even though Bonds had no political activist experience before joining the CRMW, she credited her mother with imparting a strong sense of justice in her: "She was a very strong willed, opinionated woman. I remember listening to my mother rant and rave about Buffalo Creek. . . . And

I remember hearing my mother talk a little bit about Mother Jones, and John L. Lewis and about Matewan. . . . So, a little bit of that outrage against injustices was instilled in me at an early age."[10] In the anti-MTR movement, Bonds had a reputation for speaking bluntly, motivated by an angry passion that was not palatable to all people, particular coal industry supporters. However, she was unapologetic, saying, "That's who I am. I can't apologize for that. I lost my diplomacy a long time ago."[11] She, like other grassroots activists in the movement, was the victim of threats and intimidation for speaking out against coalfield injustices, but she remained unwavering in her position.

Arguably, Judy Bonds, Larry Gibson, and Maria Gunnoe are the faces of the MTR movement. West Virginia natives with deep historical ties to the region, they, along with other people profiled in this book, have felt the negative impacts of Big Coal firsthand. All have refused to remain silent while this industry obliterates their communities. Bonds, in particular, took a firm stand on the issue and believed other people should as well. She argued, "If you do not raise your finger to stop an injustice, you're the same as that person doing the injustice."[12] She has been called a "folk celebrity" for her work with the CRMW,[13] a coalfield Erin Brockovich. However, Bonds was quick to say that she was just one of many, "a reflection" of Big Coal's impact on southern West Virginia and of the numerous people taking stands against the coal industry in this era of mountaintop removal coal mining.[14] She said, "I'm just the first one out there, because there's a lot more women that have deeper and bigger and more compelling stories to tell. . . . That's what makes it so good is that the rest of these women are now telling their stories because one woman had the courage to step out."[15]

Bonds and Gunnoe are representative of many Appalachian women who have become politically active to save their homes, communities, and the lush Appalachian Mountains literally from obliteration. They occupy an area of the country known as an energy "sacrifice zone," where the lives and environment of the few are sacrificed for the greater good of the many; in this case through the production of coal, which provides most of the electricity in the United States.[16] While they work to protect the land and quality of life, women environmental justice activists in West Virginia are cognizant that MTR is not solely an environmental issue. Rather, these women position the problems associated with MTR within a holistic framework, highlighting the political, economic, and environmental linkages to this destructive form of coal extraction.

MTR is a controversial form of coal extraction, polarizing state citizens, many of whom defend the practice and the industry, because of Big Coal's long history in West Virginia; because of the cultural belief that this area "is coal country"; and because of economic reasons, as the industry provides most of the good-paying jobs in the coalfields today. Those critical of the coal industry, particularly mountaintop removal mining, are fewer in number given the overall population in West Virginia's nine southern coal counties (Boone, Fayette, Kanawha, Nicholas, Raleigh, Logan, McDowell, Mingo, and Wyoming), which in 2007 had a combined population of 476,996, while the total number of people residing in the state was 1,812,035.[17] While working in environmental justice groups, these grassroots women activists maintain a transformative vision focused on ending the coal hegemony in West Virginia and preserving local communities and the natural environment by promoting the use of alternative energy forms. In doing so they find themselves deeply lodged within the long-standing jobs-versus-environment tensions between those who protect coal in this area and others who seek a new direction for the state. This chapter examines the material conditions of working-class West Virginia women in the age of MTR, gender ideologies shaped and utilized by the coal industry, and how women's anti-MTR activism challenges and defies established gendered prescriptions.

In the Shadow of a "Resource Curse": Material Conditions of West Virginia Women and the Hegemony of Coal

The coal industry rules supreme in the rural coalfields of southern West Virginia. In this nine-county area, the heavy manufacturing of this fossil fuel provides one of the best means of employment, with adequate wages and health benefits for many coal miners and their families. West Virginia is typically characterized as a mono-economy, reflecting the prominence of coal in the state's economy and also its long history as the most influential industry in West Virginia. While the number of mining jobs has decreased over the years with the increased mechanization of the industry, coal still employees a large number of working-class people in southern West Virginia, either directly through mining jobs or through other businesses that support mining.[18] The rest of this wage-earning population is largely employed in service-oriented occupations, many lacking health-care benefits and living wages.[19]

While the state is rich in natural resources such as coal and timber, its citizens are some of the most impoverished in the country. Currently, West

Virginia ranks as the fifth-most-impoverished state in the US, behind Kentucky, Arkansas, New Mexico, and Mississippi.[20] The highest rates of poverty are in the rural southern areas of the state, including two counties located in the southern coalfields, McDowell and Mingo, with poverty rates at 33 percent and 25.4 percent, respectively.[21] Many scholars and most anti-MTR activists connect the consistently high levels of poverty in West Virginia to the extraction of natural resources, the very basis of the state's mono-economy. Journalist Jeff Goodell claims:

> Nearly 150 years and some 13 billion tons of coal later, it's strikingly obvious that the great wealth of natural resources in West Virginia has been anything but a blessing. Rather than bringing riches, it has brought poverty, sickness, environmental devastation, and despair. By virtually every indicator of a state's economic and social well-being—educational achievement, employment rate, income level—West Virginia remains at or near the bottom of the list. Nowhere is the decline clearer than in the southern part of the state, where the promise of riches was once brightest.[22]

The adverse socioeconomic conditions Goodell notes impact many West Virginia citizens but are, perhaps, most keenly felt by working-class women in the state. Over the past decade, many studies have assessed the socioeconomic conditions of West Virginia. Some analyses focus explicitly on conditions of women, while others isolate the category of gender among other discrete variables. Surprisingly, the most influential assessment of the region, the Appalachian Regional Commission report, insufficiently addresses gender in its assessment of living conditions in Appalachia.

In 2003, the Appalachian Regional Commission, a federal program established in 1965 to assess and ameliorate persistent poverty in the region, released its annual report, *Appalachia at the Millennium: An Overview of Results from Census 2000*, based on 1990s socioeconomic data.[23] Curiously, the report has a section that segments race and ethnicity in changing socioeconomic patterns but provides no gender differential category, and provides data on gender disparities only in workforce participation rates. This oversight is consistent with the frequent omission of data on women in a good portion of social science policy research. The end result presupposes that women and men experience similar socioeconomic realities, an all-too-frequent and wholly false assumption argued against by many feminist researchers. Feminist economists Drucilla K. Barker and Susan F. Feiner draw our attention to gender biases in socioeconomic analyses, as well as the importance of making distinctions based on race, gender, class, and so forth:

> Isn't a price just a price? A market just a market? Don't men and women feel the ups and downs of economic activity equally, whether they are black or white, straight or gay? Won't a change in interest rates affect everyone the same way, regardless of gender? To all these questions feminist economists answer, "no." Gender, like race, ethnicity, class, nation, and other markers of social location, is central to our understanding of economics and economic systems. The categories of economic analysis do not express timeless truths. Economic categories and concepts, like the categories and concepts of every knowledge project, are embedded in social contexts and connected to processes of social differentiation.[24]

Indeed, concentrating on who is excluded in policy assessments can reveal just as much about hegemonic interests in certain locations and historical contexts as concentrating on who is included in these analyses. When socioeconomic studies fail to account for fundamental differences in a population, it is crucial that feminist researchers highlight gender bias, exposing the blind spots in the original study. This first step in underscoring omissions can lead to social analysis that is more thorough, informative, and inclusive.

While the ARC report fails to isolate the category of gender adequately, it does provide some useful general information on Appalachian lives. Defining Appalachia and delineating its boundaries have been the subjects of a complex, long-standing debate among those who study the region, but most current scholarship follows the ARC demarcations. In this latest ARC report, Appalachia covers 410 counties in 13 states, including all of West Virginia and portions of New York, Pennsylvania, Ohio, Maryland, Virginia, South Carolina, North Carolina, Tennessee, Kentucky, Georgia, Alabama, and Mississippi.[25] The commission also divides Appalachia into three subregions: northern Appalachia, which includes parts of New York, Pennsylvania, Maryland, Ohio, and 46 of West Virginia's 55 counties; central Appalachia, which includes 9 counties in southern West Virginia's coalfields, and portions of Kentucky, Virginia, and Tennessee; and southern Appalachia, which includes sections of Virginia, Tennessee, South Carolina, North Carolina, Georgia, Alabama, and Mississippi.[26] This study makes important distinctions between areas within the 410-county Appalachian region, which in the popular point of view is a monolithic region with uniform social and economic conditions.

The commission results, detailed by Kelvin M. Pollard, also distinguish between "transitional,""competitive,""attainment," and "distressed" counties in the region.[27] Pollard discloses that most of the "transitional" counties, those on par with national averages in some categories but lagging behind in others, are found in northern and southern Appalachia. The "competitive" counties, those closely resembling the rest of the country in social and economic indexes, are primarily in southern Appalachia. The "attainment" counties, predominantly urban areas in the region, are also on par with national averages. The "distressed" counties, located in central Appalachia, are below national averages, but also fall behind Appalachian norms in all categories.[28]

The "distressed" area of the region includes all of West Virginia's coalfield counties, which are characterized as "experiencing the greatest economic hardships."[29] Counties in the "distressed" category have per capita incomes no greater than 67 percent of the national average, and rates of poverty and unemployment that are at least 150 percent of the respective rates for the country as a whole.[30] Most households in this region experience socioeconomic hardships, and workforce participation rates are lower than national averages. Pollard reveals that in 2000, West Virginia workforce participation rates were 45 percent for women and 58 percent for men, behind the 2000 national averages of 58 percent for women and 71 percent for men.[31] These gender disparities can be attributed to the manufacturing-based economy of the state, which relies primarily on male labor. Areas reliant on heavy manufacturing typically contain stark occupational segregation based on gender. Some feminist scholars suggest that disparities based on occupational segregation and earnings speak to the value placed on women's labor in the US economy. Deborah M. Figart claims:

> Six out of ten women still work in female-dominated occupations, particularly in a growing service sector. Most women are clerical and professional specialty workers, especially African-American women who left domestic service to replace white women in offices. About eight of ten men are employed in male-dominated occupations, especially craft and managerial or administrative work. Relatively few occupations are truly integrated, as evidenced by visits to individual workplaces. The wage gap is narrower in female-dominated occupations where overall average pay is lower, although men still earn more than women in jobs such as secretary, cashier, social worker and nurse. This not only suggests that men's earnings exceed women's, but that traditionally women's work is devalued in the economy.[32]

In short, the devaluation of female labor consigns many women, particularly in areas with a large manufacturing base, to low-paying work that typically lacks health benefits and opportunities for advancement. In West Virginia, some scholars have argued this pattern was established long ago and still informs labor practices in the region today. For example, Frances S. Hensley argues that historically, industrial development in West Virginia provided jobs in "coal mines, coke plants, steel mills, machine shops, construction, and lumber mills, industries which did not, as a rule, employ women."[33] The concentration of employment in these industries "became a dominant feature of West Virginia's industrial structure and imposed long-term restrictions on employment opportunities for women."[34] These socioeconomic conditions are still influential today, rendering women more dependent upon male wages and lacking opportunities for adequate means of employment.

The ARC report reveals as well how central Appalachia, where the West Virginia coalfields are situated, also lags behind other areas in annual income. This census information indicates that in 2000 the national per capita income was $21,600, while in southern Appalachia it was $19,200 and in central Appalachia it was $14,300, just 66 percent of the national average.[35] Keeping in mind that the ARC was initiated to alleviate poverty in the region, the 2000 assessment found that poverty in Appalachia improved slightly from 1990 figures but still posed formidable obstacles, particularly for central Appalachia, where 1 in 5 people (22.1 percent) were considered poor, whereas in the southern and northern regions, 1 in 8 residents (12.8 percent) were impoverished.[36] When considering educational achievement rates between the subregions of Appalachia, Pollard reveals that in 2000, 81 percent of northern Appalachian residents, 75 percent of southern Appalachian residents, and only 64 percent of central Appalachian residents had high school degrees, while the national average was 81 percent.[37] The figures for college education were even starker. In 2000, the national average for persons holding a college degree was 25 percent, while 18 percent of northern Appalachian residents, 19 percent of southern Appalachians, and only 11 percent of those living in central Appalachia held college degrees.[38] As the ARC report reveals, central Appalachia faces formidable challenges in raising the standard of living and providing educational opportunities for the population. Although challenges impact all residents, women in central Appalachia, particularly in the coalfields, face the greatest obstacles.

Women in West Virginia, like others in the country, lack social, political, and economic equality with men. However, the socioeconomic conditions for women in this state are more troubling than for women in other parts of the country. Gender, like race, ethnicity, class, and so forth, is a fundamental category of social difference. It is important that these dissimilarities, which are embedded in our social institutions, be isolated in policy studies. Some feminist economists, such as Deborah Figart, Ellen Mutari, and Marilyn Power, promote the concept of "practice theory" when assessing the outcomes of social differences.[39] They suggest that "in practice theory, gender is treated as an 'organizing principle' of social structures rather than simply a characteristic of individuals. . . . All social structures and institutions, including the labor market and the state, are structured by gender."[40] The authors also point out that gender is just one structure of social practice, with race, ethnicity, class, and nationality being considered additional social structures.[41] However, they emphasize that the ways in which gender (or other distinguishing social markers) is structured in a particular time or place "reflects the relative dominance of different social interests."[42] Many women live in precarious socioeconomic conditions, and much work is needed to create institutional change that can provide women with greater opportunities. In the end, the Appalachian Regional Commission report does not suggest possible solutions to persistent problems in central Appalachia. The study ends by concisely reiterating the troubling information and lists several forthcoming reports aimed at analyzing demographic changes noted in the 2000 census. While the ARC report fails to sufficiently analyze gender difference, other studies focus explicitly on current conditions of women in West Virginia.

In 2002, the Institute for Women's Policy Research released *The Status of Women in West Virginia* report, which relies on data from 1997 through 2002 in assessing the social, political, and economic conditions of women in the state.[43] Barbara J. Howe, cochair for the West Virginia Advisory Committee, asserts, "The report sets forth a blueprint of where we are and where we might go to improve the status of women in the state. And if we do not address the obstacles that are keeping women from achieving their fullest potential, we will not progress as a state, for women are the majority (51.4 percent) of the population of the state."[44] Following the policy guidelines of the 1995 United Nations Fourth World Conference on Women in Beijing, the aims of these state-by-state studies is to thoroughly assess the status of women and provide solutions for improving their lives. The *Status of Women in West Virginia* report provides grades in these distinct areas: political participation, employment and earnings, social and economic autonomy, reproductive rights, and health and well-being. Feminist researchers contend that overall, West Virginia ranked forty-eighth in the nation in women's social and economic autonomy.[45] In fact, out of the five areas of assessment, West Virginia received only one passing grade, a B–, in reproductive rights. The state received D and F grades in all other categories.[46] The report states that "almost 19 percent of West Virginia women lack health insurance, and almost 17 percent live below the poverty line.... Women in the state have the lowest levels of educational attainment in the country."[47] Furthermore, this study revealed a challenging economic situation for most women in this part of the country:

> Women in West Virginia participate in the workforce much less often, earn significantly lower wages, and work as managers or professionals much less frequently than women in the nation as a whole. Their earnings in relation to men's are also lower than in most of the country. These factors combine to place West Virginia last in the nation on the employment and earnings composite index. The state receives a grade of F in this area, reflecting the inequality women experience compared with men.[48]

Not only do West Virginia women fall below the national average in these categories, overall they received the worst grades of all the Appalachian states.[49] After revealing the scores for West Virginia women in each area, Howe baldly claims, "If statistics do not lie, the status of women in West Virginia is terrible. ... Except for the reproductive rights score, which is a good score only if one is pro-choice, West Virginia would undoubtedly rank as one of the worst states in the country for women."[50]

While the Appalachian Regional Studies Commission and *Status of Women in West Virginia* reports are based on socioeconomic data from the late 1990s and early 2000s, recent reports reveal findings consistent with these earlier figures.[51] Most of the studies assessing material conditions in West Virginia suggest basic political and economic reforms to improve the status of those suffering in the state. For example, the Women's Policy Research Center, in its state-by-state analysis, claims West Virginia women would benefit from "stronger enforcement of equal opportunity laws, better political representation, adequate and affordable child care, stronger poverty reduction programs, and other policies that would help improve their status."[52] These studies, particularly those highlighting differences based on gender, race, nation, and so forth, provide a fuller picture of life in this troubled region. However, most policy studies fail to examine the root causes of the adverse socioeconomic conditions facing most West Virginians. While socioeconomic assessments are useful tools in understanding the strengths and weaknesses of West Virginia, a more transformative vision exposes the underlying causes of such immiseration.

The material and structural problems of rural central Appalachia are attributed to what Jeff Goodell calls the "resource curse,"[53] a designation that denotes a pattern of social, political, and economic problems in areas rich in natural resources. Goodell claims that "by conventional economic logic," places such as the West Virginia coalfields, the Niger Delta, Venezuela, Colombia, or the Democratic Republic of the Congo should have higher standards of living because of resource riches inherent in the natural environment of these areas.[54] In reality, these resources "curse" the land and the people in the following ways:

> Control over natural resources allows a few people to obtain tremendous wealth, giving them huge sway over the economic fortunes of the state and offering enormous opportunity for self-indulgence and corruption. At best, economies that are dependent on natural resources are unstable. When coal or gas prices are up, they're awash in cash; when prices fall, they struggle to keep the lights on in hospitals and gunfire from breaking out in the streets. This kind of economic yo-yoing leads to budgetary and financial fiascoes, in addition to leaving the government open to economic blackmail by the extraction industries: *If you don't let me mine that mountain, I'll pull out and leave you all in poverty.*[55]

Many anti-MTR activists I have spoken to over the years are well aware of these political-economic arrangements and their effects on the human and nonhuman environments of West Virginia. As such, they make links between environmental problems caused by coal operations in the state and the iniquitous social and economic conditions of West Virginia, realizing that the fundamental problems of central Appalachia must be identified as they work for transformative change in the region. This knowledge is evident in Coal River Mountain Watch's late codirector Judy Bonds's claim that "we're trying to help the state. We're trying to push the state forward, you know, to stop the destruction and to diversify the economy. We should have diversified our economy many, many, many years ago, and that's the problem. The coal industry controls everything."[56]

Omission of the iniquitous political and economic arrangements of West Virginia in most public policy assessments, particularly of the way the coal industry wields power over the state at the expense of its citizens and the natural environment, is unfortunate. The connections between the hegemony of Big Coal and the social, economic, and environmental conditions in West Virginia are more explanatory when assessing the area's problems. The deleterious influence of this elephant is a reality neatly summarized in the popular anti-MTR activist sign "Coal Keeps West Virginia Poor." This slogan is posted on an outdoor picnic shelter on Kayford Mountain, home of Larry Gibson and the site of the annual gathering of the Keepers of the Mountain, a network of people committed to ending mountaintop removal coal mining. This sign is also displayed at various direct action protests in West Virginia. Many activists cite the political system, which protects coal interests, as the biggest obstacle to creating real change in the region. This client-state relationship established so long ago still informs the political-economic arrangements of West Virginia today, to the detriment of state citizens and the Appalachian Mountains.

The coal industry has owned and controlled the state since the rise of industrialization in the nineteenth century, when coal owners moved in and seized control. Shirley Stewart Burns says, "The legacy of these acquisitions resounds today when more than two-thirds of the state's non-public land has been gobbled up by absentee landowners."[57] Focusing her study on the nine coalfield counties of West Virginia, the most distressed areas in all of Appalachia, Burns concludes that "since outside interests hold such a large amount of land in the nine-county sub-region, economic diversification is nearly non-existent there."[58] This thoroughly established pattern of ownership has resulted in increased poverty for residents, while billions of dollars in coal wealth has been transported out of the state. Chris Weiss, using the model of colonialism to assess this region's social and economic problems, asserts, "The experience in the Appalachians with land and mineral ownership patterns is that of colonial people everywhere. Outside ownership and control of natural resources prevent communities from having strong local economies."[59] It should be noted that other researchers replaced the colonialism model with the core-periphery model, developed by Immanuel Wallerstein and employed by Appalachian studies scholars such as Wilma A. Dunaway.[60] Nevertheless, this corporate hegemony thrives in West Virginia solely with the help of a state political system that ensures Big Coal's needs are met, regardless of the costs to the state's small communities. According to James O'Connor, this political-economic arrangement is endemic in capitalist economies where the state regulates the conditions of both production and distribution, and a pliable state apparatus is imperative to business interests. O'Connor says, "In terms of domestic policy, the state does little more than regulate capital's access to nature, space, land, and laborpower."[61] Indeed, state regulators in West Virginia, many of them former coal company employees, give various coal corporations carte blanche to conduct business in the state. Activists such as Ohio Valley Environmental Coalition member Maria Gunnoe have experienced the effects of this political-economic structure firsthand, particularly in encounters with the Department of Environmental Protection. Gunnoe says:

> The DEP is not there for the citizens, they're there for the coal companies, and they enable the coal companies. In some cases they even lie to the citizens in order to continue the work on the mountaintop removal site. I've been lied to many times. I've had five DEP agents stand and look at me and tell me an eroded mountain wasn't eroded. I have pictures and a lot of proof showing that it's eroded. It's like they were programmed to say—no matter what I said—that it was not eroded.[62]

In this climate, making coal companies more responsible to the communities in which they operate, and uplifting the social and economic conditions of West Virginians, has been quite difficult. However, activists continue to identify and resist the negative influence of the coal industry, while educating the public on the root causes of the destruction of the mountains and the culture of central Appalachia. Vivian Stockman, a member of the Ohio Valley Environmental Coalition, says, "It's so terribly important that we spread the word of mountaintop removal beyond Appalachia, because West Virginia's regulators and politicians seem so scared to stand up to the coal industry."[63]

The policies of the ruling elites in West Virginia are akin to those Michael Parenti defines in his discussion of the "comprador class," small groups of individuals residing in the "client state," who cooperate with outside economic interests at the expense of the majority of those occupying these regions:

> A client state is one that is open to investments on terms that are decidedly favorable to the foreign investors. In a client state, corporate investors enjoy direct subsidies and land grants, access to raw materials and cheap labor, light or nonexistent taxes, few effective labor unions, no minimum wage or child labor or occupational safety laws, and no consumer or environmental protections to speak of. The protective laws that do exist go largely unenforced.[64]

Although Parenti's discussion refers to the relationship between developing and developed countries, this model is a useful one when examining how the coal industry operates in the client state of West Virginia. The reality of this arrangement is not lost on many women fighting to end MTR and the negative influence of coal in West Virginia. Anti-MTR activist Pauline Canterbury claims the biggest obstacle to fighting MTR and the coal industry is "the state and federal government. Because all the way down the line they change the laws to protect them (coal operators) and not us. The laws are out there to protect us, but they won't abide by them, and the government doesn't make them abide by them. . . . If somebody gets ahold of something and they take it to court, then they change it. It's our government in Washington and in Charleston."[65] Despite this exploitative political-economic arrangement, some local residents, including many working-class women, continue to fight for social and environmental justice in the coalfields of southern West Virginia. Arguably, adverse material conditions precipitate the environmental justice activism of some working-class women in the state. This social phenomena is particularly noteworthy when considering how the structural component of gender has fruitfully served the coal industry over the years, and continues to be a tool used by Big Coal to maintain a committed and loyal male workforce.

Coalfield Gender Ideologies and Anti-MTR Activism in West Virginia

The coal-influenced political economy of West Virginia has uniquely influenced and utilized gender and family arrangements in the southern coalfields. Gender ideologies are particularly interesting in their connections to the material realities of women living in the area, and also in how they shape women's activism against mountaintop removal coal mining in the state. In the coalfields of West Virginia, working-class women's current anti-MTR activism is informed by the sexual division of labor that associates women with the private sphere of home and family, and men with the public arena of industrial work. Currently, some coalfield women seeking to save their homes, communities, cultural heritage, and the lush Appalachian environment from the ravages of the coal industry are influenced by entrenched gender ideologies shaped and solidified by coal in the region. However, these working-class women activists also challenge and defy separate spheres conventions through their work to end MTR. By participating in grassroots groups such as the Coal River Mountain Watch and the Ohio Valley Environmental Coalition, they publicly exert collective agency that can also be personally empowering.

In coal-rich sections of Appalachia, separate spheres ideology and its manifestation in the lives of real people existed prior to the industry's formation in the region, and some Appalachian scholars correctly note that these white, middle-class gender conventions were unavailable to the Native American, African American, and poor white women in Appalachia.[66] Regardless of their existence prior to the entrance of coal in West Virginia, the inherent class and race partialities in these social constructs, gender ideologies, and cultural notions of the best and most natural spaces for men and women became uniquely solidified with the rise of industrialization in the Western world, including in the coalfields of West Virginia.

When examining the historical roots of separate spheres ideology, Ann Crittenden argues that the social, political, and economic manifestation of these beliefs discouraged women from public participation and expanded their responsibilities within the home, while simultaneously sanctioning men's withdrawal from the domestic sphere.[67] Additionally, Crittenden reveals the intrinsic class bias connected to this gendered social construction by arguing that the cultural weight applied to domestic duties, particularly child-rearing, was more than just a "strategy to distract women from participating in public life. It was also necessary to the development of a vibrant capitalist economy. . . . The rising bourgeoisie understood that their children would have to become educated, motivated little achievers if they were going to improve or even maintain their station in life."[68] In short, the emphasis on this new family, and the roles men and women were to assume within this arrangement, was a way in which the burgeoning middle class could distinguish itself from working-class white families and families of color. This new family structure was viewed as a modern construct, signifying the progress and enlightenment of all those who conformed to its dictates. Judith Stacey argues this newly touted industrial family form became a powerful symbol for modernity, signifying a break from the largely agrarian, traditional past. She contends that in the United States,

> the modern family system arose in the nineteenth century when industrialization turned men into breadwinners and women into homemakers by separating paid work from households. Beginning first among white, middle-class people, this family pattern came to represent modernity and success. Indeed, the American way of life came to be so identified with this family form that the trade-union movement struggled for nearly a century to secure for male workers the material condition upon which it was based—the male breadwinner wage.[69]

As these modern gender ideologies and family arrangements gained traction in Western culture, many coalfield women retreated to the home, caring for husbands and children while becoming increasingly dependent upon male wages for material sustenance. Arguably, in rural areas such as the Appalachian coalfields, white middle-class social norms in gender and family were particularly influential, as many strived to conform to this model out of fear of being further seen as "backward" or "uncivilized" by those outside the region, particularly in urban areas of the country. Furthermore, these emerging ideas were utilized and emphasized by the coal industry to better control its workforce and ensure business success.

In particular, the formation of the "company town" in coalfield communities regulated and influenced the social and economic lives of residents, primarily through its use of nascent separate spheres ideologies. Over the years scholars have examined the coal camp system and its influence in Appalachian towns. John Alexander Williams, for example, has argued that these sparsely populated, remote rural areas dictated the formation of company towns where coal operators enjoyed "captive communities" to use in ways that best served their needs.[70] Williams notes how each town was segregated in terms of the race and nationality of families living in the coalfields, but does not note the dissimilar roles of women and men in these communities and how these differences were exploited by the industry.[71] Because gender is a fundamental but often overlooked social category, feminist redress of the absence of examinations of women's lives in the company town system is a crucial addition to the historical record. Mary Beth Pudup notes the importance of gender in family settlements in the coalfields, and the intrinsic economic necessity for these coal camp arrangements:

> Operators quickly learned that in a rural state like West Virginia providing housing for workers was a necessary complement to opening a mine. Operators eschewed options like housing miners in boardinghouses and paying another work force to provide services like cooking and laundry. Instead, operators both large and small chose to build company towns encouraging family settlement where wives would provide personal services to the work force. This strategy implicitly recognized the economic value of women's domestic labor.[72]

During this transformation, many West Virginia men entered the productive, public, albeit dirty and dangerous work of coal mining, gaining their cultural identity as hardworking patriarchs who risked their lives for the socioeconomic survival of their families. While men worked in exploited, unsafe working conditions, and received very little pay, they enjoyed autonomy, cultural privilege, and power at home, a sanctuary away from their public life as industrial workers. As some West Virginia women further retreated into the private sphere of home, the acceptable cultural identities as wives and mothers became more entrenched in coalfield culture. The value of women's domestic work to coal industry security and profitability are also noted by Janet W. Greene, who characterizes coal camps as women's workshops:

> Their primary work was critical to coal production: they fed the miner, washed his clothes, took care of him when sick or injured, and raised the children who would become the next generation of mineworkers. They added to the family income by performing domestic work for other families, produced goods for use in the home, and scavenged and bartered.[73]

Women's highly productive but unpaid labor for the coal industry is a fundamental component of its success in Appalachia. While some West Virginia women also worked for wages, particularly white working-class women and women of color, many public means of adequate employment were unavailable to coalfield women, and both their class and gender positions became increasingly compromised. Moreover, they received no sanctuary away from their work as wives and mothers of working-class coal miners. This arrangement served not only miners and coal operators but also early investors in this profitable resource extraction industry. Sally Ward Maggard suggests coalfield gender ideologies helped establish family patterns and systematize the coal industry in West Virginia, where coal towns had numerous "disciplined miners" and women who "provided the unpaid domestic work to support the miner labor force and increase profits for coal owners and stockholders," who, invariably, were located outside the state.[74]

While gender and family arrangements in the United States have changed since the early nineteenth century, with many more women working outside the home for wages and some men providing domestic care for their families, separate spheres ideology still has tremendous cultural and economic currency inside and outside of Appalachia. Drucilla K. Barker and Susan F. Feiner note that "despite its relatively short history, and the rather narrow cross section of the population to which the definition applies, its impact on society in the spheres of culture, politics, economics, and even psychology has been strong."[75] In sharper language, Judith Stacey highlights the idealistic nature of this family arrangement and the gendered ideology that supports it, revealing that current family systems are, in fact, much more diverse and complicated:

> The family indeed is dead, if what we mean by it is the modern family *system* in which units comprising male breadwinner and female homemaker, married couples, and their offspring dominate the land. But its ghost, the ideology of the family, survives to haunt the consciousness of all those who refuse to confront it. It is time to perform a social autopsy on the corpse of the modern family system so that we may try to lay its troublesome spirit to rest.[76]

In short, gendered social patterns have changed over the years, but these well-established, separate spheres notions about men, women, family, and work continue to inform the culture of West Virginia's coalfields. Coal operators capitalized on separate spheres ideology to influence coalfield cultural relations and increase profits when the coal industry first began operating in the state, and these ideas are still used to influence its workforce today. Mountaintop removal coal mining is a hotly contested practice in West Virginia, and some citizens work just as hard to protect Big Coal as anti-MTR activists do to stop it. Indeed, the controversy over mountaintop removal has taken the familiar path of job protection versus environmental protection, and many coalfield women choose sides in this divide while the coal industry continues to use gender to serve its own interests. Gender is particularly relevant when we consider how some middle-class and working-class women work to protect the coal industry in this era of mountaintop removal coal mining.

In 2007, the conservative West Virginia grassroots organization Friends of Coal incorporated a new weapon into its arsenal to promote the coal industry and educate the public about the industry's importance to West Virginia: the Friends of Coal Ladies Auxiliary. Friends of Coal (FOC) is a powerful front group for the West Virginia Coal Association (WVCA), even though they claim independence from the industry. For example, they use the same logo as the West Virginia Coal Association, and if one calls the number given on the FOC website to request "information or supplies," a secretary for the WVCA answers the phone. FOC is also financially supported by the WVCA and its corporate sponsors. Over the last decade, the presence and influence of Friends of Coal have strengthened, with frequent advertisements to promote the coal industry appearing on television and in local newspapers; on signs posted on residents' lawns and in the windows of local businesses; and on billboards, bumper stickers, T-shirts, and any number of places. They have inundated the region with pro-coal messages that are impossible to ignore. The FOC organization justifies its existence by asserting that West Virginia "finds itself in danger from environmental zealots," and the organization seeks to offer a "voice of reason" to the policy debates surrounding mountaintop removal coal mining, which they label "mountaintop mining," omitting "removal" to soften the public image of the practice.[77] Arguably, part of the success of this corporate front group is attributable to the ways in which it uses women to promote and protect the interest of the coal industry.

The FOC Ladies Auxiliary was initiated in 2007 by a "group of concerned women" in the private home of a Raleigh County woman.[78] According to the FOC website, the ladies auxiliary does not have "direct economic ties to coal companies," but works to "enhance the image of coal and combat some of the adverse publicity coal receives on a daily basis in the press and from many organized environmental groups."[79] The Ladies Auxiliary is self-described as an "unbiased group" whose mission is to "educate the public and raise the awareness of citizens to the benefits of coal" and its importance "as part of our national energy plan."[80] Perusing the scant amount of literature available on FOC and the Ladies Auxiliary (FOCLA) reveals that members are primarily middle-class white women whose husbands have ties to the coal industry. For example, Warren Hylton, husband of FOCLA member Patty Hylton, is a local businessman from a prominent Beckley, West Virginia, family. Warren Hylton, who recently received the Spirit of Beckley award, is described as a "business owner, civic leader, loving husband, father and advocate for the state's coal industry and its young people."[81]

FOCLA chairwoman Regina Fairchild is the wife of another Beckley businessman, J. D. Fairchild, director of sales and marketing at Terex Corporation, which produces coal mining machinery. His company recently participated in a 2009 elementary school educational campaign initiated by the FOCLA called "Coal in the Classroom."[82] The students at St. Francis elementary, a private school in Beckley, received weekly lessons on the coal industry for six weeks as part of FOCLA's educational outreach campaign. In addition to Fairchild, Billy Raney, president of the West Virginia Coal Association, spoke to the students about the importance of coal to West Virginia's economy and US energy policy. While this "Coal in the Classroom" began at a private school, it expanded into the public school system in late 2009.[83] Such educational programming is just one way in which the women relatives of coal professionals work to keep Big Coal thriving in the state. Regina Fairchild says:

> We know that the entire coal industry will benefit from an awareness we can provide in the local communities concerning coal and its role in our economic welfare. At this time, there are many special interest groups working actively to delete coal from future use. We feel it is more vital than ever to have an active, dedicated group who are willing to stand up and point out all the benefits of coal to both our nation and especially our state.[84]

This auxiliary, which is a fundamental component in the highly successful industry campaign to control the public message about coal and mountaintop removal in West Virginia, also expresses concerns over the momentum of environmental justice efforts to end MTR in the state.

While the West Virginia Coal Association relies on the work of middle-class women such as the members of the Friends of Coal Ladies Auxiliary to ensure coal's future in West Virginia, Massey Energy Corporation utilizes working-class women to ensure the loyalty of their workforce and promote the economic interests of the company in small communities throughout the coalfields. Massey Energy (now owned by Alpha Natural Resources), formerly headed by the controversial CEO Don Blankenship, is the largest producer of coal in central Appalachia, and the fourth-largest coal producer in the United States.[85] With 66 total coal mines (46 underground and 20 surface) in West Virginia, Virginia, and Kentucky, Massey reaped a $3 billion profit in 2009.[86] The company boasts 5,600 "Massey members" in central Appalachia, making them the largest private-sector employer in the region.[87] In the late 1980s Blankenship created a "Spousal Group," made up primarily of the wives of Massey coal miners, to serve on community projects throughout the region and promote the image of Massey Energy and coal throughout central Appalachia.[88]

On the Spousal Group page of Massey's website, the corporation claims "through the nature of their work, miners are a close community; cooperation, communication and trust are high priorities. Outside of the mines these same principles serve as the backbone of communities across Appalachia. At Massey, the spirit of community is also embodied by the Spousal Group."[89] The spouses of coal miners serve their local communities by engaging in "schoolbook fairs, local park improvements, senior citizen appreciation dinners and the annual Christmas Extravaganzas," among other activities.[90] Blankenship has reportedly given Spousal Groups millions of dollars over the years, viewing them as "the conduit through which these funds will be most effectively put to the best use in communities throughout our operating region."[91] By incorporating wives of coal miners and funding company-controlled and approved activities, worker solidarity and commitment is solidified, and the corporation retains a strong public profile across the coalfields. Some of these working-class Massey employee spouses view anti-MTR activists as environmental extremists, seditious "tree huggers" who are jeopardizing the economy and betraying the history of the state, and as a result these two forces have clashed in public places throughout the coalfields.

In June 2009, local environmental groups such as the Coal River Mountain Watch and the Ohio Valley Environmental Coalition, with the help of the Rainforest Action Network, staged a direct action protest at Marsh Fork Elementary School in Sundial, West Virginia, also home to many Massey coal mining operations.[92] This direct action was organized to protest mountaintop removal and coal's negative influence on the environment, particularly on climate change. The protest received national media attention, as keynote speakers included NASA climatologist James Hansen and actress/environmentalist Daryl Hannah, both arrested during the gathering. In response to this organized action, Massey CEO Don Blankenship gave many Massey employees the afternoon off from work to attend the protest and stand up for jobs and the coal industry in the region. The clash between environmental and labor interests was dramatically apparent as Massey coal miners, along with their spouses and children, staged a counterprotest at the site. Wearing the Massey-issued blue-and-orange work shirts, they chanted "Massey! Massey! Massey!" while carrying pro-Massey Energy signs. One woman's sign read "We Support Massey Energy and Massey Energy Supports Us," and another woman's read "We Love Our Coal Miners." Concern for their families and children were also displayed in another sign, "Our Families Work for Massey; Our Kids Go to This School."[93] In addition to the clash at this direct action protest, anti-MTR activists and coal miners and their supporters also collided on Kayford Mountain in Boone County during the annual July 4, 2009, Mountain Keepers Music Festival, sponsored by the Keepers of the Mountain Foundation, headed by Larry Gibson. Twenty pro-Massey residents crashed the festival, antagonizing guests with threats of violence. One angry spouse of a Massey employee expressed job security fears in the face of those critical of the industry by yelling, "You may have another way of livin', but we don't."[94]

For working-class women associated with Massey Energy miners, fighting for the coal industry is a way to protect the only opportunity to obtain livable wages for their families in the coalfields today. The middle-class FOC women seek to preserve their husbands' professional positions within this industry. Both groups are motivated by their immediate social and economic interests, and express no interest in the preservation of West Virginia's mountainous environment. As these women work to secure their class positions, secure their husbands' coal-related jobs, and promote Big Coal in West Virginia, they also symbolically embrace and conform to separate spheres ideology established long ago. Their focus on job preservation and coal industry stability is viewed as the best way to serve the interests of their families and coalfield communities. Unlike the working-class women in anti-MTR organizations, they do not defy separate spheres social confines and their connections to the industrial production of coal. In addition, the FOC women do not express environmental concerns, believing the coal industry to be good stewards of the Appalachian environment.

Carolyn E. Sachs, a premier scholar in rural and women's studies, explains the unstable situation between residents who seek to protect the natural environment and improve socioeconomic conditions for all citizens, and those who are dependent upon the offending industry and therefore fiercely protective:

> Regions dependent on mining and logging experience boom and bust cycles, high levels of poverty, and extreme sex segregation of jobs. Ownership of land and resources by outside corporate interests minimizes local control and local benefits. . . . Both the mining and timber industries increasingly substitute capital for labor, often with severe environmental consequences. These industries, attempting to increase profits, implement practices such as strip-mining and clear-cutting that result in extreme damage to the environment, rely on large-scale machinery, and use less labor than other types of mining and logging operations. Because jobs are closely tied to the exploitation of natural resources, environmental issues may be hotly contested in such communities.[95]

Anti-MTR activists are sympathetic with local residents' fears of unemployment, and most, like the FOC members and the Massey Energy supporters, have family ties to the coal industry. The targets of their activism have never been coal miners and their families, but rather the industry and the state politicians who support it. They are aware that to end the tenure of Big Coal, they have to appeal to local residents and promote alternative jobs for the coalfield economy, although this necessary coalition-building is extremely difficult when Big Coal CEOs such as Don Blankenship stoke the fires of this labor-environment conflict, playing on workers' job-loss fears.

The working-class women active in anti-MTR campaigns are influenced by traditional notions of distinct social spheres for men and women, particularly in their desire to protect their families, homes, and communities from damages wrought by MTR, yet they also challenge and transgress established coalfield gender ideologies by their very public environmental justice activism. These women are critical of the industry presence in the state, and seek to drive Big Coal from West Virginia by promoting the use of alternative energy sources. Their activism is socially, politically, and economically transgressive in that they use culturally sanctioned gender identities, such as their roles as mothers, wives, and daughters of Appalachia, in subversive, counterhegemonic ways. Rather than working for the benefit of coal-related jobs and the security of the coal industry in an era with rising environmental consciousness, they use gendered notions about women as a justification to change the political-economic hold Big Coal has on the region, to prevent the extinction of their communities, and to save the Appalachian Mountains from further devastation. They are like many women throughout the country, and indeed the world, who are active in community-based, environmental justice groups. When considering working-class women's activism against environmental problems in their communities, Celene Krauss has argued that ideologies of motherhood, in particular, have led to politicization of some environmental justice activists:

> Ideologies of motherhood, traditionally relegated to the private sphere, became political resources that these women used to initiate and justify their resistance and increasing politicization. Rejecting the separation of public and private arenas that renders invisible and insignificant the world of women's work, they developed a public, more politicized ideology of motherhood that became a resource to fight gender and class oppression.[96]

Krauss suggests that women working in environmental justice campaigns do not necessarily reject traditional ideologies of women and motherhood but, rather, reinterpret and redirect them into a source of social and political power.[97] While many of the anti-MTR activists are mothers who can be viewed as reinterpreting the traditional coalfield gender ideologies and redirecting them into political action, there are some anti-MTR activists who are not mothers or wives. Nevertheless, women, traditional gender ideologies, and political activism are frequently linked, and cited by many women activists when explaining the large presence of women in the movement. For example, former Coal River Mountain Watch codirector Judy Bonds said:

> It's a protection issue. . . . A woman just feels that she has to protect her children, and her grandchildren and her homeplace. And that's why there is so many women involved in this because we have that instinct inside of us and that stubborn streak and the convictions to protect. . . . Through the traditional people I've studied, the women has been the ones that managed things, that protected things, that basically did what they needed to do to protect their children. The mother hen syndrome.[98]

While Bonds's comments may strike some feminists as reducing women to their supposed maternal capacities, her activism ultimately challenges traditional notions of women and their place in the public, political arena. Bonds depicts anti-MTR activists as determined, driven women whose resistance is virtually an automatic reaction to the assaults on their homes and communities. Her use of the mother hen metaphor is particularly interesting, as she likens her female counterparts to fierce protectors of home and environment.

Coal River Mountain Watch member Patty Sebok uses similar metaphors when describing her commitment to protecting the community and standing up to the negative forces of coal: "I tell people . . . if you're in the woods and you see a bear and you see cubs, you know you better stay away from that mama bear. Well, I tell them I'm the proverbial mama bear."[99] Janice Nease, one of the charter members of the CRMW, also believes that many women are active in the anti-MTR movement because, unlike the women protecting the immediate interests of the coal industry in organizations such as the Friends of Coal, and through Massey Energy's Spousal Groups, women environmental justice activists "see the broad picture and the long picture. They have this long view of what's going to happen to their children, and . . . they can see ahead."[100] Nease's comments arise from concerns for the lasting social, economic, and environmental costs of coal in West Virginia.

Most members of OVEC, CRMW, and other grassroots anti-MTR groups are not only working-class white and Cherokee women—many of them wives, mothers, and grandmothers—but women whose homes and communities have been directly impacted by MTR operations. Some have no prior political experience; however, others have participated in regional reform efforts such as labor activities associated with the United Mine Workers of America Union. Some anti-MTR activists did not participate in past labor activist activities but joined these organizations because of environmental concerns. Anti-MTR activism also has a vigorous youth base, with many college students from the larger Appalachian region, both women and men, active in the fight to end MTR. Regardless of the various backgrounds of the grassroots women activists, all are involved to protect their communities, to promote alternative energy sources, to diversify the economy, and to preserve West Virginia's rich cultural heritage, which is inextricably tied to the mountainous geography. Some scholars suggest that rural women's material conditions and lack of economic opportunity have increased their political activism at the grassroots level and also reflect their strong ties to rural communities. Ann R. Tickamyer and Debra A. Henderson suggest that "the primary opportunities for and targets of women's activism often are in grassroots responses to the realities of their communities and livelihoods," particularly in the areas of "sustainable agriculture, conservation, and environmental movements."[101]

Women activists in West Virginia are engaged in formidable confrontations with the political economic power structure in the state. Despite the redoubtable power of this opposition, they keep their collective focus on community preservation foremost in group activities. When considering how her environmental justice activism helps the local community, Patty Sebok says she seeks to "turn it around so that we can have sustainable communities, save our water supply, clean up the air, and . . . we'd like to see some changes in the economics around here. . . . We want to save our communities; we want sustainable communities. . . . We want jobs."[102] Judy Bonds suggested that if "the community and the state would listen to what we say, we would already be reaping the rewards of a diverse economy. . . . What we're trying to do is force the state to quit being corrupt, quit being raped by the coal industry, stop helping the coal industry rape the state of West Virginia and the people and our children."[103] Another Coal River Mountain Watch member, Sarah Haltom, considers educating the community, particularly those who are apathetic, to be the most important aspect of her environmental justice activism, because "as hardheaded as people are, they're still seeing it; they're still hearing about it. If they see and hear about it long enough, they'll start to form their own opinions and jump off the fence, take a side."[104] The women involved in the fight to end MTR are committed activists, living in a region rich in natural resources but with limited social and economic opportunities for its citizens—particularly women. They possess a critical point of view that envisions life without coal in West Virginia. Considering the history and power of this industry in West Virginia, these women's collective activism to end the coal industry's negative influence, rather than to preserve it, is transformative and progressive.

Conclusion

Residents in the coalfields of southern West Virginia have long existed in a coal sacrifice zone as this fossil fuel has been extracted from the region. However, one could argue that the total sacrifice of the human and nonhuman communities, air, water, and land of central Appalachia that has occurred with the advent of the mountaintop removal coal mining technique has been more pronounced than in previous decades, with the region now compromised beyond repair. Noted West Virginia novelist Denise Giardina says bluntly, "Mountaintop removal is evil, and those who support it are supporting evil.... I puzzle over the modern-day difference between a terrorist and someone who supports mountaintop removal. One destroys with a bomb, the other with a fountain pen, dynamite, and a dragline. God help us."[105]

While some West Virginia women support the coal industry because of the jobs it provides in an area with few options for meaningful employment, others, particularly those whose homes have been sacrificed for cheap energy, join environmental justice organizations to stop MTR and end coal's tenure in West Virginia. Anti-MTR activists connect these social and political concerns to the preservation of Appalachia's mountains. In short, they link socioeconomic inequities to the destruction of their communities and natural environment. These activists are cognizant of both the exploitative features of the political economy of coal in Appalachia and its connection to the global environment. They are representative of many women who form or join environmental justice groups throughout the country and the world. Even though many scholars have noted that women constitute the majority of members in environmental justice groups in the United States, additional attention to their contributions by environmental justice scholars is needed. Also, environmental justice theory and activism have focused primarily on toxic pollution in urban communities of color. By highlighting the importance of gender, and focusing my analysis on impoverished rural communities in the coalfields of central Appalachia, this study widens the focus of existing environmental justice scholarship.

CHAPTER 2

Gender and Anti–Mountaintop Removal Activism: Expanding the Environmental Justice Framework

> One of the things that's really, really hard for the coal industry to accept is that a lot of us are still here . . . and we refuse to leave, and we tell. The things that we see here, we tell. . . . It would be a lot easier for them if we weren't here, if we would just die or disappear or move away.
>
> —Lorelei Scarbro

Introduction

LORELEI SCARBRO, FORMER MEMBER OF THE COAL River Mountain Watch, is one of many coalfield women who bear witness to the harmful impacts of coal operations on their communities and the natural environment. She is also among many women who work tirelessly for social, economic, and environmental sustainability and the future of the coalfield region of Appalachia. Women like Scarbro stand their ground and refuse to leave their mountain communities, despite the potential health hazards that have prompted many residents to relocate to safer areas in West Virginia. Scarbro, who joined the CRMW in 2007, is a proud West Virginian with Cherokee ancestry who was raised in rural Lincoln County. Her father was a coal miner and her mother a stay-at-home mom. Growing up in central Appalachia, Lorelei's family raised animals and grew vegetable gardens, harvesting and preserving food from their mountainous environment. In the summer the family made annual recreation treks to nearby rivers where they spent their vacations. She is deeply connected to the Appalachian environment and coalfield communities.

Shortly after graduating from high school, Scarbro married a California man and moved to Arizona, where she lived for nine years. During her years in Arizona, Scarbro never adjusted to desert surroundings and was always homesick for the mountains of West Virginia. When her marriage ended in 1989, she boarded a plane "with thirteen suitcases, three children, and my fourth on the way,"[1] to begin a new life in her familiar mountain environment. Over the years, this return to West Virginia life included raising her children, remarrying, and becoming vigorously active in public school initiatives.

Scarbro says, "When my kids went to school, I went to school." She engaged in local education politics and was a particularly vocal advocate for small, rural schools in the coalfields. Lorelei served on the PTO board as well as various "parent-school governing boards," and was a member of the Local School Improvement Council. In 2001, when the state threatened to close rural schools in her community, including Clear Fork and Marsh Fork High Schools, she joined the Citizens Preserving Marsh Fork and Clear Fork Committee, where she met anti-MTR activist Judy Bonds. Because public schools are central institutions in rural communities, some residents highlight the links between mountaintop removal coal mining, depopulation in the coalfields, public health, and the fate of local schools in their campaigns for environmental justice. When considering the population decline in some coalfield areas, Scarbro claims that in the early days of MTR, coal companies offered buyouts to residents, but today they just "poison the air and the water," making it difficult for residents to remain in their homes and to stay healthy. She links the increase in MTR, the population decline, and the fate of local schools by asserting: "As we depopulate the communities, enrollment declines; and when the enrollment declines, they can justify closing the schools that are not right in town. There's a social engineering thing that's going on here."

Once her children graduated from school, Scarbro became active in the anti-MTR movement, applying her experience in educational advocacy to this environmental justice movement. She says, "The more you become aware of what's going on around you, the more outraged you get. . . . I learned very, very quickly that if you see something that's wrong, if you dig long enough, and if you look in the right places, and talk to the right people, there's a good possibility that there's something you can do about it. That you're not totally powerless." She turned this recognition into political action by bearing witness to the social and environmental destructiveness of mountaintop removal coal mining and fighting for coalfield justice.

Women like Lorelei Scarbro who organize or join grassroots efforts to end MTR in Appalachia are representative of the larger social phenomenon of women's participation in environmental justice activism. Around the country and worldwide, poor women, working-class white women, and women of color respond collectively to threats on their homes and communities. Too often the tireless efforts of these women go unnoticed by environmental justice analyses. This is a troubling omission considering the sheer numbers of women involved in such campaigns, and that most EJ organizations emerge because women make these issues public in their communities.[2] Environmental justice has, over its thirty-five-year history, highlighted the ways in which human differences based on race and class are connected to the environment, but EJ has done a less than adequate job of highlighting the role of gender in both the effects of and the responses to social and environmental injustices.[3] This chapter reviews the historical environmental justice focus on race and class, and expands the EJ framework by centralizing gender in this analysis of women's involvement in the movement to end mountaintop removal coal mining in Appalachia. My analysis focuses strictly on environmental justice in the United States. Global connections to EJ, including women's participation, are explored in chapter 5. In examining the gendered articulations inherent in campaigns to end MTR in rural, largely white, coalfield communities, I strategically situate this evolving movement within environmental justice praxis.

Race, Class, Gender, and Anti–Mountaintop Removal Activism: Expanding the Environmental Justice Framework

In 2007, environmental scholars and practitioners debated the merits of the controversial *Break Through: From the Death of Environmentalism to the Politics of Possibility*, which poses a reenvisioning of environmental thought and practice to confront problems related to climate change. The book, born from the 2004 essay "The Death of Environmentalism: Global Warming Politics in a Post-Environmental World," ignited a firestorm in environmental circles upon its release. Authors Ted Nordhaus and Michael Shellenberger, career Washington strategists for mainstream environmental organizations, argue that the old environmental paradigm of regulation and conservationism is insufficient in addressing climate change: "The challenge of climate change is so massive, so global, and so complex that it can be overcome only if we look beyond the issue categories of the past and embrace a grand new vision for the future."[4] For some environmental justice advocates, this text appeared a welcome critical examination of the shortcomings of the regulatory approach of mainstream American environmentalism, which EJ has consistently critiqued, along with its failure to link social justice and environmentalism. However, the promise of *Break Through* is ultimately negated by its dismissal of environmental justice thought and practice, which the authors place in the category of special interests.

The issue categories in question for Nordhaus and Shellenberger are "rights-based liberalism"—feminism, civil rights, labor, and environmentalism—which they critique as "special interests" and an "old politics" that is no longer useful because "the world has changed in profound ways, but liberal interest groups have not."[5] Furthermore, they claim this "special interests" focus in American environmentalism prohibits the formation of the broad coalitions necessary to secure environmental change. At the outset, Nordhaus and Shellenberger curiously invoke Martin Luther King Jr.'s "I Have a Dream" speech by channeling its inspirational spirit to position their "breakthrough" as choices between "a politics of limits and a politics of possibility; a focus on investment and assets and a focus on regulation and deficits; and a discourse of affluence and a discourse of insecurity. And, most of all, we must choose between a resentful narrative of tragedy and a grateful narrative of overcoming."[6] In short, they argue for a transition to a clean energy economy where capitalist investment and innovation take concrete form in this "politics of possibility."

Unfortunately for environmental justice scholars and practitioners, Nordhaus and Shellenberger's directive to break the shackles of "special interests" in their plan to combat climate change assumes that under this new configuration, all people would have access to clean and healthy surroundings, similarly experiencing nature, or the environment, which in Rachel Stein's definition is "where we live, work, and play."[7] Moreover, this "breakthrough" presupposes that all people, regardless of race, class, gender, nationality, and so forth, will automatically have an equal part in the decision-making process in the transition to a green economy. Such equity should not be assumed without epistemologies that recognize the influence of political and economic structures of power on both nature's and society's most vulnerable populations. Other environmentalists have cautioned that a transition to a greener infrastructure in the United States must also be mindful of social justice. To avoid the social and environmental injustices associated with the creation and maintenance of the fossil fuel paradigm, we must ensure that society's most disadvantaged are a fundamental part of the creation of a green economy and beneficiaries of the positive outcomes promised by these initiatives. One of the most vigorous proponents of a national transition from a nonrenewable to renewable energy infrastructure, Van Jones, reveals the varied importance of social and environmental equity under a green economy:

> The task at hand is not just to win equal protection from the worst of global warming and the other negative effects that go hand in hand with ecological disaster. It is also to win equal opportunity and equal access to the bounty of the green economy, with its manifold positive opportunities. . . . If the architects of the green economy honor the principle of equal opportunity, they can also deliver help and hope to those who most need new jobs, new investments, and new opportunities.[8]

With their rejection of environmental justice as an impediment to the realization of this "politics of possibility," Nordhaus and Shellenberger fundamentally reject the connection between social justice and the environment. Without such an inclusive conceptual model, their celebrated "breakthrough" risks replicating social divisions based on race, class, gender, and so forth and hastening environmental degradation in this transition to a green economy.

A wholesale misrepresentation and dismissal of EJ thought and praxis by critics like Nordhaus and Shellenberger fails to credit the tremendous influence of environmental justice on American environmentalism. Furthermore, it negates EJ's potential at a time when neoliberal capitalism and an ineffectual environmental regulatory system exacerbate social and environmental problems. EJ's emphasis on how issues of human justice are connected to environmental justice is most crucial in this age of rapid climate change and massive disparities in income distributions throughout the world. When assessing the achievements of environmental justice, David Naguib Pellow and Robert J. Brulle claim that EJ has succeeded in framing and redefining "environmental concerns as civil rights, social justice, and human rights issues" to the point where most major environmental organizations and government agencies who focus on environmental protection cannot ignore "the issue of social equity."[9] Furthermore, EJ makes it extremely difficult for waste-management businesses to open incinerators and landfills without political contention. Pellow and Brulle also claim that, perhaps most important, EJ has broadened and redefined what constitutes the "environment" and "which populations exhibit environmental concerns."[10] These achievements of the environmental justice movement go unnoticed by Nordhaus and Shellenberger.

The authors level vigorous criticism at environmental justice scholars and practitioners, accusing the movement of exaggerating claims of environmentally compromised communities with EJ's long-standing focus on "environmental racism."[11] They claim the movement has "won no significant new environmental laws or any major civil rights legal challenges," and accuse EJ scholars and activists of suggesting that "corporate villains are deliberately poisoning communities of color—thereby committing genocide—by siting polluting facilities in poor and minority neighborhoods."[12] Like other critiques of the environmental justice movement, Nordhaus and Shellenberger take issue with the notion of "intent" and the deliberate targeting of minority communities. This focus on intent lacks an understanding of the systematic arrangements of capital and business and how these partnerships consistently impact communities of color and white working-class communities in disadvantageous ways. While one may not have a smoking gun that points to the deliberate targeting of a specific community of color by an offending business, many corporations, in order to expand and make profits, automatically target vulnerable populations as part of a de facto operational procedure. Environmental justice scholar Daniel R. Faber elaborates on this process:

> In order to bolster profits and competitiveness, businesses typically adopt strategies for the exploitation of nature that offer the path of least political resistance (and therefore the greatest opportunity for continued economic success). The less political power a community of people possesses; the fewer resources a community has to defend itself with; the lower the level of community awareness and mobilization against potential ecological threats; the more likely they are to experience arduous environmental and human health problems at the hands of capital and the state.[13]

In addition to questioning corporate intent and the targeting of minority communities, Nordhaus and Shellenberger claim that "disproportionate environmental health outcomes" cannot be attributed to intentional discrimination any more than "disproportionate economic and educational outcomes," which are due to a broader and more "complex set of historic, economic, and social causes."[14] Unfortunately, they fail to acknowledge that environmental justice is primarily based on exposing the complex connections between social and environmental injustice. Here, too, their analysis lacks an understanding of the systematic arrangements of business and capital and their impact on vulnerable communities. While rejecting the links between social and environmental justice, the authors dismiss environmental justice as being "anti-ecological."[15] They assert that "race-based environmentalism is a case study in how the *anti-ecological* logic of interest-group liberalism constricts rather than expands our concerns, and becomes complaint based—all of which make it poorly suited to dealing with large, complex, and deeply rooted social and ecological problems."[16]

The authors' critique of environmental justice exposes a shallow understanding of the historical and epistemological scaffolding that guides EJ practice. Far from being "anti-ecological," the environmental justice movement's greatest contribution is the assertion that communities suffering environmental problems such as contaminated air and water, unsafe housing, and so forth are likely experiencing entrenched socioeconomic problems as well. Thus, EJ theory and praxis seek to raise awareness about these connections and create strategies for improving conditions in disenfranchised areas. Environmental justice presents a holistic and richly complex "way of seeing" that also makes connections between the problems impacting a particular community in one location and problems similarly affecting communities across the United States and the world.[17] The ability of environmental justice to adapt to changing conditions, and to foster a greater sense of inclusion in terms of the populations and issues it confronts, is at the heart of current debates about environmental justice.

While mainstream environmentalists such as Nordhaus and Shellenberger promote the demise of environmental justice, some scholars encourage its expansion. For example, Julie Sze and Jonathan K. London have argued that as environmental justice adapts to include new populations of people and new environments, it must also maintain its "basic orientation," which is a "critical analysis of power as it plays out in the (mal)distribution of harms and opportunities related to the environment with special attention to race and class."[18] They suggest that environmental justice is currently situated at a "crossroads," a time to assess and find new ways of progressing in this era of globalization and climate change.[19] Far from being a "narrative of tragedy," environmental justice seeks to raise awareness about the connections between social and environmental injustice and, most important, to create transformative changes in afflicted communities, protecting the natural environment, and human health while creating increased socioeconomic opportunities for disenfranchised populations.

Recent calls for the expansion of the environmental justice purview arise as practitioners reflect on EJ's history and measure environmental and social needs in this era of global climate change. To understand the current state of the environmental justice movement, it is important to review specific historical points. Environmental justice, as a more inclusive, oppositional redress of the exclusionary nature of mainstream environmentalism, is rooted in civil rights thought and practice, and also in indigenous populations' concerns over the impact of colonialism.[20] These concerns and resolutions to raise awareness and resist social and environmental inequities by members of vulnerable communities are contained in the "Principles for Environmental Justice" presented at the 1991 First National People of Color Environmental Leadership Summit.[21] Because of these origins, race is a central and essential part of environmental justice thought and action. Connections to civil rights and indigenous concerns were made prior to the signing of these summit principles in the highly influential 1987 report *Toxic Wastes and Race*, produced by the United Church of Christ.[22] This study concluded that race (separate from class) is the most significant factor in decision-making processes that locate environmentally damaging businesses in vulnerable communities.[23] The report gave rise to the term "environmental racism," coined by Reverend Benjamin Chavis as a framing device for environmental justice.[24] In reflecting on the movement's racial history, EJ scholars Bunyan Bryant and Elaine Hockman suggest that while environmental justice was born out of the civil rights movement, and deeply rooted in African American history, it has encompassed a large segment of people from variously disenfranchised communities:

> Many EJM [environmental justice movement] activists began as civil rights activists, and they have brought with them their CRM [civil rights movement] organizing skills and experiences. Others moved to the EJM from the Chicano/Latino, Asian-American, Native American, or union movements. Issues of class struggle and racism were imported into the EJM.... The composition of the EJM adds another level of complexity in working effectively across cultural lines. In this movement, perhaps for one of the few times in American history, leadership by people of color—particularly at the local and regional levels—has brought together groups from a variety of racial and ethnic backgrounds to address social and environmental concerns that affected their communities.[25]

Luke Cole and Sheila Foster echo Bryant's account of the origins of this movement, and argue against an "incident-focused" history, or a history that cites a particular event situated in a particular space, such as Love Canal or Warren,

North Carolina, as the beginning of environmental justice.[26] Foster and Cole assert that EJ's development is more akin, metaphorically, to a river "fed over time by many tributaries."[27] These EJ scholars cite the civil rights movement, the anti-toxics movement, academics, Native American struggles, the labor movement, and traditional environmentalists as being the primary tributaries feeding this environmental justice river.[28] Regardless of whether we highlight civil rights, antitoxics, or indigenous struggles in our historical understanding of environmental justice, we must recognize that race has been a major framing device for EJ thought and activism, and people of color have been at the forefront of this movement.

In addition to solidifying the role of race in EJ's history, ideologies, and activism, the United Church of Christ *Toxic Wastes and Race* report has also fostered vigorous dialogue over the last twenty-three years about whether race or class is the common denominator of environmental injustice. In effect, have communities suffered social and environmental problems because they are poor, and/or because a particular area is primarily populated by people of color? Environmental justice scholars David Naguib Pellow and Robert J. Brulle suggest that environmental justice has "often focused so heavily on environmental racism as to exclude considerations of environmental inequality by class within communities of color. . . . There are scores of environmental justice conflicts that one simply cannot explain by reducing the cause solely to racism."[29] Pellow and Brulle say these "race versus class" debates have produced "methodological advances" in the study of environmental inequality and racism, but fail to realize that "environmental injustice is, and has always been, about both race and class."[30] Indeed, social identities and injustices, and their connections to the environment, are context-specific, taking shape in the environment, history, culture, and populations of a particular place in certain historical moments. It is the work of environmental justice scholars to delineate the significant social identities of environmental justice actors, as well as their connections to environmental risk in certain communities.

Environmental justice scholars Julie Sze and Jonathan K. London embrace a pluralistic, expanding environmental justice. Sze and London argue against imposing restrictive boundaries around "the concepts of environmental justice," suggesting that "scholarship in this emerging field should embrace its wide-ranging and integrative character, while remaining grounded in its political and theoretical projects to address the sources and impacts of social power disparities associated with the environment."[31] Sze and London claim that while fruitfully positioned at a "crossroads," the movement has recently expanded to include "new populations and problems, and new places and sites of analysis—specifically the relationship between the local and the global."[32] Perhaps one way of coalescing this multi-issue and multi-ethnic racial and national constituency focus, while also considering new places, is to center a critique of global capitalism and how it contributes to adverse social, political, cultural, economic, and environmental conditions for the most vulnerable populations in the world, from the Niger Delta to the coalfields of West Virginia. A critique of capitalism and its effects on the natural world could highlight the ways in which social divisions based on race, class, gender, and so forth are linked to capitalist processes, and how capitalism impacts the natural world.

David Naguib Pellow and Robert J. Brulle contend, "The use of natural resources continues to increase, regardless of the consequences on the sustainability of the ecosystem. The social result is that inequalities increase and working-class populations receive less and less material benefit from their labor. Thus, both ecological disorganization and race and class inequalities are inherent by-products of the social order."[33] Particularly in this current age of neoliberal capitalism, when climate change is threatening the life of the planet and divisions between the wealthiest and the most impoverished nations and people are increasing, it is important to situate environmental problems and social inequality within the dictates of late capitalism. This theoretical configuration has the greatest potential to address the root causes of social and environmental problems and ameliorate them. John Bellamy Foster argues:

> Capitalist economies are geared first and foremost to the growth of profits, and hence to economic growth at virtually any cost—including the exploitation and misery of the vast majority of the world's population. This rush to grow generally means rapid absorption of energy and materials and the dumping of more and more wastes into the environment—hence widening environmental degradation.[34]

Foster's claims ask us to consider the root causes of both human immiseration and environmental degradation as moored in the expansionist logic of global capitalism. This way of framing the correlations between human and environmental injustice is a workable theoretical underpinning to guide environmental justice activism. Daniel Faber suggests that an attempt to "rectify distributional inequities without attacking the fundamental processes that produce the problems in the first place focuses on symptoms rather than causes and is therefore only a partial, temporary, and necessarily incomplete and insufficient solution."[35] A critical environmental justice that is grounded in considerations of global capitalism and its impact on the natural environment and social world offers the greatest possibility to recognize the roots of both environmental and social problems and to offer more-just solutions.

As revealed in this brief discussion, environmental justice scholarship has done a tremendous job of emphasizing the importance of race, class, and nationality and their relationship to the environment. However, environmental justice has been less effective in examining how gender is connected to EJ. For example, the canon of environmental justice scholarship infrequently acknowledges the activism and importance of women in the environmental justice movement. Some EJ collections published during the past fifteen years contain the token essay about gender and its connection to environmental justice, but very few collections, and only one full-length book with a specific gender focus, exist.[36] This is surprising and unfortunate, considering that women make up 90 percent of the memberships in environmental justice groups around the country.[37] Also, biologically and socially, women are differently impacted by environmental problems. For these reasons a gendered analysis of environmental justice movements, including efforts to end mountaintop removal coal mining in Appalachia and promote the use of clean energy sources, is urgently relevant.

According to the environmental historian Nancy C. Unger, "Gender matters profoundly in environmental justice history, but understanding the role it has played is frequently lost in the sea of other influential factors including politics, and the law, and more recently, in the emphasis on race and poverty that dominates so much of the work in the field."[38] Throughout its history in the United States, poor women of color and poor white women have occupied the front lines of environmental justice activism. For example, the two major sites some consider birthplaces of the EJ movement in the US, Love Canal in New York and Warren, North Carolina, gave rise to campaigns that were spearheaded by local women and aimed at responding to toxics dumped by chemical companies in these communities. In Love Canal, Lois Gibbs and Debbie Cerrillo, who headed the Love Canal Home Owners Association, brought the largely white, working-class, suburban neighborhood's toxic past, and its impact on residents, to national attention.[39] In Warren, North Carolina, Dolly Burwell spoke out against the environmental injustice she witnessed in her rural, working-class, African American community.[40] These women are historical examples of the melding of race, class, gender, and environmental activism at the grassroots level, and many women like them are active in thousands of environmental justice groups throughout the country today, including in the coalfields of Appalachia.

These are the women Robert D. Bullard and Damu Smith call the "unsung heroes" of EJ, representing the "heart and soul of the modern environmental justice movement" while providing a "vision for environmentalism in the new millennium."[41] Rachel Stein, editor of the only existing collection of essays that examine the connections between gender, sexuality, and environmental justice activism, stresses the primary motivation for women's involvement in EJ campaigns:

> Because environmental ills strike *home* for vulnerable communities, and because women have often been responsible for that domain, women engage in these movements in order to protect and restore the well-being of families and communities threatened by environmental hazards or deprived of natural resources needed to sustain life and culture.[42]

Some women environmental justice activists who seek social justice and the protection of their homes and communities from environmental hazards frequently have little history of activism, but are propelled into political action because of direct assaults on their homes and communities. For example, anti-MTR activists Judy Bonds and Maria Gunnoe were propelled into political action because of direct assaults on their homes and communities. Other women, such as Lorelei Scarbro, apply prior advocacy experience in the civil sector to environmental justice campaigns.

When assessing the importance of women's environmental justice activism, Giovanna Di Chiro notes:

> Women active in the EJM contest and redefine discourses and practices of not only environmentalism but also of gender, racial, and class stereotyping. . . . Many women in the movement evoke deep concerns about the health and future survival of their children and communities when explaining their initial or continued involvement in fighting for environmental justice.[43]

Women working to end mountaintop removal coal mining in Appalachia express a desire to keep their families, community, and natural environment safe and healthy for present and future generations. Their activism conveys an ethics of care that mobilizes action, signifying a robust commitment to environmental justice.

Many Appalachian women participating in the anti-MTR movement became alarmed by the magnitude of MTR, and have dealt firsthand with its negative effects on their homes. Janice Nease, one of the charter members of the Coal River Mountain Watch and a retired Spanish teacher, formed the organization (along with Randy Sprouse and Freda Williams) to save the community where generations of her family have lived.[44] Nease, like Lorelei Scarbro, was active in public school politics in her community before organizing an environmental justice group to fight mountaintop removal coal mining.[45] Nease says she discovered in 1998 that coal operators were "doing it [MTR] on the mountain behind the house where I was born and raised. . . . And I was so shocked. And then I heard some people talk about what was happening, you know, to them personally, and I just, I was so riled I couldn't sleep that night."[46] She has been involved in the anti-MTR movement since her discovery. Judy Bonds, another early participant, recounted that shortly after Massey Energy began coal operations near her home in Marfork, West Virginia, she noticed these changes to her environment:

> white, gooey stuff on the bottom of the water, and then there was fish kills in which kids, my cousin's kids, and my own grandson, you know, were standing in the stream and found these dead fish. Then I started to notice as my neighbors moved out, there was coal trucks running constantly and it just devalued our property, our quality of life. . . . I was afraid for my family. I became angry. I became frustrated because I couldn't find any help.[47]

Bonds turned to the Coal River Mountain Watch in 1999 and joined the nascent anti-MTR movement. She had no prior activism experience but became one of the most visible faces in the anti-MTR movement. Winning the international Goldman Environmental Prize just four years after joining this organization reveals how publicly connected to this issue Bonds became.[48]

Patty Sebok, also a member of the Coal River Mountain Watch, has a long history of political activism, beginning with the United Mine Workers of America Union labor disputes of the 1980s, in which she supported coal miners during the Pittston strike.[49] Patty has also participated in impromptu, women-organized human chain roadblocks to stop the destructive force of coal trucks on the small roads in her community. She joined the CRMW in 2001, primarily out of concerns about coal truck traffic in her small town of Prenter, West Virginia, and a strong need to protect her family against the destructive forces of coal: "I knew, living here, that there was mountaintop removal, but I had no idea of the large scale and how bad it was, and all the things that come with it. . . . I found out later that the coal trucks were part of mountaintop removal because the mines are so far up in the mountains that the only way they can get the coal out is to truck it."[50]

Activists such as these women educate themselves on environmental issues, the intertwined workings of business, capital, and the heady maze of environmental politics. Theirs is frequently a "trial by fire" education acquired while organizing campaigns against offending coal companies. In the process they gain invaluable knowledge that assists their fight against companies and governments that create environmental hazards in their communities. Sarah Haltom, an artist and member of the Coal River Mountain Watch, highlights an increasing awareness about environmental issues when discussing her experiences with the anti-MTR movement in West Virginia:

> I knew it [MTR] was wrong the first time I saw it, and I thought, Wow, this is where I want to stay for the rest of my life, and if I don't do something, you know, I won't be able to. . . . That's kind of where my brain was at, at first. But since then it's become such a bigger issue. . . . I see it more as an entire global society issue now. . . . For the greed of many, and for the overconsumption of many, people are suffering. . . . I feel like I've gotten an education in the past year that I couldn't have gotten from college.[51]

Women such as Scarbro, Haltom, Nease, Bonds, and Sebok are very similar to other women environmental justice activists in their motivations for participating in local environmental justice campaigns. Whether situated in an urban area, the desert Southwest, or the Appalachian Mountains, these women fight to save their homes, communities, and environment from the polluting forces of industry.

Through this process of pinpointing problems, obtaining new information, and making the decision to become politically involved, environmental justice activism allows individual women and their groups to speak for themselves, self-representing in their struggles to eliminate social and environmental injustices in their communities. Members gain individual benefits from such work while simultaneously improving their communities. As Luke W. Cole and Sheila R. Foster remind us:

Residents in embattled communities both build upon their knowledge of their communities' environmental problems and acquire knowledge about the substantive and procedural aspects of environmental decision making. Their home-grown, and acquired, expertise empowers local residents and helps them to develop a grassroots base to influence environmental decision making. The community is transformed by the grassroots environmental justice groups established in the midst of environmental struggles. These groups help to transform marginal communities from passive victims to significant actors in environmental decision-making processes.[52]

Since the 1970s, women's participation in environmental protest has increased, despite the apparent neglect in assessing women's grassroots action by those who study environmental activism.[53] The centrality of gender to environmental justice thought and practice is an important part of the movement's history and its current configuration. Gender is at the heart of the anti-MTR movement in Appalachia, both in the membership of groups fighting MTR and in some campaigns created to raise awareness about the social and environmental hazards of coalfield life in this age of MTR.

Gendered Articulations of Home, Community, and Environmental Justice: The Sylvester Dustbusters and the Pennies of Promise Campaign

Women's participation in the movement to end mountaintop removal coal mining reveals a firm commitment to creating sustainable mountain communities for present and future generations. When discussing their involvement in anti-MTR activism and visions for sustainability, gendered and environmental articulations of women's participation rest on the ideological and material realities of "body," "home or household," and "community." Geographers Susan Buckingham and Rakibe Kulcur have also noted that theoretical and methodological frameworks analyzing environmental injustice have focused primarily on race and class while neglecting gender. They argue:

No society is one-dimensionally exclusive: a society which is racist and classist is likely also to be sexist and to marginalize others by age, disability or frailty. It is not enough, then, for any analysis to focus on a limited number of components of environmental injustice without an acknowledgement of wider structures of power and prejudice.[54]

Buckingham and Kulcur suggest that environmental justice theory can incorporate gender analyses by focusing on conceptions of the "body" and "household," and the ways in which they connect to larger notions of "community" and the natural world. They posit the private home, the community, and county, state, and national politics as "scales" that are imbricated and interconnected with the natural environment.[55] These associations are crucial in making the ever-important links between the local, national, and global, and also provide an effective lens through which to study the relationship between gender and environmental justice. In examining how these geographies are gendered, Buckingham and Kulcur note that extremely local positionalities such as the household cannot be detached from other broader social scales and dimensions, including those of politics, government, and business practices.[56] In effect, the private household is directly related to the public and the natural environment in complex and not so apparent ways, and gender is a central element in these connections. Buckingham and Kulcur assert that women's location in the nexus of the private household and public configuration of community brings them "into direct contact with polluting activities, and necessitates a navigation between the needs and health of the cared for, economics, time, and environmental considerations."[57] They also suggest that by examining women's environmental justice activism through focusing on the body and its links to broader configurations of household and community, we can more richly explore the gendered articulations of grassroots responses to jeopardized environments.

Buckingham and Kulcur also assert that the body is a gendered place in that both men and women are susceptible to health problems associated with contaminated environments, but men and women experience environmental problems differently. For example, women's bodies have higher fat ratios than male bodies, and because many dioxins dissolve in fat, women are particularly vulnerable to the accumulation of chemicals.[58] Furthermore, as Linda L. Layne reports, women potentially pass these toxins on to their fetuses and/or children.[59] These biological distinctions are important considerations in regard to human health, but equally important for environmental justice scholars are the ways in which the body, and biological differences between men and women and their susceptibility to environmental toxins, is linked to material realities. This distinction also complicates the essentialist cultural assumption that women's associations with nature are fundamentally rooted in biology. Buckingham and Kulcur write:

> This is not to argue that women are essentially, qua women, closer to nature, but are confronted with nature more frequently and directly by the unpaid and low-paid work they do. Similarly, we would argue that . . . it is the continued structuring of females as "different" to a male norm which results in a biological manifestation of a socio-environmental problem.[60]

Certainly, the body is the most immediate but not the only scale by which women (and men) experience nature, because we are ultimately rooted in particular socioeconomic contexts with gendered ideological and material realities.

Concerns for human health, particularly for the young, is an important part of the movement to end MTR, and these concerns are inextricably tied to notions of household and community. As we have established, the protection of household and community figures prominently in women's responses to environmental harms because the private household, historically women's domain, is a fundamental component of this larger notion of community. Rayna Rapp suggests that households, primarily political-economic entities, are "residential units within which personnel and resources get distributed and connected. Households may vary in their membership composition and in their relation to resource allocation. . . . That is, they vary systematically in their ability to hook into, accumulate, and transmit wealth, wages, or welfare."[61] Historically, women's unpaid labor—maintaining the material conditions of the household, and caring for spouses and children within this socioeconomic space—ultimately supports the public sphere by cutting reproduction costs of wage workers.[62] It has been widely noted that even with women entering the workforce in large numbers as they have over the past few decades, they are still primarily responsible for the material reproduction of the household. And because environmental ills "strike home," as Rachel Stein suggests, women are typically the first to respond and mount public reactions to them.[63]

In the anti-MTR movement, this reaction can range from making regular phone calls to the DEP to report damages to water supplies as a result of blasting, to joining a grassroots organization to fight the incursions of coal, to lobbying Congress to enact stricter environmental protections. For example, Carolyn Becker, a Coal River woman who lives next to a mountaintop removal operation, regularly calls the office of the West Virginia Department of Environmental Protection to report cracked windows and damages to her roof caused by the blasting of the Appalachian mountain behind her home, which she shares with her husband and two children. In describing life in an MTR zone, Becker says, "It's like World War III around here. They blast at least twice a day, once in the morning and once in the evening. . . . I call the DEP. I told them I've come to the conclusion that every time one goes off . . . I'm just going to call them."[64] She says that in response to her persistent phone calls, the DEP sends letters periodically that claim blasting on MTR sites poses no threat to coalfield homes. Becker, holding her most recent letter from DEP president Sandy Duncan, says, "Once every two weeks he [her husband] has to get up on the top of the house and tar. . . . This letter says blasting cannot create damages, but for some odd reason my husband has to get up on the house and tar it."[65] Becker's husband, who built their house along with his brother, has also been forced to fortify the home's foundation, replace broken windows, and landscape his yard to better handle the increased flooding around their home.

While women such as Carolyn Becker who face the daily onslaught of the effects of mountaintop removal coal mining are part of the anti-MTR movement working for the immediate protection of their households, other women engage in campaigns that tie the household to a larger sense of community. When considering the ideological and material realities of "community," it's important to acknowledge the differences among people within this political-economic space, and the ways in which "community" is situated in and connected to the natural world. Arun Agrawal and Clark C. Gibson argue:

> Communities are complex entities containing individuals differentiated by status, political and economic power, religion and social prestige, and intentions. Although some may operate harmoniously, others do not. Some see nature or the environment as something to be protected; others care only for nature's short-term use. Some have effective traditional norms; others have few. Some community members seek refuge from the government and market; others quickly embrace both.[66]

Indeed, within coalfield communities, many residents are staunchly supportive of mountaintop removal mining and other Big Coal operations because of the jobs the industry provides, and out of a belief that coalfield culture is fundamentally influenced and shaped by this industry. Some coalfield residents believe both the mountainous geography and coal mining are part of the region's culture and history, but object to the practice of mountaintop removal coal mining. Others envision an end to the tenure of coal in Appalachia, and conceptualize local culture as informed by the mountainous geography. These community members argue for the diversification of the coalfield economy and promote the production and use of renewable energy sources. These cultural distinctions among coalfield community members will be discussed in more detail in the following chapter.

In the movement to end MTR, the ways in which the private home is linked to a broader sense of community and environment are inherent in the humorously creative and effective work of the Sylvester Dustbusters. Their notable campaign also illustrates the gendered articulations inherent in sectors of the anti-MTR movement. Pauline Canterbury and Mary Miller, the duo known as the "Sylvester Dustbusters," created a way to apply the traditional housekeeping technique of dusting, or removing dust particles from the private home, to air quality protection in Sylvester, a small community in Boone County, West Virginia. Canterbury and Miller, longtime Sylvester residents, witnessed deterioration in the quality of life in their small community once coal operations increased. The Dustbusters say, "No longer could we socialize in our own back yards. Cook-outs became a thing of the past. Hanging our clothes out to dry was impossible. Coal dust blanketed everything. Our homes were covered in it. Swimming pools were polluted with it. We could no longer walk the street without coal dust blowing in our faces."[67] Many residents cite coal preparation operations in Sylvester as responsible for the chemical emissions plaguing their community over the past thirteen years.[68] Recalling this toxic history, Canterbury claims that in 1997 Elk Run Mining, owned by Massey Energy, began large-scale processing of coal produced from MTR sites, and she immediately noticed significant changes in her community.[69]

Canterbury claims that before coal mining operations increased, Sylvester was a bucolic rural town "built by people who came there, bought property, built it in order to get away from the coal camp atmosphere they were living in. It was such a wonderful town to live in. I mean, it was almost like living in Camelot."[70] The expansion of the coal processing plant resulted in widespread emissions of coal dust and other chemicals used to "clean" coal for the market. In addition, the presence of large trucks, heavy with coal, increased on the small roads of this Coal River Valley community, further contributing to compromised air quality.

Canterbury, in a letter written to the Department of Environmental Protection, says that since 1997 her community has "been a living hell of black coal dust, ever- shattering noises and broken promises, while we have watched our homes be destroyed, and respiratory illness invade our bodies, after the Department of Environmental Protection issued Elk Run Mining permit #D21-82, without considering the impact it would have on our community."[71] In an interview, Canterbury said the environmental effects of these coal operations jeopardize the health of Sylvester citizens: "It's no wonder that everybody has either bronchial trouble, laryngitis, [or] bronchitis; and cancer is very present."[72] Scientists Melissa M. Ahern and Michael Hendryx confirm these observations:

> Recent research evidence shows that persons who live in coal mining communities experience higher hospitalization rates for hypertension and lung disease, experience higher mortality rates from a variety of causes, and report higher rates of chronic illnesses and lower health status compared to other Appalachian or national residents.[73]

Since the Elk Run permit was issued in 1997, Canterbury says, coal company and state officials "left us with no alternative than to fight for our very existence, which we intend to do till Justice once again prevails."[74] Pauline Canterbury and other community members began filing complaints against Elk Run Mining with the DEP, who encouraged them to collect the evidence to prove their community was being negatively impacted by the processing plant. While residents who first issued the complaints accepted buyout offers from coal companies and moved to other locations, Canterbury and Miller refused to leave their community.[75]

Instead, they acted upon the DEP's advice. Using household paper towels and plastic bags, the "dustbusters" began collecting dust samples from the same spot in ten homes in Sylvester on a weekly basis for two and a half years—while being filmed with a video camera. Once ample physical evidence was collected, they sued Massey Energy for failure to control excessive pollution from its facilities and creating a public nuisance.[76] The 164 Sylvester residents who were part of the suit won comprehensive damages in the amount of $473,000, but Canterbury insists their "goal has never been to make money. We just didn't want them to control our community."[77] In addition to the monetary settlement, the company also had to install a dome around its Sylvester preparation plant to sequester toxic emissions. When considering her involvement in the Sylvester Dustbusters campaign, Canterbury says:

> It's hard to step back and watch everything you've worked for all your life be destroyed around you. . . . The DEP has a bad habit that they get you

involved in something to really take up your time, getting you off their backs, make you think that they're gonna do something when they don't have any intentions of doing anything. But in this case, it backfired on them.[78]

In this campaign, Canterbury and Miller embraced household work typically associated with women and applied it more broadly in their community cleanup efforts. In doing so they promoted healthy, sustainable communities for all residents living in MTR zones. As such, this campaign was deeply influenced by gendered articulations linked to the private household, the community, and the environment.

Women's environmental justice activism has sometimes been referred to as the rantings of "hysterical housewives," overly protective of their families and inordinately suspicious of the effects of business and government in their communities.[79] Giovanna Di Chiro notes that when women "make the decision to become politically active for environmental justice, they often find that their work makes them visible or identified as 'women,' and often *eccentric women*."[80] Women involved in environmental justice campaigns in the early part of the movement, such as Lois Gibbs and Dolly Burwell, emphasized their localized gendered positions as merely "housewives," speaking publicly as concerned mothers, grandmothers, daughters, and wives to the problems impacting their homes and communities.[81] One can argue that for many women involved in EJ groups throughout the country, the household is the starting point for both the recognition of the environmental problem and for creating solutions beneficial to impacted communities. In effect, a threatened household motivates many women to move outside of it and into public participation. Furthermore, in public actions such as the Sylvester Dustbusters, women improve communities by using their unique expertise, and also help shape the contours of their environmental justice participation. In examining the history of such activism, Robert Gottlieb notes that women in the past, and current EJ activists,

> became leaders in the antitoxics movement because they are often adept at a range of community leadership skills, a set of talents given little political recognition. These skills, derived from women's experiences in managing their homes, engaging in activities concerning their children's schools, and in holding their families together, have been particularly relevant in the context of a movement of neighbors and residents characteristic of the antitoxics groups.[82]

While some of these participants are what Joni Seager calls "reluctant activists" who join unexpectedly, women's participation in these movements can sometimes shape the very nature of the campaigns in which they participate.[83] Seager says that not only do women join environmental projects out of concern for the health of their families and communities, but they typically "organize around 'women's issues' of health and safety, family and children."[84] This focus is certainly apparent in the work of the Sylvester Dustbusters, but it is also central to the Pennies of Promise campaign, initiated by the Coal River Mountain Watch.

The Pennies of Promise campaign and the Sylvester Dustbusters illustrate how the movement to end MTR is framed by gendered articulations associated with women's roles in the private sphere of the household and then applied publicly to community activism. Pennies of Promise began in 2006 on the steps of the capitol building in Charleston, West Virginia, when Bo Webb and Ed Wiley brought pillowcases full of pennies to signify the start of a fund-raising campaign to build a new school for children attending Marsh Fork Elementary school in Sundial, West Virginia.[85] This school was precariously situated near Massey Energy's coal processing plant, 225 feet from a coal loading silo, and 400 yards from a leaking sludge dam 385 feet tall, leaving some residents concerned about the water and air quality within the school. In addition, some parents worried that the massive sludge dams on the mountain behind the school would give way, causing widespread floods that would be impossible for residents, particularly children, to escape.[86] Being especially concerned with the health and safety of students in the Marsh Fork Elementary school, Pennies of Promise appealed to community solidarity by stating, "In the absence of help from our elected officials, we have looked to each other for support as we are raising funds necessary to build a new school in the community ourselves."[87] The campaign urged citizens to host "house parties," become a "sister school," or make donations on their website by clicking a "Support the Kids" link.[88] In addition, the campaign consistently encouraged people to call former West Virginia governor Joe Manchin and "tell him to build a new school in the community now because coal processing plants don't belong next to elementary schools."[89] For many years Manchin resisted grassroots appeals to build a new school, arguing that any move to build a new school must come from the county school board, and not the governor's office:

As I have stated in the past, before the state can get involved in issues such as whether a school should be moved or if a new school should be built, a decision must first be made at the local level. I am encouraging the local school board to put the decision on a new school at Marsh Fork before a vote of the people of Raleigh County so they can determine the final outcome themselves.[90]

While Manchin dodged responsibility, the Raleigh County board of education claimed there were no health risks to children of Marsh Fork.[91] Pennies of Promise, assisted by Marshall University science professor Scott Simonton, who is also vice-chairman of the Environmental Quality Board, gathered scientific evidence that supported the health and safety concerns of some parents of Marsh Fork students.[92] Simonton conducted studies on toxicity levels inside Marsh Fork, collecting dust samples from seven sites within the school, including the gymnasium, hallways, and two classrooms. Simonton's tests found hazardous amounts of coal dust present in all areas, compromising air quality and placing young students at risk.[93] His official report states:

My concern about the school is that dust levels not only appear to exceed human health reference levels, but that the dust is largely made up of coal. Coal dust contains silica, trace metals, and polynuclear aromatic hydrocarbons (PAH), many of which are known human carcinogens. . . . Inhalation of coal dust is known to cause adverse health effects in humans, however, studies of coal dust toxicity are understandably mostly of adult populations. Children are particularly at risk from dust exposure in general, so it is reasonable to assume that coal dust creates an even greater risk for children than it does adults.[94]

Through the vigorous efforts of Ed Wiley and other grassroots activists armed with scientific proof of the inevitable health hazards for children of Marsh Fork Elementary, state officials finally acquiesced and agreed to build a new school. Site preparation began in June 2011, and the new school, located three miles from the existing building, is expected to open in the fall of 2012.[95]

Concern for the health of children and the safety of the schools they inhabit is a decidedly "woman's issue," and this gendered articulation is a fundamental component of the successful Pennies of Promise campaign. An initiator and public spokesperson for Pennies of Promise, Ed Wiley, is a former coal miner and coalfield resident. Ed, who picketed the governor's mansion in West Virginia many times over the Marsh Fork issue, is most famous for his walk to Washington—an effort geared toward influencing federal legislators to intervene in West Virginia state politics and obtain a new school for Marsh Fork's 220 students.[96] Media coverage of Ed's participation in the community-oriented Pennies of Promise was expressly gendered and tied to the private household in that he is identified primarily by his familial and paternalistic role as the grandfather of a Marsh Fork elementary student. Examples of article titles include "Grandpa Marches on DC for Clean Air and Safe Schools," and "Grandfather Wants Safe School for Elementary Kids." Other reports refer to Ed Wiley as a "passionate grandfather," and a "West Virginia grandfather and former coal miner."[97]

Men like Ed Wiley may have just as many concerns over community health, particularly for children, as women in the community have, but environmental historian Maril Hazlett has argued that women are more socially sanctioned to express these concerns and align themselves with movements for environmental change. Hazlett says that for men "to speak of home, health, children, nature, and vulnerable bodies" is to "voice a historically feminine protest. . . . Identified primarily with the public sphere—industrial interests, scientific research, and governmental oversight—men's strictly defined roles of fatherhood and husbanding" are used when explaining or perhaps justifying their involvement in environmental justice activism.[98] By stressing paternal roles, men become socially sanctioned to express "feminine" environmental concerns, yet in some cases their masculinity must still be stressed. A Washington, DC, independent media report was forceful in highlighting Ed's masculinity when covering his forty-day trek to Washington by stating that "Ed Wiley Could Kick Chuck Norris' Ass (For the Kids)."[99] Ed's involvement in Pennies of Promise, with its gendered, and particularly "feminine" concerns for human health, children, schools, and community, was an unlikely alliance for many people, because it challenged traditional articulations of gender and environmentalism. However, Pennies of Promise represents a successful shift in strategies in the anti-MTR campaign and has served as a way to get more people involved in the fight to end it.

Women's vigorous and extensive participation in environmental justice groups, and the gendered articulations inherent in EJ campaigns such as the Sylvester Dustbusters and Pennies of Promise, has produced debates about whether such actions can be considered part of a feminist movement. Robert Verchick argues that because environmental justice "pursues goals important to women's lives," it is not only "an environmental movement and a civil rights movement, it also describes a *women's* movement, and, I suggest, a *feminist* movement as well."[100] Verchick makes these assertions by examining the ways in which environmental justice legal techniques and history rely on feminist legal theory. However, one must consider how women in environmental justice groups self-identify or classify the work they do. It is important as well to realize that some women involved in environmental justice campaigns also have race and class concerns, cultural identities that are prime motivators in their environmental activism. The role of class is particularly evident in women's involvement to end MTR in Appalachia, because the populations most adversely impacted by coal operations in West Virginia are working-class residents.

Many women anti-MTR activists do not label their involvement as feminist; most describe themselves as people concerned about the environment and/or social justice. For example, Patty Sebok says she is a "a grassroots community activist," while Janice Nease describes herself as "a community activist with a strong environmental turn," and Judy Bonds considered herself an "environmental activist."[101] Giovanna Di Chiro labels women's participation in environmental justice an "unmarked women's movement," not only because of the sheer degree of female involvement, but also due to the reticence of many women involved in EJ movements to label themselves as "feminist," and in some cases "environmentalist."[102] Whether or not some women environmental justice activists embrace the feminist label, environmental justice scholars still have much work to do in accounting for the gendered nature of EJ activism.

Conclusion

By focusing on the ideological and material realities of the body, the household, and the community, EJ analyses can better connect gender to other human differences based on race, class, nationality, and so forth to the natural world. With such large numbers of poor and working-class white women and women of color (in rural and urban areas) collectively responding to environmental injustices, examinations of the links between gender, class, activism, and environment are a vital area of exploration. These studies can help us forge, and in some cases fortify, the critical links between theory and praxis.

In the environmental justice effort to end mountaintop removal coal mining in Appalachia, women activists are a vital part of the movement—representing in large numbers and in some cases shaping the nature of EJ campaigns.

Women like those participating in the anti-MTR movement are part of a rich history of activism in the Appalachian coalfields. Since the beginnings of this industry in West Virginia, women have joined or formed grassroots organizations aimed at ameliorating the political, economic, and social harms wrought by Big Coal. Today's anti-MTR activists, however, are different from previous women's activism in that they are not, by and large, working for reforms within the coal industry. Many of these women envision an end to coal's reign in Appalachia and work to create sustainable energy projects for their communities. They seek to protect West Virginia's lush environment and mountain culture. In their efforts to end MTR, women environmental justice activists link local culture to the natural environment, particularly its mountains. They do this at a time when many residents who support mountaintop removal, and protect coal interests in the state, increasingly link mountain culture to the history of coal production instead of the natural environment.

CHAPTER 3

Remembering the Past, Working for the Future:
West Virginia Women Fight for Sustainable
Communities and Environmental Heritage

> *Everything evolved around a mountain. . . . It gave us our sense*
> *of time, and place, and identity. And we would go there. It made*
> *you understand your connection to the universe and the creator.*
> *. . . People who never actually lived in the mountains don't*
> *understand that feeling.*

> —Janice Nease, cofounder of the Coal River
> Mountain Watch

> *Mountains are Appalachia. We are the Appalachian Mountains.*
> *We are the mountaineers, we are the pioneers. . . . My ancestors*
> *trace back on one side, on my dad's side of the family, to the*
> *1700s. They settled this area when nobody else wanted it. It was*
> *too rugged, too rough. It had no roads, no railroads, no nothing.*
> *You know our people were pioneers who came in and carved this*
> *out and now all the sudden they (coal operators and supporters)*
> *want it? Excuse me?*

> —Patti Sebok, member of the Coal River
> Mountain Watch

Introduction

IN 1998, JANICE NEASE ASSISTED RANDY SPROUSE AND
Freda Williams in the formation of the Coal River Mountain Watch in
Whitesville, West Virginia, after visiting Kayford Mountain, one of the best
places to view a mountaintop removal mining site. She was raised in the Red
Warrior coal camp near Kayford Mountain, and was appalled to learn that the

land where she grew up was being destroyed by MTR. Nease, who lived in Huntington and away from the coalfields, still had strong ties to the area, and thought the best way to protest MTR was to organize a community-based group that would monitor the coal industry and serve as a resource center for local citizens. A newly retired Spanish teacher, Nease was active in public school politics her entire career and also worked for Amnesty International in Charleston, West Virginia, for several years. She channeled her experiences in the educational system into trying to save the hardest-hit communities in the West Virginia coalfields.

Nease heard about mountaintop removal mining after Randy Sprouse, who regularly escorted friends into the mountains to hunt ginseng and other indigenous plants, informed her that a massive operation, known as mountaintop removal mining, was taking place on Kayford Mountain. She visited the site and was "shocked" by the destruction to her childhood community.[1] Nease recalls that she "heard some people talk about what was happening to them. . . . I was just so riled I couldn't sleep that night."[2] Because of her strong connection to the Kayford area, and her shock in seeing the mountain razed, she became actively involved in efforts to stop mountaintop removal coal mining in Appalachia.

In the Red Warrior coal camp, Nease grew up in a home with no indoor plumbing. The family's water source was a well outside the home, which they shared with her grandparents. By some estimates, she came of age in materially deprived conditions, as did many of her neighbors, but she warmly remembers the closeness of the mountain community:

> When you lived in the coal camps, everybody lived the same way. . . . We were definitely poor, but no one knew it. . . . It's the only time in my life that I felt . . . this communal feeling that you get when you live in the coalfields because everyone is connected. They're connected by the same history, the same culture, the same occupation. . . . It was just a wonderful life.[3]

All of Nease's male relatives, including her father, worked in the coal mines. Her paternal grandfather was part of the famous march on Blair.[4] Nease's father was working in the coal mines when he was drafted into World War II. She says that after suffering injuries in the war, he returned home to West Virginia, where he sensed a decline in coal jobs because of technological innovations in the industry. He left coal mining and moved the family out of the coal camp to nearby Chesapeake, where he began work in the auto industry.

Because of her upbringing, Nease remains strongly connected to the coalfields and to Appalachian culture, and she has worked hard over the years to preserve small communities under threat from MTR operations. While deeply rooted in her family's historical association with coal, she also views the mountains as part of her environmental heritage and works to create sustainable communities in the coalfields.[5]

Patty Sebok, a member of the CRMW, also has familial roots in the West Virginia coalfields and ties to the coal industry. Like Janice Nease, she connects central Appalachian culture to the mountainous geography. A resident of Prenter, West Virginia, in Boone County, Patty occupies a unique position in the anti-MTR movement in that she has a history of working for reforms within the coal industry, and is now active in initiatives to build environmentally sustainable communities in Appalachia, notably in the development of wind energy and diversifying the coalfield economy away from coal. Sebok, the mother of two sons and wife of ex–coal miner Butch Sebok, first engaged in political activism when she supported striking miners during the famous Pittston coal strike in 1989. Sebok was one of five hundred people arrested and jailed in 1989, and she vividly recalls her arrest, as well as the widespread media attention this direct action campaign generated:"It was an ordeal. They booked us just like we were criminals. They took a picture, mug shots, and fingerprinted us and all that. . . . CNN sent a satellite truck. I mean, it was a big deal. CSPAN. Everybody was there. They told us that we were on *Good Morning America*, but it was like, by the time we got home, we couldn't see it."[6]

In 1989 she also joined grassroots efforts targeting the dangerous presence of fast-moving coal trucks that caused a noticeable increase of dust in her neighborhood. Sebok says she immediately noticed the effects of increased mining in her community as "they (coal company workers) started flying out of there with those trucks and there was more trucks, and more dust, and they (the coal company) refused to water the roads" to prevent excess dust from polluting the community.[7] One day Sebok received a call from another Prenter woman asking her to join a protest against the coal trucks. She recalls, "I went down to see what they were doing, and we just stood in the middle of the road and blocked those trucks. And it took probably over a half a day before the state police came out on us."[8]

In 2001 Sebok joined the Coal River Mountain Watch, melding her long-standing activism against the destructive forces of coal trucks in Boone County, as well as her experience in labor campaigns, with the growing anti-MTR movement. Sebok was interested in joining the movement after making connections between nearby mountaintop removal operations and not only the increased coal truck traffic in Prenter , but also widespread flooding in the area. However, she was reluctant to join the CRMW because her husband was then working as an underground coal miner. Sebok expressed her concern to Judy Bonds, who reassured her that she could still fight Big Coal, even though her husband, Butch, was employed by the industry. As part of her activism in the anti-MTR environmental justice movement, Sebok has lobbied Charleston, South Carolina, and Washington, DC; attended numerous mine permit hearings and other community gatherings; and also traveled the country with the educational road show "Appalachian Treasures." Sebok says her organization seeks to provide information to impacted community members so they can help themselves, in addition to educating the nation "on where their power comes from and what they're actually doing when they flip that light switch, what is happening back here to us and our families."[9] While Sebok still considers herself a member of the CRMW, she is admittedly less active since her husband suffered a serious neck and spinal injury and was forced to retire from mining.

Regardless of their prior forms of political participation, or the various reasons why they joined anti-MTR efforts, the cultural history formed in this mountainous environment is important to many women fighting mountaintop removal coal mining in Appalachia. It is, indeed, a complex history where many residents are tied to the geography they inhabit. This environment influences cultural ideas and practices, yet many people are also connected to the coal industry, which has formed the economic base of West Virginia, arguably at great expense to workers, their families, and the natural environment. Assuredly, nuanced opinions about the cultural identity of the region, the role of the natural environment, and the place of the coal industry in West Virginia's cultural history and economy are articulated in public discourse in this era of mountaintop removal coal mining. Some Appalachians emphasize ties to the mountains and seek not only to eliminate MTR, but to envision a future completely free of the coal industry—a future with ecologically (and economically) sustainable communities. Others stress these same connections and seek to abolish MTR, but are not opposed to underground coal mining. A third category of citizens highlight the cultural and economic associations with the extraction of coal and hope to solidify Big Coal's position in the state. This chapter focuses on the public discourse that emphasizes West Virginia's ties to the mountainous environment, a future without coal, and cultural narratives that stress the importance of coal's history and future in the state. It ultimately reveals how this cultural history is also connected to the history of women's grassroots activism in West Virginia.

Indeed, many people living in West Virginia today are conflicted when reflecting on the environmental heritage of the state: coal or mountains? This division is dramatically captured in an exchange at the capitol building between Lorelei Scarbro and former governor Joe Manchin, as depicted in the film *Coal Country*:

> Manchin: What we're trying to do is find balance. You know that. I
> mean it's tough to find balance in an extraction state.
> Scarbro: We're the mountain state.
> Manchin: Pardon me?[10]

Of course coal and mountains have influenced the culture and economy of West Virginia, but the Appalachian Mountains are its environmental heritage, and it is this heritage that many in the anti-MTR movement highlight in this era of mountaintop removal coal mining. The Appalachian Mountains are 300–500 million years old, and have the potential of an even longer life if mountaintop removal mining is halted.[11] This belief guides many of the environmental justice activists fighting the adverse effects of coal and mountaintop removal mining in West Virginia today.

The importance of mountains to West Virginia's cultural history is not only stressed by the environmental justice activism of women such as Janice Nease and Patty Sebok, but that importance is also discernibly connected to the long history of women's social protest in Appalachia. Most notably, women have joined coal industry reform campaigns, assisting the United Mine Workers of America (UMWA), and primarily male miners, in their fights for unionization and better compensation and working conditions. They have also been active in anti-strip-mining efforts that have largely sought to preserve underground mining jobs while also pointing out the environmental effects of strip-mining on Appalachian homesteads and landscapes. Many women in the anti-MTR movement envision and work for a future without coal in their communities, focusing on what Janice Nease calls "the long view."[12] They are aware of the centrality of coal in West Virginia's economy, but focus less on coal employment and working conditions and more on building sustainable communities. In doing so, their activism seeks to protect the Appalachian Mountains and their environmental heritage. This environmental justice activism faces great opposition from some coalfield residents and industry supporters, who link West Virginia's history and environmental heritage to coal and work just as hard to protect coal industry interests in the region.

Women Anti-MTR Activists on the Continuum of Appalachian Resistance and American Environmentalism

Throughout its history, Appalachia has been a place of contradictions, a site of great social, economic, and environmental exploitation by industry but also a region where residents individually and collectively resist these injustices. More than thirty years ago, Thomas Plaut observed that "Appalachian history is full of rebellions and rebels: of men and women who demand . . . that their existence be recognized. From mine wars to roving pickets, Mother Jones to Widow Combs, Black Lung and Brown Lung movements, Appalachians have fought domination."[13] West Virginia novelist Ann Pancake captures the current manifestations of this rebellious spirit in the main character in the anti-MTR novel *Strange as This Weather Has Been*. Lace, who joins an environmental justice organization after watching the mountains disappear around her, says, "The best way to fight them is to refuse to leave. Stay in their way—that's the only language they can hear. We are from here, it says. This is our place, it says. Listen here, it says. We exist."[14] Lace is a fictional version of many of the women active in the anti-MTR movement today; women who are links in the historical chain of Appalachian social protest. Even though this region has been the site of vigorous grassroots movements, this is not to suggest that the majority of residents speak out against injustice, individually or collectively, or join organizations to improve conditions in their homes and communities. In the West Virginia coalfields today there are many residents who actively oppose MTR, and the negative influence of the coal industry, while other residents have no opinion, or actively defend the practice and Big Coal's presence in the region.

John Gaventa draws our attention to the dichotomous conditions of what he calls "quiescence and rebellion" in Appalachia, where many residents are socially, politically, and economically disenfranchised but do not resist oppressive conditions.[15] Gaventa's work poses this fundamental question: Why do some people in Appalachia speak out and actively resist oppressive forces such as Big Coal, while others remain silent and inactive? He suggests that dialectical conditions in oppressed communities in the Appalachian coalfields buttress this dichotomy of action and inaction:

If the interests of A and B are contrary, and if A (individual, group, class) ex-
ercises power for the protection of its interests, then it will also be to A's advantage if the power can be used to generate and maintain quiescence of B
(individual, group, class) upon B's interests. In the process, the dimensions
of power and powerlessness may be viewed as interrelated and accumulative
in nature, such that each dimension serves to re-enforce the strength of the
other.[16]

This dialectical pattern has long been a part of Appalachian culture and, arguably, culture in any location where massive social and economic inequalities
exist. Janice Nease affirms this quiescent tendency, claiming one of the biggest
obstacles in ending MTR is organizing community members because residents have been "under the boot of the coal industry . . . so they still see themselves as unable to do anything about that. But also they were raised with this
idea that you didn't do anything to hurt your neighbor. And it's still ingrained
in you . . . it's still ingrained in me."[17] In this climate, motivating residents to
stand up to Big Coal is formidably difficult, which makes the robust rebellions
of the past and the current fight against MTR all the more impressive.

In addition to cultural attitudes and a history of oppression as reasons for
inaction, Silas House and Jason Howard suggest that coal companies wage
successful media campaigns to garner public support while stoking job-loss
fears:

Many Appalachians find it difficult to oppose this practice because of the
coal industry's long history of convincing people that to protest any form of
mining is to oppose an industry that has long been a major supplier of jobs
within the region. . . . Some Appalachians tend to believe that speaking out
against any form of mining is biting the hand that feeds them.[18]

Indeed, Big Coal controls the message in the coalfields of Appalachia, promoting their interests in newspapers, TV commercials, workplaces, and schools,
as will be discussed later in the chapter. While many people protect and defend the forces of Big Coal in Appalachia, there are, of course, many residents
who fight these interests, envisioning environmentally sustainable communities with diverse economies. These residents, many of them women, are firmly
situated on the historical trajectory of grassroots Appalachian activism. Current efforts depart, however, from previous women's activism against the coal
industry in that much of the current resistance visualizes a future without coal

in Appalachia, focusing less on industry reforms. Anti-MTR efforts highlight concepts of sustainable communities and link West Virginia's environmental heritage to the mountains, whereas earlier forms of activism promoted the importance of coal jobs and strong families in reformation actions. In short, an environmental consciousness, not prominent in most of the prior grassroots initiatives, drives anticoal efforts today.

When historically assessing Appalachian women's activism, Karaleah S. Reichart argues that the cultural identity of the coalfields was largely formed by the coal industry and organized protest against its abuses, and women have assumed an active presence in many initiatives. She claims:

> Varied actions of women in labor activism and industrial conflict have played an important role in the development of the coal industry across the region. . . . Appalachian women have historically been involved in nonviolent picket line demonstrations, boycotts of company stores, businesses, and local government offices, and organizing and implementing food distribution systems during strikes.[19]

When considering women's involvement in organized resistance, their work in labor initiatives has a long history, and is most documented by regional scholars. Women participants in labor union efforts engaged in what Virginia Seitz calls "proxy" activism, working primarily in the interests of male jobs and working conditions.[20] As such, women's resistance was reformative, protecting the gender and class positions of male relatives working in the inherently exploitative coal industry. While securing and strengthening male jobs against the forces of coal, these women sought to maintain and improve their own gender and class-based positions in the private context of home and family, envisioning strong jobs in the coal industry as a way to build and sustain healthy communities. These labor reformers were influenced by long-established UMWA activities, and critiques of the coal industry did not encompass or include an environmental preservationist perspective. Two recent historical examples of women's involvement in industry reformist activism in the Appalachian coalfields illustrate the focus on jobs and family: the Brookside and Pittston strikes of 1973 and 1989, respectively.

The Brookside mining strike in Harlan County, Kentucky, is one of the most noted industry and labor conflicts in Appalachian history, famously chronicled in Barbara Kopple's Academy Award–winning documentary *Harlan County USA*. Miners at the Brookside mine walked off the job in efforts to unionize the mine.[21] As Kopple's documentary highlights, women were at the forefront of this strike, peopling picket lines, planning strike activities, organizing participants, negotiating with union officials, and talking with the press. The Brookside mining strike was headed by women who faced both public and family criticism while striving to ensure better working conditions for their male coal mining relatives.[22] In one revealing scene from Kopple's documentary, Norman Yarborough, president of the Eastover Mining Company, which owned the Brookside mine, is asked to reflect on the role of coalfield women in this strike: "Well, they've certainly played a big role in it. I would hate to think that my wife would play this kind of role.... There's been some conduct that I don't like to think that our American women have to revert to."[23] Yarborough's assessment calls into question women participants' femininity and moral character in their fight for coalfield justice, revealing the difficulties for Appalachian women assuming public activist positions in their communities.

Sally Ward Maggard notes that women living in Brookside in the early 1970s had limited job opportunities and therefore occupied precarious positions, being dependent upon male wages in working-class coalfield homes.[24] Maggard contends that the participation of these Appalachian women who mobilized to protect family resources reflected "their class interests as these interacted with their gender interests."[25] While Brookside women sought to reform the coal industry to protect the private interests of jobs and family, this participation was tied to their situatedness in coalfield communities. Maggard argues:

> Affective ties to a spouse on strike, links to families with UMWA histories, a shared community history, personal experiences, and a belief in the UMWA as a progressive force for Harlan County all contributed to women's involvement in the strike. These reflect a web of family, community, and economic experiences and networks that have political consequences.[26]

For women in the Brookside strike seeking reforms within the coal industry, their gender interests intersected with the material conditions of working-class life, and their vigorous participation was woven into family and community history as tied to coal jobs. As will be discussed later, the Brookside strike took place during a resurgence of environmental thought and action in the United States. However, Brookside, Kentucky, being one of the last places in the coalfields to obtain a union, logically focused solely on the goal of organizing the workforce to improve job conditions and strengthen coal-field families.

In what was perhaps the last of the great industry and labor battles in the Appalachian coalfields, the 1989 Pittston strike, women also took center stage, working on reforms for mostly male relatives, but also for the wages of coal mining women who by 1989 were employed in mining jobs. Most women participants in the Pittston strike were organized by the United Mine Workers of America Union (UMWA), working within one of the UMWA Family Auxiliaries in the coalfields.[27] The strike was called in response to Pittston Coal Company's decision to cut health benefits for retired coal miners, because of overtime and Sunday work requirements for present employees, and because of the use of nonunion miners in mines represented by the UMWA.[28] Women in the Pittston strike engaged in activities associated with the Brook-side strike, but most notably organized under the name Daughters of Mother Jones, a nod to past women coalfield activists. Karen Beckwith notes that overall, the collective action of the Pittston strike was "gender-inclusive, and its expression was primarily in terms of a collective class identity based on claims about family and community."[29] Beckwith suggests that despite the vigorous participation of women in the strike, class identity superseded and perhaps muted gender identity positions:

> The union's strike rhetoric—silent with specific reference to women, or to women as directly empowered and as central to the strike—provided little space within which activist women themselves could establish a discourse of women's collective identity. . . . "Community" and "family" were presented as comprehensive concepts, enveloping—and accurately so—all strike activists. Within the strike discourse's presentation of a unified, homogeneous community in solidarity, however, women's specificity and grounding for a working-class women's collective identity were subsumed.[30]

The Pittston coal strike was a reformist effort to fight for better treatment of past and present coal industry employees. The ten-month strike that began in April 1989 used women's activism in particular ways, primarily in the service of protecting male underground mining jobs. The protection of these jobs was seen as a way to support coalfield families and build stronger communities. As such, this industry reform effort was obviously not geared toward the direct improvement of the mountainous environment. Together, these Brookside and Pittston examples illustrate the connections between gender and class interests and locations as tied to underground coal mining jobs, families, and a vision of community linked to coal. The Pittston coal strike occurred during a time of great backlash against the environmental gains secured in the 1960s and 1970s—a decade in which the focus became "material living standards" and "economic security" and the jobs-versus-environment debate was particularly keen.[31] The early 1990s witnessed governmental retrenchment on environmental regulation, and the conservative backlash against environmentalism was growing.[32] In this context, the industry reformist orientation of women's activism is best understood and most distinguished from grassroots efforts today.

When examining the continuum of Appalachian women's protest, today's anti-MTR movement has its roots most firmly planted in the anti-strip-mining efforts of the 1960s and 1970s because these grassroots initiatives, while not situating environmental concerns prominently, did convey an environmental consciousness through expressed concerns for jobs, family, and private property. Large-scale strip-mining began in Appalachia in the 1950s after the creation of new technologies to mine more coal with fewer workers, making it more profitable for companies in coalfield communities.[33] Strip-mining and mountaintop removal coal mining are both forms of surface mining, but strip-mining is far less destructive to coalfield communities and the environment. Coal River Mountain Watch member Judy Bonds distinguished early surface mining from MTR by classifying the latter as "strip-mining on steroids."[34] Large-scale strip-mining involved making cuts in the earth to uncover a coal seam, while dumping the dirt and rock produced during the process back into the previous cut, continuing this process as the operation proceeded.[35] There is an obvious difference between making cuts on ridges with machinery and using the potent mixture of amyl nitrate and fuel oil to blast away entire mountain formations to extract coal.

Ronald Eller argues that the introduction of these new technologies in the 1950s not only left the Appalachian environment scarred, but led to massive unemployment for underground miners: "Rural families could see the truckloads of coal that poured from expanding strip mine operations while their sons and daughters were forced to migrate out of state for jobs and while those who remained struggled to survive on charity and government handouts."[36] In organizations such as the Appalachian Group to Save the Land and People (AGSLP), regional residents fought for coal industry reforms that would protect underground mining jobs and better regulate surface mining practices to lessen the environmental costs.[37] Strip-mining operations occurred in coalfields throughout the Appalachian region but were most fiercely contested in Kentucky.[38]

Women were active in all aspects of the anti-strip-mining campaigns, including lobbying local and national legislative bodies, working for legal reforms, keeping the issues alive in their communities, and direct action protests such as placing their bodies in front of bulldozers to stop the stripping of hillsides.[39] In fact, one of the most visible symbols of the commitment to end strip-mining came in the form of a sixty-one-year-old Kentucky woman, Ollie Combs, who was publicly signified by her marital status as "Widow Combs."[40] Combs, a member of the AGSLP, lived in a small cabin in Clear Creek Valley, Kentucky, with her four sons, and worried that local strip-mine operations would permanently alter her twenty-acre property, endangering the lives of her family.[41] Around Thanksgiving in 1965, when the operations began, Combs climbed upon the ridge by her house and stood in front of bulldozers to stop their operations. She was subsequently arrested, and local newspapers carried dramatic pictures of this older woman being carried away in handcuffs, and then eating her Thanksgiving meal in the county jail, garnering a lot of attention for the anti-strip-mining campaigns.[42]

Direct action protests by women continued during the campaign when, in January 1972, a group of seven women in Knotts County, Kentucky, occupied a strip mine, standing in front of bulldozers to sabotage the operations. One of the participants, Mary Beth Bingman, says that although the movement to end strip-mining was not successful, "there is some value in the kind of direct confrontation we took. We helped publicize the issue of strip mining and may have served as an inspiration to other people in various struggles. . . . Our action, along with the many other early anti–strip mining protests, undoubtedly helped to lay the groundwork for later efforts."[43] Their actions resulted in the Surface Mining Control and Reclamation Act, federal legislation passed in 1977 designed to regulate surface mining in the region. Some women involved in the anti-strip-mining campaigns have also taken a stand against MTR. For example, Coal River Mountain Watch cofounder Freda Williams recalls writing letters to the editors in the 1960s and 1970s protesting strip-mining in Appalachia. When reflecting upon her involvement in both the anti-strip-mining and anti-MTR efforts, Williams says, "I'm definitely trying to protect the environment, but I consider myself an activist first and foremost. . . . My drive stems from growing up in the coalfields. My dad was a union organizer. I've always been involved with injustice in the coalfields all my life."[44]

Williams's rationale reflects her ties to older forms of activism in Appalachia as she prefers being called an activist rather than an environmentalist. In this sense she is a notable bridge between past and present grassroots campaigns in the coalfields. While participants in the anti-strip-mining campaigns had concerns over the impact this new form of coal extraction had on the natural world, environmental concerns were largely secondary to labor concerns. Ultimately, they wanted strip-mining outlawed to protect underground mining jobs as well as the private property of coalfield residents. In his study of the opposition to strip-mining in Ohio, Pennsylvania, Kentucky, and West Virginia, Chad Montrie describes the priorities of people in organizations fighting strip-mining:

> These critics expressed dislike for stripping in aesthetic terms, as a concern for the conservation of valuable mineral and timber resources, and as a matter of preserving the ecological integrity of the hills. But they were more likely to bemoan the damage done by strip mining to farmland and homesteads, as well as the loss of jobs in an economically depressed region.[45]

The anti-strip-mining campaigns, although focused on saving jobs and preserving private property, did convey a nascent organized awareness and commitment to protecting the natural world. However, this environmental consciousness was much weaker than we see in today's movement to end mountaintop removal coal mining in Appalachia, which focuses on West Virginia's postcoal possibilities, emphasizing environmentally and economically sustainable mountain communities.

These anti-strip-mining campaigns, in which women throughout Appalachia participated, occurred during a resurgence in environmental thought and action in the United States—a post–Rachel Carson age when people raised awareness about environmental issues in newly energized ways. Environmental historian Benjamin Kline has noted that the widespread social changes in the 1960s fostered increased public concern with environmental issues, and the environmental movement grew alongside the women's movement, antiwar activism, and civil rights.[46] These social transitions also sowed the seeds for environmental justice thought and practice, which, as previously noted, arose in the 1970s as the environmental movement began to mature.[47] In the 1960s, many national groups were formed, such as the League of Conservation Voters, Friends of the Earth, and Environmental Action; and major environmental laws were passed, including the

Wilderness Act of 1964.[48] Also, the first Earth Day celebration took place in 1970, with twenty million participants.[49] Kline stresses that this new environmental energy was also a product of increasing public anger, as Americans had "daily reminders of the deteriorating condition of the environment, in both rural and urban areas, as well as alarming reports of humanity's wasteful behavior."[50] Residents of coalfield communities in Appalachia were also concerned with mining's impact on the natural world, but these concerns were tempered by considerations for employment and the protection of their homes and the lands on which they were situated.

Today, the environmental justice movement to end mountaintop removal coal mining in Appalachia, and women's exuberant participation in it, focuses less on the reformations of the coal industry in terms of employment and working conditions for coal miners, since this mechanized form of mining has dramatically cut the number of coal jobs in the region. Janice Nease claims that many coalfield residents oppose MTR but refuse to speak out against the practice because they have relatives working in the coal industry, even though coal jobs have declined considerably over the past three decades.[51] To illustrate, in 1970, coal mining in West Virginia supplied 45,261 jobs; while in 1996, 16,794 worked in coal mining jobs; and in 2009, 11,506 jobs were in coal production.[52] Considering this decline, Nease says those who do not speak out against MTR are "still trying to protect jobs that don't exist."[53] In addition to using less labor power than traditional forms of mining, or strip-mining, MTR is much more devastating to the natural environment than early surface mining operations. While environmental justice efforts to end mountaintop removal mining, and women's participation in these campaigns, detail destruction to homes and families, efforts are more focused on the preservation and health of coalfield communities, as well as the Appalachian environment.

Arguably, there is currently more national public awareness and commitment to environmental issues in this era of climate change than in the 1960s and 1970s when strip-mining operations were commonplace. In the first decade of this new era, green discourse has increased as many people are concerned about climate change and thus more receptive to environmental thought and action. Benjamin Kline has called this "the century of the environment."[54] In this context, anti-MTR activists seek an end to MTR, and a future without Big Coal and fossil fuels, as they promote the development of alternative energy sources to build sustainable communities creating economic diversity in the coalfields of Appalachia.

Environmental Justice and a Postcoal Future: Renewable Natural Resources and Green Energy in West Virginia

The logo for the Coal River Mountain Watch is a large blue eye, whose center is a green mountain chain topped by a bright sun. Accompanying this logo is the slogan "Remembering the Past, Working for the Future."[55] The first part of this motto is a historical awareness of the social, political, and environmental problems of the state as well as the legacy of grassroots activism in West Virginia. The second half of the catchphrase reveals the organization's commitment to making transformative changes that will benefit West Virginia citizens and the natural environment. The group's mission is "to stop the destruction of our communities and environment by mountaintop removal mining, to improve the quality of life in our area and to help rebuild sustainable communities."[56] Similar sentiments are expressed by OVEC, whose broader mission is to "organize and maintain a diverse grassroots organization dedicated to the improvement and preservation of the environment through education, grassroots organizing and coalition building, leadership, development and media outreach."[57] Its logo is a large tree that sits on top of the group's acronym, OVEC, which is painted green. Groups such as the CRMW and OVEC in West Virginia have these primary goals: to stop the socially and environmentally destructive influence of coal, to diversify the economy, and to foster sustainable communities.

Many women in the anti-MTR movement lodge critiques of coal as environmental justice activists who are part of a national and international movement that seeks to raise awareness about climate change and the impact of fossil fuels on the environment. In particular, they seek to draw attention to the destructive force of coal at the production end of the energy chain. OVEC member Maria Gunnoe exposes environmental problems impacting coalfield communities, drawing attention to the urgent need for sustainable communities located near these production zones:

> People around here are swiggin' down contaminated water all day long, every day. The health effects are sometimes long term. It's usually pancreatic cancer of some kind or liver disease, or kidney stones, gallstones—digestive tract problems. And then, too, people's breathing. The blasting is killin' people—just smothering them to death through breathin' all of the dust. The computers and electronics and stuff in my house stay completely packed up with black coal dirt and rock dust together. Why do they expect

us to just take this. . . . It's flat-out wrong to do people like this. . . . How can you do me like this in the name of jobs?[58]

Anti-MTR activists like Gunnoe fight to change the social, economic, and environmental conditions of their communities for both present and future generations. Many women in West Virginia promote economic diversity and healthy communities through sustainable development of the area's renewable natural resources and the promotion of green energy projects. In doing so they advocate an ecological "partnership ethic," conceived by Carolyn Merchant as an "idea that people are helpers, partners, and colleagues and that people and nature are equally important to each other. If both people and nature are acknowledged as actors, we have the possibility of a mutually beneficial situation."[59] Furthermore, Merchant suggests this partnership "entails a viable relationship between a human community and a nonhuman community in a particular place, a place in which connections to the larger world are recognized through economic and ecological exchanges."[60] This ecological ethic is at work in mountain communities today, as some residents draw our attention away from fossil fuel extraction and onto more environmentally sustainable economic endeavors, including the economic development of renewable natural resources and wind energy.

Many activists view the cultivation of natural resources, such as medicinal plants and timber, as an alternative to the economic reliance on coal, the state's most lauded, but finite, natural resource. Highlighting the sustainable cultivation of indigenous plants is a way to transfer the economic message away from coal industry jobs and to the promotion of economic diversity. Ginseng, a medicinal plant used for centuries in Asia and North America, grows in all fifty-five counties of West Virginia, and the harvesting of it is a state-regulated activity, whereby residents are able to dig their own ginseng from September 1 to November 30 every year.[61] "Ginsenging," known by locals as "sangin," has a long history in the Appalachian region. In some West Virginia communities such as Coal River, digging ginseng is a fundamental part of local culture and, in Anthony P. Cavender's words, "represents an intimate, harmonious relationship between the people and the environment as much as an economic activity."[62] This medicinal herb—used to improve physical vitality and to treat a wide range of afflictions, including digestive problems and hypertension—is certainly profitable, as it sells for $300 a pound. According to the West Virginia Department of Forestry, in 2002, 6,400 pounds of ginseng were extracted in West Virginia, worth $2 million.[63] CRMW activist Patty

Sebok maintains that MTR is threatening these indigenous plants, and she hopes her organization's efforts can curtail the threat and provide economic alternatives to the extraction of coal:

> There's other things growing here . . . medicinal plants, the ginseng, black cohosh, yellow root, all the things that are being destroyed. . . . That's another thing we're trying to revive that might come under sustainable communities. That, I mean, as much as the price of ginseng and cohosh and stuff is up, why can't we stop destroying it, and have businesses out of that?[64]

Black cohosh, another renewable resource promoted by local activists, has been used for centuries by healers and doctors to treat fever, arthritis, and women's health issues, including menstrual and menopausal symptoms and reproductive diseases.[65] There are many such roots and herbs growing naturally in the mountainous landscapes of West Virginia. The production of these renewable natural resources, when combined with other environmental assets, can provide viable economic alternatives to the destructive force of MTR.

The discourse on medicinal plants and economic plans for their cultivation ties into a long history of folk medicine practices in the Appalachian region and women's connection to them. Furthermore, in many cultures throughout history, women have been healers, cultivating and utilizing natural plants in folk medicine practices.[66] In the Appalachian region this connection is duly noted, most recently in an extensive study of current folk medicine uses in Appalachia. Over ten years, Anthony P. Cavender visited many Appalachia towns, asking residents to identify people in their communities who were especially knowledgeable about folk medicine. His informant population of 660 people was overwhelmingly made up of women at a total of 473, with just 187 males. Cavender argues that this unintentional bias "aligns with the generally accepted observation that women have traditionally served as the primary care givers in families," and thus have the most knowledge about traditional herbal remedies for common maladies such as colds, flu, burns, warts, depression, sunburn, and so forth.[67] The bias also speaks to women's expertise, and the ways in which folk traditions are passed down by family members with similar knowledge and skills. Cavender elaborates on this long-established connection between medicinal plants, healing, and women:

> Conventional wisdom has it that women were the primary sources of botanical medicine knowledge since they were largely responsible for family

health care. Many communities had men or women known as "yarb doctors" or "herb doctors," who were recognized as being exceptionally well versed in the knowledge of medicinal plants. Women often served as both yarb doctors and granny midwives.[68]

This link between Appalachian forest plants, women, and healing is an interesting connection, especially in light of current efforts by some environmental justice activists promoting the economic cultivation of renewable indigenous resources. With this gendered natural history in mind, and current calls for economic diversity that promote the use of other natural resources, it is important to engage in ecologically sustainable ways of growing and harvesting indigenous plants. This stance is in keeping with Carolyn Merchant's partnership ethic in that it "makes visible the connections between people and the environment in an effort to find new cultural and economic forms that fulfill vital needs, provide security, and enhance the quality of life without degrading the local or global environment."[69] If the cultivation and exchange of renewable natural resources is vigorously pursued in West Virginia, it can serve as one alternative to the ecologically unsustainable practice of coal extraction.

In addition to the use of native Appalachian plants, some activists promote the economic development of West Virginia's expansive forests and the valuable timber currently destroyed by MTR. The first step in the MTR process is to clear trees and other vegetation from the permitted site. Instead of using the trees from MTR sites productively, coal companies burn them in their haste to extract the coal and deliver it to national markets. Coal River Mountain Watch member Patty Sebok says, "Why can't we have furniture stores with all the wood that's being razed? A lot of this wood doesn't even leave here, and it's on a mountaintop removal site, but they don't want to wait. They slash it and burn it."[70] While the extraction of timber can be environmentally problematic, this renewable resource can be managed in sustainable and economically just ways.

Even more important for economic diversification and building environmentally sustainable communities is the development of wind projects in West Virginia. Renewable wind energy has been utilized for centuries and is currently the fastest-growing energy source in the world. Some environmentalists claim that "the potential for wind power is so huge that coal-, oil- and natural gas–fired power plants could be retired."[71] Wind energy has many advantages over fossil fuel–based sources, and is considered "environmentally benign," generating no chemical emissions or major land disturbances.[72]

However, it is not without controversy. Some proposed wind sites are opposed for aesthetic reasons, as residents cannot abide the presence of wind turbines in their home vistas and worry about the impact on property values.[73] The siting of wind generating equipment is also protested because of its impact on bird populations.[74] In late 2009, a federal judge's ruling halted the construction of a 122-turbine project, known as the Beech Creek project, in Greenbrier County, West Virginia, because of its potential impact on the endangered Indiana bat.[75] Despite this setback, wind energy development is growing in West Virginia, particularly in the central and eastern portions of the state, which have been classified as "6 and 7" sites, the highest rankings areas can receive for wind generation potential.[76] Because of the high elevations, these state sites consistently have powerful wind velocity and the capacity to house large-scale electricity generation operations.[77] In 2009, West Virginia installed 330 megawatts of wind power, the only state in the Southeast to do so besides Tennessee, which created 29 megawatts. To place this in a national perspective, Texas had the highest wind megawatt installation with 9,410, and California followed at 2,749, while New York installed 1,274 megawatts, and Massachusetts 15.[78]

In the coalfields of Boone County a coalition of forces, including the Coal River Mountain Watch; Appalachian Voices, a regional organization; and WindLogics, a national wind development modeling firm, have proposed the Coal River Mountain Wind Farm as a source of alternative energy in the southern region of the state. This plan is being contested, as Massey Energy has requested permits to mine Coal River Mountain using MTR. Area resident and CRMW member Lorelei Scarbro says, "Our concern today is our homes, our environment, and the sustainability of the environment. The house I live in and raised my children in, which my husband built—and he is buried in the family cemetery next door—would be in danger from this mine. The wind farm would preserve the mountain."[79] Predictably, Big Coal forces contest the proposal because they realize the threat green energy development poses for enterprises reliant on the extraction and sale of nonrenewable fossil fuels. Patty Sebok counters Big Coal's opposition to the wind project by saying, "They like to tell everyone that you can't produce electricity without coal, but at the same time they say, well, the windmills are not going to make enough wind to see a difference. Well, if it's not, why are they fighting it?"[80]

The Coal River Mountain Wind Farm is, indeed, a viable economic alternative. A WindLogics cooperative study on wind energy production contains data on the economic benefits of this alternative. During construction of the wind farm, $20 million a year would be generated in local spending, creating more than 200 construction jobs. In addition, after construction, $2 million a year in direct spending would be generated, and 40–50 permanent operation and maintenance jobs could be created. The local tax base would also benefit, as the project would provide $400,000 annually in state tax revenue and $3 million in county tax revenue. Developers of this project claim it has the potential to provide the city of Beckley and all of Raleigh County with electricity generated by clean, wind energy.[81]

Developers of the Coal River Mountain Wind Farm project acknowledge coal's historical connection to the economic development of West Virginia, but focus our attention on the present: "Appalachian coal has fueled the nation for over a century, but it is a non-renewable resource and will run out some day. . . . In contrast, a wind farm will produce energy for as long as the wind blows."[82] There are other wind farms operating in West Virginia, including one in Tucker County that contains forty-four turbines covering approximately seven miles.[83] Even though wind energy is contested in West Virginia and other locations throughout the country, it is a growing form of energy that can provide economic and environmental sustainability to communities negatively impacted by fossil fuel production and consumption. These local gains, of course, have global implications as we work to move away from the fossil fuel paradigm to greener alternatives, realizing Merchant's "partnership ethic" by bringing "humans and nonhuman nature into a dynamically balanced, more nearly equal relationship with each other."[84] If we do not make concerted efforts to develop a green economy, we further peril the planet and place our communities in long-lasting economic jeopardy. However, we must also ensure a transition to a greener economy that is mindful of social justice issues. Van Jones, for example, cautions against the private sector controlling such development, advocating more state control through these changes:

> Unless the government helps to steer jobs and investment in new directions, those who most need the benefits of a new, green economy are highly unlikely to get them. If the best of the green wave bypasses the most disadvantaged urban and rural communities, then low-income and marginalized places will miss out altogether on their one shot in this new century at a glorious rebirth.[85]

Wind energy has an exciting future in West Virginia in the coalfields and beyond. This shift to greener energy sources is welcomed by many coalfield residents, whose homes and communities are currently being destroyed by mountaintop removal coal mining.

West Virginia activists and their supporters are posing tangible solutions to the current crisis in coalfield communities throughout Appalachia. They foster systematic changes that can save towns from extinction and protect West Virginia's lush, mountainous environment. In doing so they promote the use of renewable natural resources to facilitate the end of Big Coal's tenure over the people and the environment of West Virginia. This fight to end MTR, and the ways in which it envisions a future without this industry, exposes interesting cultural notions about the history and environmental heritage of West Virginia. The environmental justice efforts that seek economic diversification and sustainable communities in the coalfields highlight West Virginia's environmental heritage as connected to mountains, whereas the coal industry actively promotes the cultural idea that the environmental heritage is coal and the industry that extracts it for national electricity generation.

West Virginia's Environmental Heritage: Coal or Mountains?

In May 2007 I traveled west on Route 3 in West Virginia to the offices of the CRMW in Whitesville. In the town of Surveyor, I passed a billboard with white lettering on a black background that read "Stop Destroying My Mountains," signed "God." The next day, when traveling the same route, I was disturbed by the sign's overnight alteration. Someone had scaled the billboard and, using white spray paint, had crossed out the original message and changed the signer from "God" to "Tree Huggers," an obvious message to environmental justice activists. In addition, driving through Beckley during this visit, I saw a sticker on a car with a picture of a coal miner urinating on a "tree hugger." The vandalism of this public sign, and the widespread presence of antienvironmentalist cultural artifacts, reveals how coal industry proponents denigrate grassroots activists. The cultural climate in the coalfields today labels most people who oppose MTR as extremists seeking to destroy West Virginia's economy and cultural ties to coal. These messages also speak to the divisiveness created by mountaintop removal coal mining. West Virginia has a strong contingent of grassroots activists fighting to save the mountains and small communities and to promote new economic enterprises, such as alternative energy projects. In addition, many pro-industry forces—coal employees, state political leaders, and some residents—continue to serve Big Coal interests at the expense of state citizens and the natural environment. These divisions inherently call into question whether mountains or coal is most connected to West Virginia's cultural history and environmental heritage. Thomas Heyd argues that "heritage" is

> something fundamentally shared in common, perhaps by all those who belong to a nation, ideological affiliation, or other affinity group. . . . As such heritage belongs to some group in a trans-temporal manner; it is something to be enjoyed not only by certain people in this generation, but also by the relevant set of people across time, possibly for indefinitely long future periods.[86]

Heyd suggests that this definition also implies that heritage is something to be protected before being passed on to the future.[87] For anti-MTR environmental justice activists it is the mountains that are "trans-temporal," capable of being enjoyed now and into the future. Because of this future promise, the mountains differ from coal, a finite fossil fuel resource whose production and consumption threaten human and nonhuman natures.

The defining marker of the Appalachian region is, of course, the expansive Appalachian mountain chain. Mountains are inextricably tied to the history, culture, and environment of this area. This ancient land formation extends from northern Georgia to southern Maine. Mountain residents, particularly in the southern and central Appalachians, express personal ties to the surrounding landscape, and many thus have great difficulty leaving the area for other environments. This cultural, environmental phenomenon has existed in the region for generations. For example, in 1905, author and folklorist Emma Bell Miles explained:

> Only a superficial observer could fail to understand that the mountain people really love their wilderness—love it for its beauty, for its freedom. . . . Nothing less than the charm of their stern motherland could hold them here. . . . Occasionally a whole starved-out family will emigrate westward, and, having settled, will spend years in simply waiting for a chance to sell out and move back again.[88]

This sentiment is still expressed today by those living in the region. When I first began research in West Virginia in 1998, one evening I enjoyed dinner at a Charleston restaurant. The waiter, a West Virginian who had just moved back to the state from Pennsylvania, told me he had to return because "I missed *my* mountains." In addition to a sense of longing and ownership of the natural landscape, many people in Appalachia, particularly in West Virginia, express the sense of being comforted and protected by the enveloping mountains in which they live. For example, West Virginia poet Maggie Anderson says:

> I know, of course, that the mountains can narrow our horizons, lower our ceilings, and hold us in, both literally and metaphorically. But I must also admit that these hills comfort me. Perhaps because of their great age (the range of mountains that makes up the Appalachian region from Georgia to Maine is two hundred million years old), the hills provide a sense of history and, therefore, of implicit continuance. The fact of their long past suggests the possibility of a long future.[89]

Anderson wrote this in the mid-1990s—a decade that saw the rise and expansion of mountaintop removal coal mining in West Virginia. While Anderson is optimistic in her belief that a long history ensures a long future, many grassroots activists in West Virginia worry that if mountaintop removal mining does not end, people in Appalachia will lose the source of their comfort and devotion, the sublime mountainous landscape. Other Appalachian writers, including Doris Diosa Davenport, describe the mountains as active and alive, and mountain inhabitants as also alive in a connected partnership. She suggests the mountains "are always 'doing something' and the ripples of that infinitesimal motion run through these valleys, run through me . . . the connections renewed in the air, the dirt, the trees; the sky and earth. . . . I am bound to these hills in a timeless, absolute fact of being."[90] Davenport highlights the timeless and almost spiritual relationships between people and the environment they inhabit in Appalachian mountain communities. Considering the ways in which human and nonhuman natures are conceptually connected in this cultural context, it is not surprising that environmental activists in West Virginia are keenly aware of how the mountainous landscape is part of their environmental heritage, and why they fight to protect the mountains.

Patty Sebok, a longtime member of the Coal River Mountain Watch, expresses the views of many in West Virginia concerning the historic and cultural significance of the mountains:

Mountains *are* Appalachia. We *are* the Appalachian Mountains. We are the mountaineers, we are the pioneers. . . . My ancestors trace back on one side, on my dad's side of the family, to the 1700s. They settled this area when nobody else wanted it. It was too rugged, too rough. It had no roads, no railroads, no nothing. You know, our people were pioneers who came in and carved this out, and now all the sudden they (coal operators and supporters) want it? Excuse me?[91]

Sebok's comments call into question the real owner of this natural landscape, and reveal, by invoking the history of settlement, the danger of losing this environmental space to current political-industrial forces. Like most white Americans with European roots, the land Sebok currently protects was originally occupied by numerous Native American tribes, who were forced off the land to make way for white settlers, African slaves, and free blacks. Nevertheless, Sebok's familiar ties to the Appalachian Mountains is an important incentive for her work in protecting this landscape. Janice Nease claims mountains are also important to her family history:

It [Kayford Mountain] gave us our sense of time, and place, and identity. And we would go there. If you were happy, you were in the mountains to celebrate. . . . It made you understand your connection to the universe and to the creator. And we went there when we were very sad, for solace. The mountain would, you know, replenish you.[92]

With the Appalachian Mountains falling prey to MTR, activists increasingly and consistently highlight the cultural link to their environmental heritage. They remind people that mountains—not the coal industry—define the region. Asserting their connection with land, culture, and history in the destructive era of mountaintop removal coal mining, CRMW member Lorelei Scarbro says simply, "We don't live where they mine coal. They mine coal where we live."[93] Scarbro's comments expose what defines West Virginia culture for many environmental activists in the region, and privileges long-standing Appalachian communities over coal extraction. The connections between mountains and environmental heritage made by many anti-MTR women are echoed by West Virginia novelist Denise Giardina, who considers mountaintop removal coal mining a crime. She argues that MTR is the environmental counterpoint to the Holocaust. It's the landscape, to the earth, what the Holocaust was to destroying people. These are some of the oldest mountains in the world, so whether you believe the earth is 6,000 years old or several million, they are still among the first mountains . . . so mountaintop removal is a violation of everything I believe in, both religiously and in terms of how I think people should be treated.[94]

Giardina's assessment of the impact of MTR on this ancient landscape also connects people to this environment, suggesting that the maltreatment of the mountains is equivalent and concomitant with the destruction of human communities nestled within the valleys of the Appalachian Mountains. This human and nonhuman nature connection constitutes the region's environmental heritage in the eyes of many MTR opponents, and strongly influences their fight to end MTR. These people consistently link their culture with the mountains that surround them, not with coal and the industry that produces it.

While many residents and anti-MTR activists see West Virginia culture as forever tied to mountains, business interests claim that West Virginia culture has long been shaped by the coal industry because of its historical economic primacy in the state. A conscious effort on the part of business and state politicians supportive of the coal industry stresses the industrial connections between coal and West Virginia, and for many residents of the state, coal defines the culture. One can read sentiments such as "West Virginia *is* coal country" on billboards, T-shirts, and public signs throughout the state. In addition to these pro-coal cultural artifacts, proponents control the message in the coalfields, using the media in effective ways to garner citizen support. Renku Sen states:

In an environment of dwindling media diversity and democracy, it is extremely difficult for grassroots community organizers who want to affect deep social change to get their stories heard. . . . Mainstream media are generally acknowledged to be politically conservative, not in party affiliation but in their unwillingness to put forth major challenges to the current political and economic system.[95]

This is certainly the case in West Virginia, as the interests of coal proponents are overwhelming served in the mainstream media, while the interests of mountain defenders are hardly represented, and in many cases denigrated as environmental extremism.

A powerful trio linking coal to West Virginia's history, culture, and environment in the mainstream media are the West Virginia Coal Association (WVCA), particularly through their Friends of Coal Campaigns, Massey Energy, and WalkerCat, makers of industrial machinery. Their media messages link coal to jobs, family, community, history, and heritage in Appalachia.

In addition to the use of commercials airing on West Virginia television that support Big Coal, the West Virginia Coal Association, sometimes under the name of their media outreach group, Friends of Coal (FOC), distributes yard signs, T-shirts, and bumper stickers to citizen supporters as part of its well-funded propaganda campaign. In the 2006 WVCA publication *Coal Facts*, the Friends of Coal group asserts that "it is likely that no state and industry are as closely identified with one another as West Virginia and coal."[96] FOC says the state is "full of people who understand and appreciate the value and the importance of the coal industry to the Mountain State and its people. . . . These people have always been around. But they have never before been organized into a cohesive force capable of demonstrating just how many West Virginians are directly and indirectly involved with the coal industry."[97] The WVCA sponsors commercials on local television, and even provides ringtones for coal supporters to purchase. In one available ringtone, a group of singers promotes coal in exuberant voices, exclaiming: "Coal is West Virginia. Coal is me and you. Coal is West Virginia, we've got a job to do. Coal is energy, we need energy. Coal is West Virginia."[98] This brief song highlights work and the energy-producing purpose of this fossil fuel, while also connecting the industry to the state, and its inhabitants, a casual yet ubiquitous way to spread the message about coal's ties to West Virginia.

Massey Energy (now owned by Alpha Natural Resources) also uses the mainstream media to promote its interests in West Virginia. In fact, Massey's presence saturates the state coalfields. A typical Massey television commercial promotes the company as valuable community members, while emphasizing economic messages about jobs and the need for coal-produced energy. For example, a recent Massey television advertisement, "More than Coal," boasts:

> At Massey we produce more than coal. We create opportunities—opportunities for American energy independence, and opportunities for our

members, their families, and for our communities. That's why Massey Energy is expanding every day, opening new mines every month, and creating hundreds of new, good-paying jobs. And Massey continues to support our hometowns to enhance our quality of life. Why? Because we live here, too. Massey Energy. Doing the right thing with Energy.[99]

While the text is read, a young Massey miner (wearing the signature blue-and-orange uniform) is shown leaving his comfortable middle-class home for work, as his wife and child walk him to the door. This commercial explicitly targets young men with families and promotes the possibility of economic security and material advantages that come with being a member of Massey's team. Other images that flash on the screen during this commercial include firemen at a local station, young women walking through a college campus, and children on a playground.[100] These shots emphasize the point that Massey Energy is situated in local communities who benefit from their presence. These advertisements are powerful messages in an economically depressed region like the coalfields of West Virginia, and along with the media outreach of the West Virginia Coal Association, help support the interests of Big Coal in these areas.

WalkerCat also has a strong presence in coalfield culture, and frequently sponsors ads along with the WVCA. Recent television commercials exalt the West Virginia coal miner working an MTR site, positioning him as a good steward of the state's natural environment. In their ad "Clean Green Coal," WalkerCat presents scenic pictures of reclaimed MTR sites, full of natural life, interspersed with pictures of a miner operating dragline equipment. The text, set to blues music, contends:

> West Virginia's mountains and ridge tops have provided America with jobs and energy from coal. These beautiful green areas represent the final stage of mining. Our miners have maintained the rugged West Virginia character of their homeland through the almost artistic use of their equipment. West Virginia's citizens and hardworking miners deserve credit and praise for preserving our mountain character. That's a cleaner and greener West Virginia coal.[101]

In addition to exalting coal miners as good stewards of the mountainous environment, the ad makes strong connections between coal mining and the culture and history of West Virginia, presenting responsible mountaintop removal mining as producing "green" coal. These commercials are powerful public relations tools, and undoubtedly successful in garnering public support for coal interests. Coal River Mountain Watch member Judy Bonds suggested that the mainstream media, more than anything else, is used to obtain support for Big coal, and to foster opposition to environmental justice messages: "I've always said that if we had the money to produce commercials on prime-time TV, this battle would be over with."[102] Even though Big Coal controls the message in the coalfields, activists have used the mainstream media as much as budgets will allow and, more important, have developed other ways to raise awareness about the impact of MTR on the mountains and the communities within them.

Rinku Sen suggests that activist groups "cannot afford to avoid the main-stream media," because they "have a responsibility to try to influence the coverage of our issues."[103] However, she argues that progressive groups must have well-planned strategies that use media in dynamic ways.[104] While not having multimillion-dollar budgets to buy television or radio advertising, anti-MTR environmental justice groups such as the Coal River Mountain Watch and the Ohio Valley Environmental Coalition use a number of media to fight Big Coal. They produce and distribute newsletters such as OVEC's *Winds of Change* and CRMW's *Messenger*. These organizations also utilize consistent and vigorous letter-to-the-editor writing campaigns in mainstream newspapers such as the *Raleigh Register-Herald* and the *Charleston Gazette*. In addition, they regularly engage in phone campaigns geared toward getting mountain defenders to call local, regional, and federal politicians with their concerns over the impact of MTR and the need for greater coal industry regulation. Websites such as the slick and highly interactive I Love Mountains are also used, in addition to the social media site Facebook, which is helpful in spreading the pro-mountain, anticoal message and in organizing large groups of people to participate in campaigns. Through these efforts to educate the public and stop mountaintop removal, activists consistently link West Virginia's environmental heritage to the mountains that envelop coalfield communities. They do so in a cultural climate where the interests of Big Coal are powerfully supported.

The short answer to the question posed in the subhead at the beginning of this section (West Virginia's Environmental Heritage: Coal or Mountains?) is: both. Coal is undeniably a major part of West Virginia's history, economy, culture, and environment. Certain industries do influence the culture of particular areas, and to a large extent this is the case in West Virginia, but one must note the impact of that influence and question the efficacy of such arrangements, particularly in regions ruled by extractive businesses. The coal industry, despite the jobs created, has not been a positive influence in West Virginia. It has reaped billions of dollars of profit over the years in the second-most-impoverished state in the country. It continues to enjoy record profits through the increased use of mountaintop removal coal mining, while controlling media messages suggesting that coal defines the state's history, culture, and environmental heritage. For many state residents, the environmental heritage is solidly linked to mountains, and thus the practice of MTR is disturbingly unacceptable. They seek to preserve the mountainous environment and build sustainable communities through green energy and economic development.

Conclusion

For many women in the anti-MTR movement, there is a way to remember the past and work for the future to improve the social, economic, and environmental conditions in the state. Women's participation in social justice efforts in Appalachia has a robust history, and many anti-MTR activists embrace and acknowledge this past as they work to create economic diversification and environmentally sustainable communities in the coalfields today. This environmental justice activism is fairly new, but considering coal's long history of social and environment exploitation in central Appalachia, it is arguably one of the best sites to highlight the connections between social protest and economic and environmental concerns. In fighting to end mountaintop removal coal mining and envisioning a future without coal, many women also promote the richness of Appalachian culture as tied to the mountains. Recognizing that environmental degradation and social exploitation frequently go hand in hand, they seek to raise awareness about the ways in which people in Appalachia are also victims of cruel cultural stereotypes that ultimately serve, and in many ways justify, the continued exploitation of West Virginia's environment and culture. Some members of the Coal River Mountain Watch, for example, wear T-shirts that read "Save the Endangered Hillbilly," playing on the mainstream environmental legislation geared toward protecting jeopardized animals by applying it to mountain people whose homes and culture are under threat by MTR. This reclamation of the hillbilly stereotype can serve as a formidable weapon to preserve mountains and Appalachian culture. Examining the hillbilly image, so strongly attached to Appalachia, and West Virginians in particular, can also provide fruitful paths to examine the ways in which this stereotype is connected to gender and racial formations in the coalfields.

CHAPTER 4

Saving the Endangered Hillbilly: Appalachian Stereotypes and Cultural Identity in the Anti– Mountaintop Removal Movement

> *And the hillbilly, it's always been okay to make fun of them, and still today is not recognized as the racial and class issue that it is. . . . I'm hillbilly to the core, but don't call me no stupid hillbilly. I don't think there's such a thing. Hillbillies are absolutely the most resilient people on U.S. soil. We can live through anything, and we've proved it because we've lived through the rise and fall of the coal industry many times.*

> —Maria Gunnoe, community organizer for the Ohio Valley Environmental Coalition, and 2009 recipient of the Goldman Environmental Prize

Introduction

IN 2001 MARIA GUNNOE, SELF-DESCRIBED "HILLBILLY to the core," lived a quietly domestic life with her husband, a professional masonry worker, and their children in Bob White, West Virginia.[1] The couple was active in the kids' school activities, particularly the football team. Gunnoe, who had no prior activist experience, was oblivious to nascent coal operations in her neighborhood, failing to notice mining permit announcements in the local newspaper that would literally change the landscape beneath her: "I didn't look at them. I didn't know I needed to. I was really naive about what they even meant."[2] Gunnoe's naïveté ended that year when her home was flooded three times, wiping out access to the main highway and altering the physical contours of her property. She recalls that the water "came from all directions," and because she has lived here her entire life, she instinctively knew that "something wasn't right with this."[3] Since 2001 her home has flooded numerous times, and in 2004 was covered with toxic sludge, cutting off her water supply and forcing the family to rely on bottled water for cooking and drinking. Gunnoe has since learned that in 2000, a year before the flooding began, a twelve-hundred-acre mountaintop removal operation began above her home, which is situated on a ten-story valley fill that contains two toxic slurry ponds capturing mining waste.[4]

These events prompted Gunnoe to join the Ohio Valley Environmental Coalition, working as a community organizer to protect nearby coalfield communities. Gunnoe spends her days talking with local community members, getting their stories out to local, national, and international media, and trying to preserve neighboring towns such as Lindytown and Twilight. In Gunnoe's community in Boone County, West Virginia, people who occupy lands without owning the mineral rights beneath them are accused of trespassing and forced off the land by coal companies. Those who do own those rights are accepting company buyouts and relocating, while others refuse to move. The community houses that are vacated are typically burned or used for company purposes in what Gunnoe describes as a growing "mining complex."[5] When she is not working in her local community encouraging people to stay and fight the encroachment of Big Coal, Gunnoe travels the state and the country, talking about coalfield injustices and rallying support to end MTR and promote the use of alternative energy.

Like other women environmental justice activists in the anti-MTR movement, Gunnoe has strong family ties to the Appalachian Mountains and works to preserve the culture and environment from the destructive forces of coal. She hopes her activism will ultimately benefit future generations who live in these small, rural communities. When Gunnoe talks about her ties to these mountains, she emphasizes her Cherokee grandparents and great-grandparents as instrumental in passing on knowledge about the natural environment, and also instilling in her a sense of pride in mountain culture. Gunnoe's family moved to central Appalachia in the early 1800s after escaping the forced removal of Cherokee people in Georgia, settling in West Virginia.[6] In the 1950s her Cherokee grandfather bought the land where Gunnoe now lives, and she credits her grandfather and her great-grandmother with teaching her to value and rely on the environment by identifying and gathering edible mountain plants. She says, "It's our culture. We go into these mountains; we're mountain people, that's what we do."[7] Gunnoe claims that most of the places her grandparents took her, and other places in the mountains where her family used to gather, are now lost to encroaching mining operations. She believes her community, family history, and culture are being destroyed along with the natural mountainous environment in which they are situated.

In addition to fostering respect for the Appalachian environment, Gunnoe inherited a strong sense of community from her great-grandmother Minnie, who lived to the age of 106 after raising not only seven children of her own, but forty-two neighborhood kids who were orphaned for various reasons. This grandmother, who lived in Buffalo Creek, organized the children she cared for into an efficient and self-sustaining community. Gunnoe says Minnie was "absolutely the backbone of that entire operation, working as smoothly as it did. She was like the drill sergeant, if you will."[8] Gunnoe's upbringing in West Virginia taught her to love and value the natural environment and instilled a sense of community that no doubt fuels her environmental justice activism. She recalls studying a West Virginia history book during her school years that defined a mountaineer as "a steward of the land, of community, an active community member. . . . It really defined the mountaineer in a way that made me proud."[9] Gunnoe enthusiastically refers to herself as a "mountaineer" and a "hillbilly," adopting the terms as part of her cultural identity. As such, she considers herself a fierce defender of the Appalachian Mountains and culture.

The term "hillbilly" is an inveterate, white racial construction in American culture. The grassroots women participating in the anti-MTR movement are primarily white, working-class women. All of the women are white except Lorelei Scarbro and Maria Gunnoe, who both claim a partial Native American racial identity because of their Cherokee grandparents. These coalfield women are situated in a state whose residents also are primarily white and working-class, although historically, race, ethnicity, and nationality differences have interesting links to the coalfield economy and culture. Currently, West Virginia is considered one of the most racially homogeneous states in the country along with Maine and Vermont.[10] In 2009, the U.S. Census Bureau indicated that 94.5 percent of West Virginians were white, 3.6 percent where African American, .07 percent were Asian, and 1.1 percent were Latino.[11] This racial homogeneity explains the overwhelming presence of white people in the movement to end MTR. Because West Virginia is largely white, and the grassroots component of the anti-MTR movement primarily consists of white women, racial distinctions intersect with class and gender in important ways in coalfield culture. Examining cultural stereotypes of Appalachians, particularly the long-standing "hillbilly," and situating this symbol within cultural studies scholarship on whiteness, reveals complex racial and class-based identities that have interesting environmental justice connections.

Actions such as Maria Gunnoe's adoption of the racially marked mountaineer identity, and even the ostensibly derogatory term "hillbilly," are a fundamental cultural component of the environmental justice activism against mountaintop removal coal mining. This is a notable distinction, given that environmental justice activism emerged out of communities of color in this country, while the anti-MTR environmental justice movement is borne out of mostly white, rural, working-class communities in Appalachia. This movement seeks to foster cultural pride and a sense of history among Appalachians, while convincing those living outside the region that this is a valuable culture and environment worth saving. One of the most intriguing slogans in the movement, emblazoned on T-shirts and protest signs, reads "Save the Endangered Hillbilly," a directive encouraging people to consider the human costs of mountaintop removal along with the environmental toll on Appalachia. This directive constitutes the cultural reclamation of the pejorative term "hillbilly," with its racial, class, and gendered implications. Moreover, the directive can be read as an environmental justice call to action with an inherent critique of mainstream environmentalism, and also an aggressive move by the activists to situate themselves within American environmental politics. The reclamation of "hillbilly" is ultimately used as a cultural tool in the fight against MTR and highlights interesting ways in which race, class, and gender are part of mountain culture and the anti-MTR movement.

Appalachian Cultural Stereotypes: Gender, the Ideology of "Appalachia," and American Awareness of Mountaintop Removal Mining

Over the years, many residents and scholars of Appalachia have noted the disturbingly predictable ways the word "Appalachia" evokes stereotypical notions about the region's inhabitants. It is difficult to escape the idea of Appalachia as a historically troubled region where ostensibly poor, culturally backward, violent, and sexually deviant people reside in substandard social and economic conditions of their own creation. One doesn't have to look too hard to find examples of these formulaic notions; they are evidenced in politics, popular culture, literature, journalism, and in academic production.[12] This long-standing cultural "othering" of Appalachia is a distinct part of the American imagination and serves to easily dismiss the region's residents, prohibiting a complex understanding of the problems facing Appalachia, including mountaintop removal coal mining. Some activists believe that this persistent cultural denigration of Appalachians exacerbates the region's problems and prevents people within and outside Appalachia from fighting for better conditions in this area. While all Appalachian people are victim to belittling stereotypes, these notions are particularly problematic for West Virginians, who inhabit the only state whose borders fall entirely within the geographically and politically designated Appalachian region of the United States.

Current popular examples of dyslogistic ideas of West Virginians are numerous. For example, a widely available Abercrombie & Fitch T-shirt contains a cartographic outline of the state and reads "West Virginia: It's All Relative." This cultural artifact plays upon the derogatory casting of West Virginians as an incestuous population where most residents' familial relations are attributed to inbreeding reproductive practices. In another example, a recent casting call for the horror film *Shelter*, starring Julianne Moore, sought West Virginia mountain people who had unusual body types and facial features, in an effort to present images of Appalachian people as contained in other popular movies such as *Deliverance* and *The Hills Have Eyes*.[13] Even though the images contained in these popular movies are also derived from stereotypes, the filmmakers were insistent on locating these types of people, ultimately reifying existing notions of Appalachians through their unwillingness to challenge or question conventional notions about the region.

Donna Belajac, owner of the casting company contracted to hire paid extras, explained her rationale: "Some of these 'holler' people—because they are insular and clannish, and they don't leave their area—there is literally inbreeding, and the people there often have a different kind of look. That's what we're trying to get."[14] The idea of West Virginians as culturally backward, inbreeding people is conveyed by popular films like *Shelter*, reliant on degrading stereotypes that are, by and large, perfectly acceptable in mainstream American culture. After hearing about this particularly egregious example, former West Virginia governor Joe Manchin demanded an apology from the makers of the film.[15]

Unfortunately, mean-spirited conceptions of West Virginians are not conveyed only through consumer products such as T-shirts and films, but are also expressed by high-ranking American politicians. In 2008, while addressing the National Press Club in Washington, DC, then vice president Dick Cheney reflected upon his family heritage, joking to the crowd that he had "Cheneys" on both sides of his family, and "we don't even live in West Virginia."[16] These recent examples convey the idea of West Virginians as primitive, backwoods people, with incest as the prominent theme running through these derogatory cultural utterances. Such ideas not only demean those targeted, but also cast Appalachians as outside of mainstream America. These acceptable formulaic ideas prevent people from acquiring a complex understanding of Appalachian history, culture, and the systematic problems currently facing the region.

While both Appalachian men and women are victims of stereotyping, women are represented, historically, in culturally specific ways. When considering the types of Appalachian women depicted in American culture, Sally Ward Maggard maintains that women in the Appalachian Mountains are frequently cast in romantic ways that emphasize "enigmatic but talented" women adept at folk art such as quilting, spinning wool, and playing dulcimers.[17] These women are viewed in popular consciousness as "quiet caretakers of an idealized rural life."[18] Such notions connect women to a largely agrarian past, as if Appalachia and the people who reside there are stuck in time, remnants of a preindustrialized, bygone era. Maggard says the other prominent stereotype of Appalachian women employs "degrading" images of voluptuous, vapid mountain women perceived in popular culture characters such as Daisy Mae, Daisy Duke, and Elly Mae.[19] These representations highlight young, beautiful, highly sexualized women who are pretty to look at, and easily manipulated because of an apparent lack of intellectual wherewithal.

The opposite of this particular cultural representation is the Appalachian "Granny," an aging, wise woman who is "wiry" and "wrinkled," and perfectly content to live a poor, rural existence rather than aspiring to an upper-middle-class lifestyle.[20] While these images differentiate Appalachian women, Maggard suggests that on the whole they cast mountain women as "standing outside of or apart from the rest of America. They are counterpoints to the modern world, representing either a simpler rural life or a ridiculous fringe population of deficient, mysterious characters."[21] These images suggest Appalachia is monolithically rural, although, just like the rest of the country, central Appalachia contains urban and suburban areas as well. In addition, these stereotypes of Appalachian women render them incapable of independent public participation, even though we know that historically Appalachian women have been at the forefront of organized movements that draw attention to problems confronting the region and have worked toward solutions to improve their mountain communities.

Women in the anti-MTR movement do not conform to conventional notions about Appalachian women. They are not "quiet caretakers" or women who exist solely in the private sphere, caring only for their families. They are women actively engaged in environmental politics, working hard to save the

Appalachian Mountains and the communities nestled within them. Nor do they fit the oversexed and dumb image of the Appalachian woman, or the august granny who stubbornly clings to agrarian ways in the face of rapid industrialization. The women fighting mountaintop removal coal mining are Goldman Environmental Prize winners, ex–labor activists, retired teachers, visual artists, former Pizza Hut waitresses, mothers, and wives of coal miners. In short, they are a varied group of working-class white and Native American women who are proud of their Appalachian heritage and work tirelessly to create sustainable mountain communities.

Considering the saturation of stereotypes of Appalachia in the popular American imagination, Elizabeth S. D. Engelhardt argues that a feminist analysis in Appalachian studies scholarship can provide illustrative ways to challenge stereotypical assumptions about Appalachia, particularly Appalachian women. She encourages us to "dance away from Granny and Elly May" by framing our discussions of women in Appalachia in a way that "does not let stereotypes dictate the terms of analysis—but that instead thinks in complicated ways about the social hierarchies that intersect and shape individual lives."[22] Furthermore, Engelhardt argues that an Appalachian feminist analysis has the potential to reveal the complex "power dynamics" between those being stereotyped and those stereotyping, allowing us to better understand the connections between individuals and the institutions in which they are embedded.[23] A critical analysis of the role of representations of Appalachia and their function in American culture is vital because of the entrenchment of these oversimplified conceptions in the United States, and what they reveal about the intersections of race, class, gender, and environment in Appalachia and beyond. However, before we fully examine these social locations, it is important to note the history of cultural ideologies about Appalachia.

David C. Hsiung correctly suggests that Appalachian residents are not the only victims of stereotyping, but calls into question the makeup of the invidious characterizations of Appalachians. He argues that "every stereotype has some basis in truth, but the danger comes when stereotypes make it easy to generalize and paint everyone with the same brush. . . . Do examples of poverty, violence, illiteracy, inbreeding, and laziness exist in Appalachia? Certainly, but that does not mean the entire region should be characterized by such terms."[24] While Hsiung calls our attention to the pitfalls of relying on formulaic notions to define entire groups, other scholars provide insight into how Appalachian stereotypes are connected to American culture. Ronald D.

Eller suggests that Appalachia may be America's most maligned region, even replacing the southern part of the United States, which has risen culturally and economically in recent years.[25] Eller argues that Appalachia has always been part of the "mythical South," but continues to "languish backstage in the American drama, still dressed, in the popular mind at least, in the garments of backwardness, violence, poverty, and hopelessness once associated with the South as a whole. No other region of the United States today plays the role of the 'other America' quite so persistently as Appalachia"[26] Indeed, these negative cultural notions of Appalachians have persisted for generations, and are thus thoroughly ingrained in American culture. Jill M. Fraley writes:

> In the American imagination, Appalachia exists as a wholly formed entity, one created by generations of stereotypes and condescension. In the American imagination, Appalachia is no place to go on vacation. Appalachia is a place to avoid, perhaps even a place to fear. Appalachia is dirty, ugly, unkempt, and decidedly different from the rest of the country. . . . Appalachia is a place to escape from, not a place to live.[27]

Because these ideas have such a long history in American culture, and plentiful examples of the troubling ways Appalachia is viewed in the public imagination exist, the circulation of these cultural myths are solidified and continually re-created in the American imagination with too few challenges.

When examining Appalachian stereotypes and the functions they serve in American culture, many scholars invoke Henry D. Shapiro's work on "the idea of Appalachia," a social construction developed in the nineteenth century to "explain" those living in the southern mountain region of the United States.[28] Shapiro argues that the creation of the "idea of Appalachia" attempted to "understand [a] reality perceived in a particular way from a particular point of view."[29] In other words, this idea of Appalachia is a product of the nineteenth-century, white, middle-class, urban imagination. Shapiro says these ideological social constructions about Appalachia developed between 1870 and 1900, in post–Civil war America when industrialization was increasing and concomitant social values were formed and solidified. He suggests Appalachia served a vital function in this creation, and continues to help define American culture by representing the "other" America—apart from mainstream, middle-class life. Hence this notion of the Appalachian "other," or a "strange land" with "peculiar people," conveniently served as an example of what the rest of the country was not, and more important, should not be.[30]

Other scholars, such as Allen Batteau, call the ideological processes of this cultural creation the "invention of Appalachia," suggesting, like Shapiro, that this social construction is primarily a "creature of the urban imagination."[31] The creation of Appalachia in the American imagination is indeed a convenient tool that supports existing cultural binaries of urban/rural, rich/poor, culture/nature, and their attendant positive and negative associations.[32] The urban is defined by what it is not, the rural; while the rich are defined by their opposite, the poor; and culture exists because it has separated from nature in the Western imagination. These ideas, largely the creation of nineteenth-century "local color" writers and travelers from northeastern urban centers, preclude a nuanced understanding of Appalachia and its residents, and are fundamentally designed to define and promote white, urban, middle-class, industrial culture.[33]

Anthony Harkins notes the efficacies of local color writing based in Appalachia for travel writers and those consuming these fanciful texts in urban areas:

> Their vision was of a picturesque landscape and colorful, even quirky men and women oddly out of step with modern society. More of a curiosity than a concern, this fictionalized Appalachia served primarily to point out the benefits of advanced civilization and to offer northern urbanites a welcome sojourn in a mysterious (but ultimately safe) wilderness from which they could return refreshed to their place in the cosmopolitan social order.[34]

Harkins suggests that during this time in American history and culture, images of mountain women reflected the merging of ideas about "poor whites" and "backwoods pioneers" into a new image of the "poor mountaineer," and Appalachian women were depicted in stock ways: "The beautiful but ignorant mountain lass; the overworked and crudely attired drudge who struggles to care for her oversized family; or ... the bonneted, toothless crone who lives out her remaining years smoking a corncob pipe awash in a haze of melancholia."[35] These local color ideas and their rendering of mountain people as isolated, poor, backward, and violent people who threatened American modernity and progress were solidified in the American psyche by the turn of the twentieth century.[36] Ronald L. Lewis argues that this "fictional representation became accepted and then reified as 'history' by subsequent reporters, scholars, and policy makers," creating a mythical Appalachia.[37] He suggests that if we are to look beyond these myths and examine Appalachia's economic evolution, "it is clear that much of Appalachia was neither unusually isolated, physically or culturally, nor was its population uniformly more homogeneous than that of other sections of rural America."[38]

Appalachian studies scholarship has done a tremendous job of pointing out the ways in which these prominent cultural notions about Appalachian people, particularly the ostensible backwardness, isolation, and social homogeneity of the population, are myths that fail to recognize the diversity of the region. Dwight Billings claims that "while the peoples and cultures in the Appalachian Mountains are decidedly plural, outside the region in the arts, the academy, and popular culture, many representations of them now, as for the past one hundred years, are often monolithic, pejorative, and unquestioned."[39] Indeed, much of Appalachian studies scholarship seeks to debunk these cultural myths and provide a deeper, more nuanced cultural history of the region. The work of historians is particularly helpful in revealing that although poor and working-class whites have made up the majority of the population of Appalachia for a long time, it is important to note the presence of people and communities of color and their ties to Appalachia.

Studies by Wilma A. Dunaway and Joe William Trotter Jr., in particular, highlight the economic and cultural diversity of Appalachia in an effort to redress prominent notions about cultural homogeneity and isolation. For example, Dunaway's examination of preindustrial Appalachia positions it as a peripheral region of a capitalist world system, supplying raw materials in a global market, a trend one can argue continued with the rise of the coal industry in parts of West Virginia. Dunaway's work successfully complicates the long-standing notion of Appalachia as an isolated rural, agrarian space, untouched by outside cultural and economic interests. Her work also examines racial diversity in Appalachia by analyzing the social conflicts and harmony among white settlers, slaves and free blacks, and mountain whites during this period.[40] In addition, Joe Trotter highlights the ethnic and racial diversity of the region as he points to the diverse labor force of coal miners in West Virginia from 1915 to 1932. Trotter's work demonstrates that in the early days of coal mining in West Virginia, whites of European descent, foreign-born Europeans, and blacks worked together and lived together, although in highly segregated fashion, in the coalfields of West Virginia.[41]

Texts such as *Blacks in Appalachia*, by William H. Turner and Edward J. Cabbell, highlight African American life in Appalachia in the early twentieth century, while John C. Inscoe's *Appalachians and Race* examines the mountain South from slavery to segregation.[42] While today whites overwhelmingly constitute the majority of West Virginia's population, this state, and other areas in central Appalachia, has an interesting and diverse history that is absent in prevalent cultural notions of the region as racially and ethnically homogeneous. And it is important to note that many people of color, from African Americans to Native Americans, and ethnically and nationally differentiated people such as Jews and Irish Americans, also have strong ties to Appalachia.

Many in the movement to end mountaintop removal coal mining embrace Appalachia's rich cultural history and expose these stereotypes as simplistic ideas preventing people, both inside and outside of the region, from stopping a mining practice that is decimating not only the Appalachian mountain chain, but also its culture and history. Kentucky novelist Silas House highlights the cultural diversity and history of Appalachia, connecting this rich past to the present fight against mountaintop removal coal mining, effectively utilizing this diversity as a unifying tool in the fight to end MTR:

> We come from people who were the first people in these mountains, the Cherokees, Shawnees, the Crow, the Mingo. We come from the tough Scots-Irish who came to settle it next, and the Italians and Germans who worked like dogs to make their way in the world and the black men and women who were brought here on ships to be slaves and later sent here on trains to work for half-scale down in the mines.... We are a true melting pot of strong peoples, a culture of immigrants, all joining strengths to become Appalachians, and in the past we haven't backed down, so this time we can't back down either.[43]

House questions the apathy within Appalachia over mountaintop removal mining, which he views as both an environmental and a cultural problem. He promotes the concept of a "conscious heart," where residents embrace their cultural heritage, defy belittling stereotypes, and stand up against forces that threaten the culture and environment of Appalachia today. While Appalachian writers and activists such as Silas House encourage Appalachians to understand this cultural history and use it as a way to embolden anti-MTR efforts, West Virginia novelist and activist Denise Giardina encourages people to be mindful of the ways in which Appalachian problems are American problems as well. Giardina agrees that the idea of Appalachian otherness is a fundamental component of mainstream American consciousness when she suggests:

It is convenient, this habit of relegating Appalachia to the margins of national life. For if the situation should turn out otherwise, if the mountains are populated by average Americans with concerns common to the country at large, then the blame for our problems would have to be located elsewhere. The nation's view of Appalachia and itself would have to change.[44]

Giardina's observations situate Appalachia within America, suggesting that material problems facing the region, from poverty to low education levels to weak local governments to mountaintop removal mining, are American problems as well. The social construction of Appalachia, and the stereotypes by which the region and its people are marked as "other" in American culture, not only preclude a complex understanding of these problems, but also fail to see the ways in which the rest of the country benefits from these cultural misrepresentations. Relying on stereotypes prevents the rest of the country from seeing the contributions of Appalachia, hindering an adequate assessment of central Appalachia's material challenges: poverty, weak local governments, low education levels, and environmental problems such as mountaintop removal coal mining.

Many people who oppose mountaintop removal mining are aware of the widespread use of derogatory notions of Appalachians, and argue that they are convenient tools in the exploitation of the Appalachian environment and culture. Revealing an awareness of popular stereotypes, Coal River Mountain Watch cofounder Janice Nease reminds us of the material base of these cultural notions and the industrial interests they serve:

> Appalachia is not a woe-begotten place filled with illiterate people lost in poverty. . . . This is a common stereotype created by the land barons and the out of state corporations that robbed the people of their land and mineral rights. . . . This image is used to strip us of our humanity so that no one will feel obligated to care about us. For them, we are throwaway people.[45]

Other activists echo Nease's assessment of the connections between stereotyping and the socioeconomic and environmental exploitation of West Virginia, lamenting the lackluster mainstream media coverage of mountaintop removal coal mining and the anti-MTR movement. In 2006, for example, mountaintop removal coal mining and the civil disobedience against Big Coal was voted the tenth-most-underreported story by the American media.[46] Ohio Valley Environmental Coalition community organizer Maria Gunnoe believes, "The reason it's ignored is because we are who we are. We're hillbillies from south-ern West Virginia, and it's okay to do this to a subhuman culture of people, which is the way the biggest part of the world looks at us."[47] Scholars such as Jill M. Fraley also make connections between the disparaging cultural views of Appalachia, economic exploitation, and the systematic poverty in this age of mountaintop removal coal mining:

> The great attack on the Appalachian Mountains continues unabated pre-cisely because the public consciousness does not value Appalachia. Through 150 years of stereotypes, Appalachia has been rendered a place outside nor-mal American life. Just as stereotypes have been used around the world to aid in economic domination of other minority groups, the iconic image of Ap-palachian poverty serves to justify economic domination of Appalachia by the coal industry. A region with one of the most valuable deposits of natural resources in the world continues to be one of the poorest areas—doomed by a colonial economy created and maintained by the coal industry.[48]

Fraley argues that environmental, cultural, and economic problems in Appa-lachia are easily ignored by the general American public precisely because the region is "othered" in the American imagination. The late Judy Bonds, former Coal River Mountain Watch codirector, consistently suggested that cultural stereotypes have conveniently "made us the sacrifice zone," because "why would anyone care about a bunch of hillbillies."[49] Bonds further described the con-nection between cultural stereotypes and economic processes in the coalfields by saying, "We are living with domestic terrorism from these coal barons, and our lapdog politicians are working hand in hand with corporations that put them in place to destroy our children's world. They think we're a bunch of ig-norant hillbillies, but you don't have to be very smart to figure that one out, do you?"[50] Cultural stereotyping and social economic exploitation can be viewed as effective partners that render a region unworthy of help and protection, fa-cilitating the rapid cultural and environmental abuses present in the coalfields of West Virginia today.

The prevailing adjectives used to describe Appalachian people, from *violent* to *culturally backward* to *sexually deviant*, are notions deeply rooted in American culture. For some people living outside of Appalachia, these cultural messages can justify or make palatable the social, political, and environmental exploita-tion in West Virginia today. For some insiders these stereotypes are internalized, and can partially explain the reluctance to speak out against coalfield injustice, a social process discussed more fully in the next section. While I have provided a general discussion of Appalachian stereotypes, I wish to isolate what is perhaps the most prevalent Appalachian cultural symbol: the "hillbilly." Examinations of the long-lasting hillbilly stereotype can provide complex understandings of race, particularly whiteness as a racial category, and environmental connections to this popular image, which are important considerations in our understanding of how and why some anti-MTR activists embrace this term as an inclusive symbol of cultural identification and unity.

Appalachian Cultural Identity in the Anti-MTR Movement:
Race, Class, and the West Virginia "Hillbilly"

Inherent in the movement to end mountaintop removal is the cultural reclamation of the West Virginia "hillbilly" as a way to identify mountain people and instill cultural pride in coalfield residents. In the popular American imagination, the "hillbilly" is a contemptuous symbol of cultural backwardness or, in some cases, comedic buffoonery. Anti-MTR activists realize that "hillbilly" is decidedly depreciatory, but adopt and redefine what it means to be a "hillbilly" into a source of cultural pride. For many of these activist women, a hillbilly is a person who lives in the Appalachian Mountains, and who values and protects the history and environment of mountain communities. Judy Bonds stated, "I'm proud to be called a hillbilly.... It's what you use before the word 'hillbilly' that we have a problem with. You know, it's the derogatory statement of dumb, lazy, stupid, hillbilly, ignorant, inbred hillbilly.... It's all those adjectives that you put on it that makes it the bad word."[51] Maria Gunnoe, an OVEC community organizer, also values the term as a sense of cultural pride while realizing its pejorative associations in American culture:

> It's always been okay to make fun of them, and still today is not recognized as the racial and class issue that it is.... I'm hillbilly to the core, but don't call me no stupid hillbilly.... Hillbillies are absolutely the most resilient people on U.S. soil. We can live through anything, and we've proved it because we've lived through the rise and fall of the coal industry many times.[52]

As will be discussed later in this chapter, Appalachia women such as Judy Bonds and Maria Gunnoe emphasized what they perceived to be the positive connotations of the word as signifiers of historical, cultural and environmental connections to this region.

The dualism of the term "hillbilly" is perhaps the most fascinating aspect of this examination of Appalachian stereotypes. On the one hand, "hillbilly" is a pejorative and fundamentally classist term applied to poor whites in Appalachia as a way to distinguish this rural, working-class white population from urban, suburban, and middle-class whites. On the other hand, it evokes a regional and environmental identity that some activists actively fighting mountaintop removal coal mining have reclaimed as a cultural identity marker tied to the history and environment of Appalachia. Anthony Harkins argues that historically, "hillbilly" "incorporates both 'otherness' and self-identification," and in some "oppositionally dualistic way, southern mountain folk both denounced it as a vicious slur and embraced it in defense of their value system and in celebration of their cultural heritage."[53]

However, not all scholars agree that reclamation of invidious terms is a positive step in instilling cultural pride, or in making transformative changes in the Appalachian region. For example, Elizabeth S. D. Engelhardt says, "Looking for a positive spin on a negative stereotype only reinforces the power of the stereotype. In theoretical terms, a concept is never deconstructed by focusing on its opposite; doing so merely reinforces the binary and the structures of power it supports."[54] Engelhardt's ideas on the reclamation of negative cultural stereotypes, and the terms used to define and describe them, insufficiently acknowledge race and class differences among people or their connection to the natural environmental spaces they occupy. Furthermore, Engelhardt's criticism also fails to note social object and subject positions and the power dynamics inherent in these cultural arrangements.

This reclaiming and redefining of the hillbilly cultural stereotype is akin to the tendency of some African Americans' usage of the term "nigger" or "niggah," or when parts of the gay community embrace "queer" to self-identify and foster a sense of community. By doing so, the subjects using the term acknowledge (perhaps unwittingly) the pejorative originations of the word and use it as a tool to foster a social collective among disenfranchised populations. Susan Sarnoff acknowledges the reality that stereotypes internalized by minority groups often create a sense of inferiority that can be overcome only "by changing the social landscape, enabling citizens to see 'their own kind' succeed without giving up traditions and cultural connections."[55] Adopting and redefining "hillbilly" does not reinforce the oppression of coalfield citizens; rather, it can be a term of individual and collective empowerment. By embracing "hillbilly," West Virginia activists are asserting a racial and classed identity situated in the mountainous environment of Appalachia that distinguishes them from urban and suburban white, middle-class society. In self-identifying as hillbillies, they reclaim and redefine the term as a way to showcase and protect mountain culture in the anti-MTR movement. The hillbilly is an interesting cultural symbol containing many of the stereotypical notions about Appalachian people discussed in the previous section, and serves similar functions in American culture. This pejorative term, and the images it conjures, has a long history and thus provides productive ways for examining race and class implications of Appalachian stereotypes.

While the term "hillbilly" is applied to both women and men, it has masculine connotations arising from its gender-specific etymology, where a "hillbilly" is primarily a male, "southern Appalachian resident."[56] The term originated around 1900, formed by combining the word "hill" with the masculine proper name "Billy" or "Billie."[57] Other sources define it more generally as "a person from a backwoods or other remote area, especially from the mountains of the southern U.S."[58] While the term is gendered, the first component of the name, "hill," denotes a mountainous environmental region in the southern part of the country. It is a word specific to the region of Appalachia and the southern mountains in most definitions, although it is typically applied to poor and working-class whites throughout the country. John Hartigan Jr. explains:

> Though "hillbilly" imagery is caustically active from California to Washington, D.C., it has burrowed most deeply into Appalachia, where concentrations of poverty and illiteracy have long nourished its most disparaging connotations. Residents feel the impact of stereotypes that construe them as "backward," lazy, and dangerous. This region has been exploited for over a hundred years by various corporate interests and government agencies, producing a degrading dynamic of dependence that continues to this day, highlighted by rampant environmental destruction caused by ongoing mining operations.[59]

In noting the various referents of the hillbilly image, Hartigan's work reminds us how the use of stereotypes of Appalachian people is connected to systematic social and economic conditions in the region. Because the term has specific referents, it cannot be used interchangeably with similar cultural terms such as "white trash" and "redneck." In examining these distinctions, Hartigan asserts that "'hillbilly' applies to a social landscape reminiscent of the terrain covered by 'redneck,' but with greater regional specificity and perhaps more historical depth and coherence. . . . But its usage also depicts a social collective, in a manner contrary to 'white trash,' a term that inscribes severe social isolation."[60] Interestingly, it is the region-specific location and sense of collective identity that are most attractive to anti-MTR activists and employed in their work to end MTR. While Hartigan specifies the ways in which the term is specific to Appalachia and indicates a sense of social collectivity, other scholars trace its cultural roots by revealing the race- and class-based connotations inherent in this popular American symbol.

Anthony Harkins suggests the "hillbilly" image in the popular imagination has historical roots in the colonial era and represents the amalgamation of the "rural rube," "poor whites" of the southern backcountry, and people residing in the southern mountain regions of the United States. Similar to general stereotypes of Appalachian people, Harkins writes that the hillbilly became iconic in the early 1900s. He goes on to state, "Consistently used by middle-class economic interests to denigrate working-class southern whites ... and to define the benefits of advanced civilization through negative counterexample, the term and idea have also been used to challenge the generally unquestioned acceptance and legitimacy of 'modernity' and 'progress.'"[61] Even though other cultural slurs, such as "white trash" and "redneck," are frequently used to identify white, and primarily southern, people, Harkins, like John Hartigan, suggests that "hillbilly" has the longest history and is the most widespread in American culture.[62] When considering the function of this cultural image during its inception in the popular American imagination, Harkins highlights the class-based nature of this Appalachian stereotype:

> "The hillbilly" served the dual and seemingly contradictory purposes of allowing the "mainstream," or generally nonrural, middle-class white, American audience to imagine a romanticized past, while simultaneously enabling that same audience to recommit itself to modernity by caricaturing the negative aspects of premodern, uncivilized society.[63]

Walter Precourt also reveals the class-based conceptions of "hillbilly" by linking the stereotype with notions of Appalachian poverty, tracing the history to economic changes in nineteenth-century America as Appalachia, and other parts of the country, increasingly shifted from a largely agrarian to an industrial, market-based economy. Precourt suggests that with the change from agricultural production to heavy industry such as coal mining, a new regulation of labor was required. He asserts that denigrating the residents of the area with hillbilly stereotypes related to poverty helped cast industrialists as forces trying to uplift the ostensibly ignorant, uncivilized people of the region. Precourt argues that these early socioeconomic arrangements molded the hillbilly stereotype that persists today.[64]

So far we have established that the hillbilly is gendered through its etymological origins, and both Harkins and Precourt situate the hillbilly image as a fundamentally class-based symbol with origins in the rise of industrialization in late nineteenth-century America. Indeed, cultural slurs aimed at white people are typically class-based because it is mainly poor whites and working-class whites who are racially marked and named; middle-class and upper-middle-class people are less frequently racially denoted as white because their subject positions are considered normative and therefore race is typically unspecified. However, it is also important to examine and isolate the ways in which this stereotype is raced as primarily a white social construct.

Some critical race scholars contend that whiteness is a racial and social category that shapes white people's lives in ways that are typically unnamed and outside the realm of social consideration.[65] In American culture, whiteness is typically unspecified, occupying a normative social position by which other nonwhite people are compared and evaluated. Ruth Frankenberg asserts that although unnamed and unmarked, whiteness is also a "cultural practice," "a location of structural advantage," and "a standpoint—a place from which white people look at the world."[66] Woody Doane echoes Frankenberg's notion of whiteness as occupying a culturally normative position that reveals the structural dominance of white racial identity and practice:

> As a sociopolitically and numerically dominant group, whites in the United States have used their political and cultural hegemony to shape the racial order and racial understandings of American society. . . . White-dominated racial understandings have generally focused upon the characteristics (i.e., "differences") of subordinate groups rather than the nature of whiteness. This emphasis by whites upon the racial "other" has gone hand in hand with the politically constructed role of whiteness as the "unexamined center" of American society.[67]

Doane suggests that because of these "white-dominated racial understandings," whites feel less culturally or socially different as they go about their everyday lives, and are much less likely to experience significant disadvantages based on race.[68] Moreover, by being unmarked and unnamed, whiteness demonstrates its dominant position in the racial hierarchy. Ruth Frankenberg argues that whiteness is, indeed, a "set of locations that are historically, socially, politically, and culturally produced and, moreover, are intrinsically linked to unfolding relations of domination."[69] It is this hegemony of whiteness and inferred dominance that scholars such as Frankenberg urge us to note when considering race relations. For these reasons, whiteness must be placed upon the racial trajectory in our analyses of social, cultural, and political power, because if we speak of whiteness and name it as a racialized position, we productively "assign *everyone* a place in the relations of racism."[70]

While it is important to specify and study whiteness, other scholars caution that we must not let these studies "further marginalize the experiences of groups long left out of the historical record," particularly people of color.[71] In addition, it is important to be aware of the potentially negative effects of white racial reclamation when it becomes what Woody Doane calls a "defensive assertion," evidenced by white supremacist groups such as the Ku Klux Klan or anti-immigration forces.[72] We must be mindful of these potential pitfalls in marking whiteness as a racial category in our attempts to reveal white racial dominance, and the ways in which other identity markers such as class and gender intersect with race in American culture.

While whiteness is a normative racial position that enjoys structural privilege that should be identified and acknowledged, it is equally important to recognize the differences in this category of "whites." Whiteness does include certain cultural, political, and economic structural advantages that are less available to nonwhite people. However, white people do not equally enjoy these benefits. For example, Mab Segrest suggests that whiteness is not a "monolithic" category, and some groups of white people can be considered "less white" than others, meaning they do not fully enjoy the social, cultural, and political privileges of the straight, middle-class, WASP representatives of normative whiteness.[73] Segrest argues, "If whiteness is a signifier of power and condition of access in U.S. culture, then women are less white than men, gay people less white than straight people, poor people less white than rich people, Jews than Christians, and so forth."[74] This is an important distinction. The women environmental justice activists in the anti-MTR campaigns are white and Native American working-class women. They live and work in a marginalized region of the United States—marginalized not primarily by race, but by the material realities and conceptions of class in American culture. Their class and gendered positions therefore render them "less white" in the popular racial imagination.

Anthony Harkins suggests that the hillbilly's white racial status can offer interesting insights into "internal conceptual divisions" within white America.[75]

He points out that because hillbillies are seen as "one hundred percent" Protestant Americans of Anglo-Saxon descent, "middle-class white Americans could see these people as a fascinating and exotic 'other' akin to Native Americans or Blacks, while at the same time sympathize with them as poorer and less modern versions of themselves."[76] Hence, "hillbilly" has long been viewed in American culture as the "white other," frequently despised and ridiculed but at times in need of salvation and intervention from middle and upper-middle-class whites with social reformation proclivities. Furthermore, Harkins says mainstream American media can produce images of white "poverty," "ignorance," and "backwardness" without raising crimes of bigotry and racism.[77] In effect, stereotypes of poor whites are largely acceptable in a culture that is arguably less comfortable expressing pejorative ideas about other socially disadvantaged groups based on race, gender, and sexuality. Part of the problem is that class is virtually invisible in the United States; we do not have an adequate language for productively assessing and understanding the ways in which class is relevant in American culture.

Gregory Mantsios argues that "people in the United States don't like to talk about class. . . . We don't speak about class privileges, or class oppression, or the class nature of society."[78] Mantsios suggests that prominent myths about class—that we live in a classless society, or all Americans are middle class, or that everyone has equal opportunities acquired through merit and hard work—prevent the development of a sufficient analysis of class in the United States.[79] Michael Zwieg says the result of such myths is that people from the "underclass" are depicted as "lazy, damaged, scary enough so that we want to stay out of their neighborhoods. The poor are beneath the supposed vast middle class, who work hard and play by the rules, making a life through hard work and sacrifice."[80] Zweig says the poor are separated from the rest of society in a way that encourages and allows "everyone else to treat them in dehumanizing ways. The actual facts of poor people's lives become irrelevant when the poor take on a social and psychological role in the popular imagination. They stop being people and become symbols, freighted with the baggage of fear and loathing."[81] We desperately need to recognize that like race and gender, class is a fundamental structural component of American culture. Without such a critical understanding, stereotypical ideas about poor and working-class people justifying their disenfranchisement will continue to be accepted and circulated in American culture. When we consider the ways in which "hillbilly" is used as a dehumanizing term for Appalachians, it is practically impossible to separate the links between class and race in this inveterate stereotypical construction of Appalachian identity.

Like Anthony Harkins, John Hartigan Jr. also highlights the class and race associations of white cultural identity by asserting that derogatory terms such as "hillbilly" are, indeed, marked forms of racial identity that reflect "distinct forms of social positioning and cultural representations that lead us further in understanding how white racial identity operates."[82] Hence "hillbilly" is ultimately a "form of difference marked off from the privileges and powers of whiteness, each demarcating an inside and outside to 'mainstream' white society."[83] Ultimately, class-based, white racial identities such as "hillbilly" effectively serve to, as Matt Wray suggests, position these groups as "not quite white" in racialized social locations.[84] These class and race dimensions of "hillbilly" are important to note when examining the reclamation of this term by some anti–mountaintop removal mining activists. They reveal notable cultural dynamics anchored by the intersections of human differences based on race, gender, and class. The class and race dimensions also have interesting environmental connections, as the hillbilly is not only raced and classed in the American imagination but is also linked closely with nature in negative ways. However, some members of the anti-MTR movement reclaim and redefine "hillbilly" more positively as someone who values and protects the culture and natural environment of the Appalachian coalfields.

Reclaiming the Hillbilly: Environmental Connections to
Appalachian Stereotypes

We have established that Appalachian stereotypes, in particular the hillbilly, are the products of the middle-class, urban American imagination and contain race and class cultural considerations. These stereotypes also have environmental connections to the idea of Appalachian "otherness," and to existing tensions between environmental justice and mainstream American environmentalism. Hillbillies are more closely aligned with nature in a culture that some would argue does not value nature. Because nature is undervalued and denigrated, the close association of humans to nature is inherently negative. "Hillbillies," who are considered inbred, culturally unsophisticated, and ruled by emotion rather than rationality, are clearly located on the nature side of the well-established culture/nature binary that ecofeminists argue is an ideological bedrock of Western culture.[85] Ecofeminist thought asserts that capitalist, patriarchal forces that rely on the oppression of women, the poor, and people of color also negatively impact nonhuman nature. Ynestra King argues that the "systematic denigration of working-class people and people of color, women, and animals is connected to the basic dualism that lies at the root of Western civilization: nature vs. culture."[86] Karen Warren claims there are crucial connections between what she calls the "unjustified domination" of these human groups and the "unjustified domination of nature."[87] For these reasons, King, Warren, and other ecofeminists insist that nature is a feminist issue.

In ecofeminist thought, this oppression of nature and nonhuman nature operates according to capitalist patriarchal impulses that devalue, but also rely on, the domination of the environment and disenfranchised populations. These processes of domination are ideologically supported by numerous binarisms: culture/nature, reason/emotion, master/slave, civilized/primitive, male/female, white/black, public/private, and so forth.[88] One part of the binary construction is valued and supported and, in effect, constructed through the negation and devaluing of the other half of the dualism. One is civilized because one has negated the primitive; one is reasonable because one is able to subdue the emotional; one is cultured because one has transcended nature. A noticeable by-product of Western culture's reliance on ideological binaries is that subordinated groups are more linked to nature (as opposed to culture) than other populations. Greta Gaard suggests that in Western culture, disenfranchised groups are frequently depicted as more "naturalized" and "animalized" than people with social, economic, and political power.[89] This cultural tendency is witnessed in a number of areas, such as calling Native Americans "savages," or linking African Americans, and other racially and ethnically differentiated groups, with animals such as monkeys or baboons. The end result is that if you culturally devalue and denigrate the population viewed as inferior or closer to nature, then the oppression and exploitation of these devalued groups is ideologically and materially justified.

Anthony Harkins notes that Appalachian "hillbillies" are identified as closely tied to nature, as evidenced by the use of descriptors such as "brush ape," "ridge runner," and "briar hopper."[90] In addition, the persistent association of West Virginians with inbreeding reproductive practices suggests this population has not transcended the crude, primitive impulses of nature by engaging in deviant, backward, and animalistic sexual behavior. This ideology also positions Appalachian women as persistently pregnant, producing far too many children while they are chained to the domestic sphere and treated like slaves by their hillbilly husbands.[91] Herbert Reid and Betsy Taylor argue that this "national Otherization of the hillbilly icon" contains "embodied qualities of male violence, natural wildness, genetic degeneration, uncontrollable sexuality, improvidence, and lack of self-disciplined will."[92] They argue that ultimately the otherization of the hillbilly is a *"spatial and temporal* reframing of eco-class positionality" that effectively locates Appalachian people and the environmental spaces they inhabit at the periphery of American life.[93]

These entrenched stereotypical ideas and assumptions have led some women in the anti-MTR movement to suggest that cultural denigration makes the exploitation of Appalachian communities and the environment possible in this age of mountaintop removal coal mining. Coal River Mountain Watch member Patty Sebok believes that a majority of the American population thinks, "You're an ignorant hillbilly; it's all right to destroy you and your home."[94] We can recall Maria Gunnoe's perception that West Virginians are considered a *"subhuman* culture," or as Janice Nease says, "throwaway" people inhabiting what Judy Bonds suggested is a "sacrifice zone" of cultural and environmental degradation. Indeed, the links between both cultural and environmental annihilation are succinctly summarized in Judy Bonds's accusation that Big Coal has "robbed us of our humanity, misinterpreted our culture, maligned our heritage."[95]

When populations are viewed as outside of mainstream American culture, culturally backward, or too connected to nature, it becomes difficult to garner support from outside the region. When considering the impact of MTR on mountain communities, and the absence of robust national concern for problems confronting Appalachia, West Virginia novelist Ann Pancake points to a failure in mainstream America to recognize and accept that the area of the coalfields of West Virginia is "a unique culture, an important culture, and it has a lot of values being lost on the rest of the culture. . . . More people perceive it not as a culture that has value, but as a hillbilly, white-trash kind of culture. So they don't think it is worth preserving. This wouldn't be going on if it was in some middle-class, white, neighborhood in California."[96] Casting Appalachian people as uncivilized, too close to nature, and fundamentally lacking in culture has the effect of justifying the cultural and environmental destruction caused by mountaintop removal coal mining, making it difficult to garner robust outside support to stop it.

While Appalachian stereotypes suggest that West Virginians are closely associated with nature, and are, in fact, hillbillies in need of culture and civilization, activists in the anti-MTR movement have a divergent conception of "hillbilly" and the human-nature connection. As indicated earlier in this chapter, part of the fight to end mountaintop removal coal mining contains an effort to instill cultural pride in West Virginians because many activists believe that just as their mountains are being destroyed, so is local Appalachian culture. This cultural pride rests on redefining and reclaiming the "hillbilly," and also reconceptualizing the human-nature connection in a more positive manner. This reclamation effectively challenges the prevailing Western notion that being close to nature is an inherently debased position. Rather, the human-nature connection is conceived as potentially harmonious, not based on dominance and exploitation, but where mountain people live in partnership with nature. Sylvester "Dustbuster" Pauline Canterbury connects the mountains while culturally self-identifying as "hillbilly" when she says simply: "Mountains are the culture here. We're hillbillies. I'm proud to be a hillbilly."[97] Canterbury's cultural reclamation firmly positions hillbillies in the Appalachian Mountains, conveying a sense of belonging and pride in her history and culture. Like Pauline Canterbury, former Coal River Mountain Watch codirector Judy Bonds said:

> I'm proud to be called a hillbilly—we *are* reclaiming the word "hillbilly." . . . A "hillbilly" is a person that lives in the hills and loves the hills. . . . We live in our mountains, our mountains surround us and they are who we are, and we're who we are because of those hills, those hollers. What's in those mountains that causes us to be who we are, that we survived off of for generations.[98]

She pointed out that some local residents "gather things that their ancestors have gathered for years. They'll go into that mountain to gather yellowroot or ginseng or medicinal herbs or just to be a part of that mountain. . . . You're part of that mountain because you know what that mountain holds for you. . . . That's what makes the hillbilly."[99] Bonds's cultural pride in the reclamation of this term explains how coalfield communities are situated in their natural environment, a part of the human and nonhuman life of the mountains. Her definition also speaks to the history behind these communities, and their ability to survive in and with nature. Coal River Mountain Watch member Lorelei Scarbro also reclaims this hillbilly stereotype, and highlights this notion of survival by saying, "We're hillbillies, and you certainly can't be hillbillies without the hills. Mountains to me have all those things in them that we could survive on should we choose to or should we have to."[100] Scarbro recalls identifying and collecting local herbs, nuts, and berries with her Cherokee grandmother when she was a child. To Scarbro, a hillbilly is someone who lives in this mountainous environment and has knowledge of how to survive and support oneself while also valuing and being a part of this ecosystem.

Coal River Mountain Watch cofounder Janice Nease says, "The real Appalachia is lush green mountains, deep ancient forests, ice cold trout streams, small hill farms, and little mountain communities filled with unpretentious working-class people. . . . Their roots run deep into mountain soil, deeper than corporate greed or political corruption."[101] Nease's definition, like those of many other women in the anti-MTR movement, counters stereotypes of Appalachians, identifying this culture as tied to the natural environment as part of their long family history in the mountains.

The anti-MTR movement slogan "Save the Endangered Hillbilly" is a class- and race-based sentiment that simultaneously reclaims the hillbilly as a source of cultural identification while also situating the hillbilly within the natural environment. The fight to save the hillbilly and his or her environment also positions this movement firmly within both environmental justice and mainstream environmental discourse, revealing the existing tensions between these forms of American environmentalism. This slogan is an obvious play on the Endangered Species Act, a centerpiece of American environmental reform and protection and, for some, a symbol of the values of mainstream environmental thought and action. The Endangered Species Act (ESA), passed by the Nixon administration in 1973, is geared toward saving animal and plant species in immediate threat of extinction, and also protecting other groups of animals and plants deemed vulnerable to extinction. The ESA legislates the importation and exportation of species contained on the list, and also prohibits federal agencies, or any existing entity receiving assistance through a federal agency, from destroying habitats of species. This legislation involves a periodic review process for determining and reviewing species currently on the list, or those considered for inclusion and protection.[102] The Endangered Species Act has been successful in protecting near extinct and vulnerable animal and plant populations, and used strategically by mainstream environmentalists to protect wilderness and other natural areas from industrial use.

William Cronon argues that "those hoping to defend pristine wilderness have had to rely on a single endangered species like the spotted owl to gain legal standing for their case—thereby making the full power of the sacred land inhere in a singly numinous organism whose habitat then becomes the object of intense debate about appropriate management and use."[103] It is indeed interesting that some members of the anti-MTR movement assert the "hillbilly" as a human species in threat of extinction and in need of environmental protection in this age of mountaintop removal coal mining. Through their "Save the Endangered Hillbilly" directive, they are advocating the preservation of mountain people and culture as well as their natural mountain habitat. In this sense, they place themselves within mainstream environmental discourse and legislation, while simultaneously revealing the tensions that exist between mainstream environmentalism and environmental justice.

The ESA, and the way it is used, contributes to popular notions about mainstream environmentalists and environmental legislation being geared toward protecting plant and animal life at the cost of society's most disenfranchised human populations. Recall chapter 3's discussion of wind energy projects in the West Virginia coalfields, and how the Beech Creek wind farm, the largest one proposed in the state, was nixed by a federal judge in Maryland who ruled the project threatened the vulnerable Indiana bat population in West Virginia. For many people living in ground zero of mountaintop removal coal extraction, green energy projects such as wind farms are a promising alternative to razing entire mountain chains, dislocating human and nonhuman nature in the process. Washington, Rosier, and Goodall argue:

> Some environmental justice activists and scholars have suggested that the class and race (affluent and white) of leaders of twentieth-century conservation and wilderness movements has hampered them from recognizing the impact of modern industrial society on minority and ethnic communities, which some may have perceived to be part of the threatening environment rather than its victims.[104]

Indeed, because environmental justice scholars and practitioners seek to draw attention to the connections between the subordination of disenfranchised groups and the natural environment, they are frequently accused of being anthropocentric, caring less about nature and more about people who inhabit the environment. For example, environmental scholar Kevin DeLuca reasons:

> The main concern of the environmental justice movement is humans. The nonhuman is only of interest insofar as it affects humans. . . . Although the environmental justice movement is often concerned to clean up the environment, at other times it is content to support practices that harm the environment and the nonhuman in support of some human concern, frequently jobs. Never is the environmental justice movement primarily concerned with wilderness.[105]

Environmental justice is a response to the workings of mainstream environmentalists, which they accuse of being inadequately attentive to human health in environmentally jeopardized communities. Environmental justice activists have interpreted this bias or omission as indicative of an environmental movement largely concerned with wilderness protection and indifferent to human difference based on race, class, or gender.[106] These tensions are sometimes apparent in the movement to end mountaintop removal coal mining in Appalachia. In the early days of Judy Bonds's involvement with the Coal River Mountain Watch, she was critical of mainstream environmentalism and their slow response in taking a position against MTR. Bonds asserted:

> It's time to bring humans back into the environmental movement. . . . You can't separate social and environmental injustice. You find most of these injustices is in low income communities, and communities with people of color. . . . It's hard to explain to Appalachian people why they should care about seals when their home is getting blasted. You have to make the nationals understand that yes, there is a cycle of life, we understand that, but the average person living in a bad environment doesn't see that.[107]

Another activist who once lived in the now decimated town of Blair, West Virginia, Patricia Bragg, says, "We know the quality of life we hold so dear is weighed against the progress of the country . . . but we're paying for that progress. People raise millions to save whales and walruses and birds, but the state doesn't lift a hand to save the most precious thing in the world, a person's way of life."[108] Bragg, whose name is on the first major litigation aimed at ending MTR, *Bragg vs. Robertson*, expresses a common environmental justice sentiment that highlights the persistent tensions between mainstream environmentalism, with their large staffs and well-funded projects, and environmental justice activism, which is community-based and primarily reliant on local, regional, and federal grant funding.

While the comments made by Bonds and Bragg contain anthropocentric values that many mainstream environmentalists would find disturbing, gender, race, and class differences among people often preclude the luxury of caring solely about the nonhuman environment. In effect, when basic material needs are not met, and one's culture, history, and livelihood are under threat, people in poor white communities and communities of color cannot be expected to divorce the human and nonhuman environments in the expression of their concerns. However, through their call to "Save the Endangered

Hillbilly," the anti-MTR movement is successful in linking sustainable human communities to the preservation and sustainability of nonhuman communities through their emphasis on "hillbillies" situated in the lush Appalachian Mountains. Many people active in the movement see the human and nonhuman environments as connected and interrelated, a point lost on many environmentalists such as Kevin DeLuca. However, even DeLuca must admit that environmental justice has

> changed government policies and laws and has helped specific communities protect their homeplaces from the depredations of corporate polluters. For its many successes, for its dedication, and for its effective redress of race and class discrimination, the environmental justice movement is to be celebrated. . . . The environmental justice movement has also challenged and transformed the environmental movement, especially with respect to its focus on wilderness and nonhuman nature.[109]

Through its activism and theoretical considerations, the EJ movement has prompted mainstream environmentalists to make better connections between the human and nonhuman worlds, to not ignore human social relations, differences, and conditions in their efforts to protect the natural environment. In David E. Camacho's view, the problem is that the mainstream environmental movement "has not fully recognized the fact that social inequality and imbalances of power contribute to the environmental degradation, resource depletion, pollution, and environmental hazards that disproportionately impact people of color along with poor and working-class whites."[110] However, Camacho notices that the large national organizations are perhaps beginning to understand the need for environmental justice and supporting EJ organizations with "technical advice, expert testimony, direct financial assistance, fundraising, research, and legal assistance."[111]

Judy Bonds once asserted that "environmental justice is for people who are living in communities that have to deal with the impacts of a polluting industry, and that's what we're looking at. . . . It's how the environmental movement has changed over the years."[112] Bonds suggested that although we typically picture a white, "upper-middle-class type person" when we think of an environmentalist, more disenfranchised people are becoming increasingly environmentally aware.[113] She said, "You are finding more and more people that are redefined as environmentalists through the need to be, not because it's aesthetics, it's the need for clean air, clean water, and a place to live . . . that makes people environmentalists."[114] She maintained that the environmental move-ment has "changed, and we'll continue to morph into the environmental justice movement more as we go along."[115] Whether or not human justice becomes a central component of mainstream environmentalism, we are, as Camacho suggests, seeing an increase in national support for local environmental jus-tice initiatives, including the movement to end mountaintop removal coal mining in Appalachia. Washington, Rosier, and Goodall argue that rather than a neatly polarized division between mainstream environmentalism and environmental justice, "the reality is most often a continuum with the many positions and many ambivalences of the stands and strategies that both indi-viduals and movements take. The consequences are continual tensions within the movement between the priorities of social justice and ecological goals."[116]

Over the past decade, the anti-MTR movement has drawn the attention of various national environmental organizations. Some are part of the Group of Ten, the largest environmental organizations in the country, while others occupy a more fringe position in the national environmental scene. In 2003 the Sierra Club, included in the Group of Ten designation, established a represen-tative in the coalfields, Bill Price, a former coal company employee who lost his home in the 2001 floods in Boone County. Price is part of the Sierra Club's environmental justice wing and works to raise awareness about coal issues and collect information from community members harmed by coal company practices. In these efforts, Price connects human social differences based on race, class, and gender to adverse environmental conditions in the coalfields and beyond.[117] The Sierra Club's involvement in the anti-MTR movement is part of their "Beyond Coal" initiatives.[118] The other Group of Ten environ-mental organization that is speaking out against MTR and offering support to the movement is the National Resources Defense Council fund, which primarily provides legal and scientific expertise to environmental issues and actions. The NRDC has a "No More Mountaintop Removal" campaign as part of their "Clean Energy Future" program.[119] Both the Sierra Club and the National Resources Defense Council have been active in mainstream Ameri-can environmental politics since 1892 and 1970, respectively.[120]

These large mainstream organizations provide personnel and professional expertise, while the smaller national and international organizations encour-age civil disobedience and direct action in their push to end MTR. Earth First! sponsors the Mountain Justice Summer (MJS) campaign in West Vir-ginia, Virginia, Tennessee, and Kentucky. MJS, which began in 2005, provides an activist camp every summer in one of the states most affected by MTR, educating volunteers about coal industry issues and grassroots environmental activism.[121] Ending mountaintop removal is one of the top priorities of Earth First!, which formed in 1979 "in response to a lethargic, compromising, and increasingly corporate environmental community," and is focused on "front-line, direct action" to fight global environmental problems.[122] The group "Mountain Justice" was created to support the MJS campaign in Appalachia.

The other major environmental group supportive of anti-MTR efforts is the international Rainforest Action Network (RAN), headquartered in San Francisco with offices in Japan and Canada.[123] RAN refers to MTR as an "American tragedy," and considers its members "savvy environmental agitators" who believe that to confront the most pressing global environmental problems, "aggressive action must be taken immediately to leave a safe and secure world for our children."[124] RAN sponsors the campaign Climate Ground Zero, which comprises a group of experienced direct action environmental activists who live in Rock Creek, West Virginia. Climate Ground Zero engages in protests such as occupying trees slated to be clear-cut to facilitate mountaintop removal operations, and sit-ins at coal company offices, the state and federal department of environmental protection, and banks who fund Big Coal endeavors in Appalachia. The anti-MTR movement has grown tremendously over the past decade and encompasses an interesting mix of environmental justice organizations, large mainstream environmental organizations, and smaller national and international organizations. This outside assistance is welcomed by many activists in West Virginia, and their ability to garner this robust support speaks to the strength of local environmental justice initiatives by coalfield residents who fight to end MTR in Appalachia.

As anti-MTR activists work to "save the endangered hillbilly," they effectively center human justice within the larger environmental framework, and call attention to the historical disconnections between concerns for the health of the nonhuman environment and social justice issues. This slogan reclaims and redefines the historically pejorative term "hillbilly," using this image as cultural self-identification to foster pride in coalfield history and culture as tied to the mountainous geography and environment. In this effort they resist and defy the stereotypical assumptions about Appalachian mountain people as "backward," "primitive" white people who are too close to nature to become "civilized." On the contrary, these Appalachian people contest the stereotypes through their public participation in efforts to stop the destruction of their rural coalfield communities.

Conclusion

Cultural aspects of the anti–mountaintop removal coal mining movement are crucial considerations to understanding the connections between long-standing notions of Appalachian "otherness," particularly race and class implications of the term "hillbilly." In addition, analysis of Appalachian activism should note the ways in which this region, and the people who live there, are maligned in the American imagination and used to facilitate ideas of white, middle-class, urban America. It is equally important to examine the ways in which Appalachian people counter these prevalent notions and fight to change cultural, political, economic, and environmental conditions in their communities. They exert collective agency by countering and reclaiming stereotypical notions about the Appalachian "hillbilly," repositioning this symbol as a person embedded in the mountains who values and protects the natural environment and mountain culture. As such, they situate their efforts within national environmental discourse and action, and also within environmental justice action, by calling attention to the endangered "hillbilly" living in a threatened habitat.

While entrenched in Appalachian and American culture, anti-MTR activists are also aware of the global implications of mountaintop removal coal mining and the environmental justice efforts to end it. One of the many reasons this movement is so successful is that it consistently makes those ever-important links between the local and the global. Activists note the international implications of coal production and consumption in a world environment adversely impacted by climate changes and reliance on fossil fuels. Finally, they recognize and support similar environmental justice campaigns that promote the use of alternative energy sources to create sustainable global communities, particularly for the most disenfranchised populations.

Picture of lush mountains in central Appalachia along Route 19 in Nicholas County, West Virginia (2011).
Photo by: Tyler Underwood.

A view of Kayford Mountain, taken in 1998 when organizing against MTR began in West Virginia.
Photo by: Joyce M. Barry.

The Coal River Mountain Watch office in Whitesville, West Virginia.
Photo by: Joyce M. Barry.

Mountain mural painted by Sarah Haltom on the office of the Coal River Mountain Watch in Whitesville, West Virginia. The mural was defaced by unknown pro-coal forces that painted yellow bulldozers on the side of the mountain. CRMW members responded by painting people chained to the bulldozers and carrying signs with anticoal messages. *Photo by: Joyce M. Barry.*

Graffiti wars between pro-coal and anticoal forces in Whitesville, West Virginia. The mountain mural, painted by Sarah Haltom, was vandalized by someone who painted yellow bulldozers on the mural. CRMW members responded by painting pictures of activists holding anticoal protest signs. *Photo by: Joyce M. Barry.*

Janice Nease participating in a May 2004 protest directed at Massey Energy. Massey's shareholders and board of directors were holding their annual meeting in Charleston, West Virginia. Here Nease poses as a member of the Massey board of directors behind bars for crimes committed against the people and environment of Appalachia. *Photo by: Vivian Stockman.*

Patty Sebok, member of the Coal River Mountain Watch, masquerades as a Massey Energy board of directors member jailed for crimes committed against the people and environment of Appalachia (Charleston, West Virginia, 2004). *Photo by: Vivian Stockman.*

Judy Bonds being interviewed in the Coal River Valley, West Virginia (2006).
Photo by: Vivian Stockman.

Lindytown in Boone County, West Virginia. Neighborhood homes are acquired by coal companies expanding their operations. Once homes located near MTR sites are obtained, they are boarded up and eventually bulldozed and burned. *Photo by: Joyce M. Barry.*

Lorelei Scarbro, former member of the Coal River Mountain Watch and founder of the Boone Raleigh Community Group in West Virginia. Scarbro speaks on the steps of the Environmental Protection Agency in Washington, DC, during Appalachia Rising (2010). *Photo by: Joyce M. Barry.*

The Sylvester Dustbusters, Pauline Canterbury (*left*) and Mary Miller, protesting the impact of Big Coal on local communities. *Photo by: Vivian Stockman.*

Ohio Valley Environmental Coalition member Maria Gunnoe (with Larry Gibson, *left*) on the steps of the Environmental Protection Agency in Washington, DC, during Appalachia Rising (2010). *Photo by: Joyce M. Barry.*

Billboard on Route 3, Surveyor, West Virginia. These public signs reveal the competing interests in the coalfields in this era of MTR. On the left, local anti-MTR activists featured a sign suggesting mountains are divine creations. The billboard to the right is an ad by the ICG coal company used to recruit workers for new mining operations in West Virginia. *Photo by: Joyce M. Barry.*

CHAPTER 5

Situating the Particular and the Universal: Gender,
Environmental Justice, and Mountaintop Removal
in a Global Context

> *It's become such a bigger issue. . . . I see it more as an entire
> global, society issue now. . . . For the greed of many, and for
> the overconsumption of many, people are suffering. And entire
> ecosystems are being destroyed.*
>
> —Sarah Haltom, artist and former office manager
> of the Coal River Mountain Watch

Introduction

IN 2001, SARAH HALTOM MOVED FROM CLEVELAND,
Ohio, to West Virginia. Haltom's paternal ancestry is situated in Boone
County, and she frequently visited the area during her childhood in Cleveland.
At the age of ten, she had a particularly vivid dream where she was in West
Virginia during the fall, walking on the side of a mountain, when she spotted
an orange house with a yellow door. Over the years, she experienced recurring
dreams in which she was trying to find this colorful house. Shortly after moving to West Virginia, Haltom's father, Bo Webb, a vigorous participant in the
anti–mountaintop removal mining movement, took her to Kayford Mountain
to witness the environmental destruction caused by razing mountains to extract coal. Haltom recalls, "I'm looking at all the MTR destruction going on
up there, and we were coming around a little curve in the road, and I looked
over on the side of the hill, and there were all these houses over there, and my
house was sitting there." Haltom was shocked to discover the house of her
dreams on Kayford Mountain in West Virginia, and she says, "It kind of made

me feel like it was some sort of sign, that that was where I was supposed to be." Since then she has participated in the anti-MTR movement, volunteering as an office manager for the Coal River Mountain Watch. In addition to her father, Haltom's husband, Vernon, is also very active in the anti-MTR movement. Haltom, who was never politically engaged before relocating to West Virginia, credits her father and husband with educating her about MTR in West Virginia. She says, "I knew it was wrong the first time I saw it, and I thought . . . This is where I want to stay for the rest of my life."[1]

During the summer of 2005, Haltom painted a mural of mountains on the cinder-blocked side of the Coal River Mountain Watch office in Whitesville. This mural has become a physical marker for the contestation over coal extraction in Boone County, and the call for sustainable energy production and consumption. Haltom says that while she was painting the mural, many people drove by the building paying compliments and offering encouragement, while others were angered and honked their horns. She says one such passenger drove down the alley where she was working and said, "Hey, if you don't watch out, we're gonna blow that one up too." Over the years, Haltom's mural has fallen prey to graffiti "artists" who have painted bulldozers and draglines on the side of her mural mountain, familiar equipment on mountaintop removal mining sites. Haltom countered this alteration by painting people holding signs reading "Stop Mountaintop Removal" and "There's no such thing as cheap energy." This artistic battle continues on the CRMW office building.

Haltom, who gave birth to her first child in 2010, still volunteers with the Coal River Mountain Watch, even though she has relocated to Princeton, West Virginia, to pursue a BA in art at Concord College. In 2009 she and her husband, Vernon, were arrested in Boone County, along with actress Daryl Hannah and climatologist James Hansen, while protesting mountaintop removal coal mining. Like many activists in the anti-MTR movement, she makes connections between the extraction of coal in Appalachia and the worldwide consumption of fossil fuels to power the global economy. She says, "Everybody, including myself, is adding to the problem by, you know, using energy. And there's gotta be a better way. . . . Fossil fuels aren't going to be here forever. And if we don't start making the transition now . . . when are we ever going to?" Haltom's positioning of MTR as part of the global environment is in concert with the overall anti-MTR perspective. Activists are focused on the preservation of their coalfield communities at the site of coal extraction, and know the production and consumption of fossil fuels has global health and safety implications for the human and nonhuman environments.

Thus, the anti-MTR movement is situated in the particular context of the coalfields of Appalachia, but also within a more universal call to address climate change, its impact on the world's most disadvantaged populations, and the need to transition from energy derived from fossil fuels to energy derived from renewable sources. Some environmentalists are calling the central Appalachian coalfields "ground zero" for climate change because this area produces an abundance of coal.[2] While Big Coal promotes national energy security and economic prosperity through the extraction of coal, and the development of clean coal technologies to "green" this fossil fuel, many anti-MTR activists advocate a shift away from the use of fossil fuels altogether. In doing so they are part of the environmental justice transition from place-based, American environmental politics to global environmental justice activism. Because many of the most active opponents to MTR in West Virginia are women, they represent the feminized nature of environmental protest in the United States and beyond. This chapter examines Big Coal within the context of the neoliberal political economy, highlighting the connections between the worldwide consumption of coal and its production in West Virginia. In addition, I explore the articulations of and links between locally situated US environmental justice practice and global environmental justice theory and praxis, discussing the significance of gender in EJ activism and the shift away from fossil fuels.

"Black Is the New Green": Neoliberalism, Climate Change, and the Production and Consumption of "Clean" Coal

The rise of mountaintop removal coal mining in Appalachia is most productively situated within the context of climate change and the rise of neoliberal economic policies that contribute to social injustices and adverse environmental conditions around the world. Climate change is the most pressing social and environmental issue today. The continued production and consumption of fossil fuels such as coal, oil, and gas on a worldwide level will hasten the impact of climate change on the human and nonhuman environments. When considering climate change and the use of fossil fuels such as coal, the discourse focuses primarily on the consumption and the emission of coal into the earth's atmosphere. Less frequently considered are the production zones of these energy sources and the people and the environment impacted in these areas.

While it is crucial to mitigate the effects of coal consumption on the environment, we must also be aware of the politically transformative possibilities of linking social and environmental conditions in local production areas with the more global sites of consumption. This is accomplished theoretically through David Harvey's suggestion to adopt "critical ways to think about how differences in ecological, cultural, economic, political, and social conditions get produced. . . . And we also need ways to evaluate the justice/injustice of the differences so produced."[3] An understanding of the neoliberal, political-economic forces that shape the global environment is essential to thinking critically about the differences Harvey notes and to developing solutions to improve environmental conditions that most adversely impact disenfranchised populations. Such a materialist theoretical framework reveals how social and environmental differences are produced and sustained across local, regional, national, and international axes.

Gwyn Kirk says a materialist perspective "identifies economic and political institutions as the perpetrators of ecologically unsound investment" and enables us to understand "connections across lines of race, class, and nation, and to build alliances across these lines of difference."[4] It is in this context that I seek to situate the social, political, and environmental problems of mountaintop removal coal mining. Big Coal is a powerful corporate force in the global economy. Coal companies operate in the most economically efficient manner possible, producing and selling a product accountable for the increase of carbon emissions into the earth's atmosphere, greatly contributing to climate change. Understanding the neoliberal context out of which the industry operates is crucial to connecting social and environmental problems on multiples scales, as well as the environmental justice activism addressing these issues.

Beginning in the 1980s, large-scale economic restructuring, typically termed "globalization," strengthened the private sector while weakening governmental power, labor movements, consumer protections, environmental regulations, and other perceived impediments to the flow of free market capitalism. Daniel R. Faber and Deborah McCarthy argue that globalization has led to a "general increase in the rate of exploitation of both working people (human nature) and the environment (mother nature), as witnessed by the assaults on labor, the ecology movement and the welfare state."[5] Faber and McCarthy claim that the "rise of neo-liberals committed to less governmental control of industry . . . have become hegemonic."[6] They suggest that in this neoliberal context, global and domestic markets are more competitive and "*cost minimization* strategies now lie at the heart of business strategies for *profit maximization* for all nations. Greater efficiency . . . becomes more important precisely because it leads to more profits."[7] This means expenditures for labor, environmental regulation, worker health and safety, and other regulatory mechanisms are considered too costly, cutting into corporate profits under global trade arrangements.

Under this neoliberal economic restructuring, disenfranchised populations around the globe suffer the most along with the natural environment. For example, Faber and McCarthy say that to keep costs low and profits high, corporations rely on "ecologically unsustainable forms of production, which disproportionately impact communities of color and lower income members of the working-class sectors, which are underrepresented in the traditional environmental movement."[8] When considering the impact on the natural world, the authors argue that "increased rates of environmental exploitation are being achieved by such measures as extracting greater quantities of natural resources of greater quality more quickly and at less cost."[9] Indeed, these political-economic trends facilitate and exacerbate the social and environmental injustices associated with recent disasters such as the Gulf Coast oil spill, the coal ash spill in Tennessee, and the leveling of mountains in central Appalachia. After all, a massive dragline and other construction equipment can produce more coal at lower costs, and in less time, than conventional underground coal mining. Vandana Shiva urges us to bear in mind the human and environmental costs of these arrangements: "Globalization and free trade decimate the conditions for productive, creative employment by enclosing the commons, which are necessary for the sustenance of life. The anti-life dimensions of economic globalization are rooted in the fact that capital exchange is taking the place of living processes and the rights of corporations are displacing those of living people."[10] In this neoliberal context, Big Coal is working overtime, spending millions to protect its economic interests around the globe, relying heavily on the use of "green" rhetoric to garner support for its operations.

In 2008 the American coal industry shifted its strategy of promoting coal interests in the United States and beyond, moving away from climate change denials to the promotion of technological innovation designed to make the consumption of coal more environmentally friendly or "clean." The change was precipitated by intensifying public concern over global warming, and impending US congressional action on climate change legislation. *New York Times* environmental journalist Melanie Warner suggests Big Coal is currently "in a fight for its survival,"[11] an assessment shared by the late Coal River Mountain Watch codirector Judy Bonds, who said, "The coal industry senses that it's in its last throes. It's like a dying animal, and it's scratching and clawing, reaching out any way it can."[12]

Journalists and activists may sense chinks in Big Coal's armor, but the production and consumption of coal is still big business, albeit a very dirty one. With roughly 600 coal-fired power plants in the United States, in 2007 coal provided 48.5 percent of the country's electricity.[13] In this same year, the United States accounted for 25.7 percent of the world's total of coal-fired electricity, second only to China, who produced a world total of 32.3 percent.[14] US coal-fired power plants generating electricity account for 36 percent of the country's total production of CO_2, the main culprit in climate change.[15] Figures from 2004 show that with such large-scale coal consumption, the United States was responsible for 35.8 percent of the world totals for CO_2 emissions, a larger percentage of emissions than all sources in Africa, South America, and Central America combined.[16]

To protect their economic interests, Big Coal's primary weapon in their new "clean coal" campaign is the industry front group American Coalition for Clean Coal Electricity (ACCCE), formed in 2008 to promote the consumption of coal.[17] Big Coal's current strategy heavily utilizes the ACCCE, which touts the abundance and affordability of coal and the industry's ability to make this fossil fuel more "green" through clean coal technologies that have yet to be created and utilized. Their mission statement reads:

> The American Coalition for Clean Coal Electricity (ACCCE) advocates for public policies that advance environmental improvement, economic prosperity, and energy security. ACCCE believes that the robust utilization of coal—America's most abundant energy source—is essential to providing affordable, reliable electricity for millions of US consumers and a growing domestic economy. Further, ACCCE is committed to continued and enhanced US leadership in developing and deploying new advanced clean coal technologies that protect and improve the environment.[18]

Concerns for the environment are invoked twice in this mission statement, as ACCCE links environmental concern with mining coal and improving the economy. These points are plentiful in their literature, which asserts that coal

is an integral part of the American energy and economic structure, and is particularly vital in the current economic recession:

> As Americans we all want a reliable supply of electricity for our homes ... in
> our offices and shops ... and our factories and farms. And we want a clean
> environment. Moreover in today's challenging times, we need energy costs
> to remain affordable. The American Coalition for Clean Coal Electricity is
> committed to the idea that America can have the affordable, reliable elec-
> tricity we need ... with the clean environment we want.[19]

In Big Coal's ACCCE public relations campaign, with its generic wording and
ostensible environmental concerns, America can have it all: fossil fuel energy
production, a good economy, cheap electricity, and a healthy environment for
everyone.

This information is certainly contested by the national Citizens Coal
Council, a network of numerous environmental justice groups from nine
states where coal is produced.[20] This grassroots network, which includes the
Coal River Mountain Watch and the Ohio Valley Environmental Coalition,
challenges coal industry practices by working to protect people and the environment. The Citizens Coal Council maintains that historically the industry
has "disregarded the health and safety of people and the environment. The entire coal cycle—from extraction through the disposal of power plant waste—
impacts the health and safety of people as well as the environment. Its legacy
of polluted streams, devastated landscapes, and chronic poverty can be seen
from Appalachia to the Southwest."[21] Coal River Mountain Watch cofounder
Janice Nease questions the economic efficacies of "clean" coal, saying, "It's not
cheap to the people who live where it's extracted. And it's not cheap to the
people who breathe the emissions. ... There is no such thing as cheap electricity."[22] Despite these realities, Big Coal continues to promote its economic
and political interests with a message markedly different from its prior focus
of denying the realities of climate change.

In the 1990s, as scientific findings and warnings about the existence of
climate change became more numerous, Big Coal and its supporters were
frontrunners in climate change denial. In 1988 the United Nations created
the Intergovernmental Panel on Climate Change, which Pulitzer Prize-
winning journalist Ross Gelbspan calls the "largest and most rigorously peer-
reviewed scientific collaboration in history."[23] This panel of 2,000 scientists
from 100 countries reported its findings to the UN in 1995, declaring that

climate change exists and is caused by human activities.[24] To counter this scientific evidence, organizations such as the Western Fuels Association, a group of coal-burning electric utilities and cooperatives, sought to undermine the science of climate change, positioning the findings as theory rather than fact.[25] In addition, the corporate alliance Global Climate Coalition took on the moniker of global climate concerns while working to obfuscate and muddle the science of climate change.[26] Other organizations, such as the Greening Earth Society, which is funded largely by Big Coal, unabashedly promoted the idea that global warming is healthy for the planet in that it promotes the growth of trees and vegetation.[27]

Since the mid-1990s, denying climate change has become increasingly more difficult as the materiality of the global climate crisis becomes more apparent in many parts of the world. As such, Big Coal's new message claims that emissions generated by burning this fossil fuel can be offset through the use of clean coal technologies. In one of their recent promotions, the ACCCE promises to meet the "CO_2 challenge" through carbon capture technology, which has the potential to render coal a green energy source. The ACCCE claims, "There has never been an environmental challenge facing the coal-based electricity sector for which technology has not provided the ultimate solution."[28] Peabody Coal, the world's largest coal company, with expanding markets in Asia and Australia, boasts that through global partnerships, they are "making black the new green."[29] The promotion of coal, and the diffusion of this industry, is concomitant with a capitalist ethos, which some argue creates environmental instability.

John Bellamy Foster says that culturally, we fail to recognize the "ecological basis of the human condition," and the "full human dependence on nature undoubtedly has to do with the expansionist logic of the capitalist system that makes the accumulation of wealth in the form of capital the supreme end of society."[30] Terry Townsend solidifies the environmental connection by asserting that "capitalism, an economic and political system based on the never-ending expansion of production of commodities for sale, is incompatible with the basic ecological cycles of the planet."[31] In making black the new green, Big Coal argues that the federal government will have to partially subsidize the creation of clean coal technology. ACCCE recommendations include building 124 new power plants that use the technology, which they claim will create 150,000 new jobs.[32] In this push for clean energy, Big Coal is promoting two technological strategies: carbon capture and storage, and coal-to-liquid technology, both designed to decrease carbon emissions in the consumption of coal.

In carbon capture and storage (CCS), CO_2 is isolated at the point of large-scale production, compressed, and pumped underground or stored in massive carbon-capture facilities.[33] Theoretically, CCS can reduce emissions by 90 percent, but the cost associated with changing the way coal-burning power plants operate is exorbitant and efficiency is not guaranteed.[34] Some industry critics argue that CCS technology promises clean coal and a greener environment but is ultimately "counting on a fix for climate change that is at best uncertain and at worst unworkable."[35] Industry watchdog Jeff Goodell calls Big Coal's carbon capture and storage proposals a "pipe dream," noting there is no "single commercial coal-fired power plant in the world that captures and buries its carbon emissions," because the "process is far too complicated and expensive. But the coal industry knew it didn't need to have a real solution—it could just tout the promise of new technology, without actually changing a thing."[36]

The other technological fix promoted by Big Coal is liquefied coal for use in motor vehicles and aircraft, as opposed to the current use of oil and gas to power these transmissions. Coal-to-liquid technological proposals are lauded as not only beneficial to curbing climate change, but also to ensure US energy security. Bradford Plummer notes that the coal industry has "latched onto the 'energy security craze' by casting itself as the answer to US oil dependency."[37] Plummer suggests that the coal industry rationale is that since the United States sits on vast coal reserves, why not utilize liquid coal "instead of tossing money at the House of Saud?"[38] However, the US Energy Department suggests that coal-to-liquid fuel could generate twice the carbon emissions of gasoline, but coal proponents argue these emissions could be captured and stored underground, similar to emissions from coal-fired power plants.[39] Whether being used in aircraft or domestic vehicles, or at large-scale coal-fired power plants, Big Coal promises a green future through the use of costly technologies that have yet to be developed. Environmental theorist John Bellamy Foster says, "All of the hoped-for carbon capture and sequestration technologies are designed to get around the emissions problem, allowing the carbon-based economy to continue as before unchanged. None of these technologies are remotely practical at present and may never be."[40]

Many environmentalists claim that clean coal is the ultimate oxymoron. Al Gore, for example, says, "Clean coal is like a healthy cigarette. It does not exist."[41] During some of her public presentations Judy Bonds passed out a bag of coal, asking those who believed it was clean to remove it from the bag and rub it on their hands and faces.

While clean coal technologies promised by Big Coal may not be economically or environmentally feasible, they are politically expedient, appealing to Republicans as well as Democrats. Both parties receive large donations from the coal industry to promote their interests on Capitol Hill. Marianne Lavelle says that in the 2008 election cycle, Republican candidate John McCain received $302,474 from Big Coal, while Barack Obama garnered $241,870. Republican Kentucky senator Mitch McConnell was a close third, receiving $235,350.[42] Big Coal's clean coal campaigns provide a middle ground for politicians to navigate, particularly the promise of carbon capture and storage, which, some argue,

> appeals to politicians reluctant to limit the use of coal. Coal is the dirtiest of fossil fuels, and burning it releases roughly twice as much carbon dioxide as burning natural gas. The world will struggle to cut greenhouse-gas emissions dramatically if it continues to burn coal as it does today. Yet burning coal is one of the cheapest ways to generate power. In America, Australia, China, Germany and India coal provides half or more of the power supply and lots of jobs. Rejecting cheap, indigenous fuel for job cuts and international energy markets is seen, naturally enough, as political suicide. CCS offers a way out of this impasse.[43]

Indeed, the promise of this technological fix became a big part of Barack Obama's presidential campaign. In a campaign stop in Virginia, Obama said, "This is America. We figured out how to put a man on the moon in ten years. You can't tell me we can't figure out how to burn coal that we mine right here in the United States of America and make it work."[44] The 2009 American Clean Energy and Security Act, which passed the House but stalled in the Senate, provided $1 billion in clean coal research and all told, $60 billion in support for Big Coal, "far more than the aid given to wind, solar, and all other forms of renewable energy combined."[45] This bill does not contain adequate steps to cut emissions quickly enough to curb the most devastating consequences of climate change. However, it does include measures to improve American energy efficiency, and for some represents a first step in creating "the framework for a low-carbon economy," even though it lacks a robust commitment to the development of alternative energy sources.[46] Big Coal's change in strategy before the climate change legislation proved fruitful, given the large governmental subsidies received in the American Clean Energy and Security Act. Environmental justice scholar David Naguib Pellow reminds us of the human and environmental costs of the collusion of business and government in this neoliberal era:

> Social inequality between social classes and racial groups is rising, the labor movement is weak, environmental protection is seriously threatened, and the rights of citizens are being stripped away. . . . Many states have simply shifted their focus away from public welfare approaches toward the support of privatization and a broader neoliberal agenda, thus adopting a corporate form. That orientation reveals the influence and reach of the ideology of privatization and therefore serves to strengthen the position of TNCs.[47]

Ohio Valley Environmental Coalition organizer Maria Gunnoe, as someone directly impacted by these political-economic arrangements, is frustrated by the current reliance on fossil fuels and the inadequate commitment to alternative energy development. She says, "Our government has planned a carbon future for us and we should, as a people, think about how that's gonna impact our kids, our water. . . . It's not a promising future."[48] Even though these neoliberal arrangements have adverse material consequences for the most vulnerable populations, and negatively impact planetary health, business and government continue to operate in the most economically and politically efficient manner possible.

For many environmental justice activists in the anti-MTR movement, the effects of coal consumption are important, and raising awareness of the human health and environmental hazards of using coal as an energy source is a big part of their work to end mountaintop removal coal mining in West Virginia. However, it is interesting to note that if clean coal technologies were not the "pipe dream" Jeff Goodell suggests, and the industry were able to burn coal with decreased CO_2 emissions that create global warming, nothing would change at the production site of coal in Appalachia and elsewhere, because the demand for coal would not decrease along with efficiency mechanisms. John Bellamy Foster reminds us:

> As economic growth occurs in carbon-based capitalist economies the demand for fossil fuels rises as well. Mere increased energy efficiency—as opposed to the actual development of alternative forms of energy—is unable to do much to arrest this process in the face of increasing demand. . . . High demand for fossil fuel use is also encouraged by the high profits to be obtained from this, inducing capital to structure the energy economy around fossil fuels (a reality that is now deeply entrenched).[49]

Indeed, if carbon capture-and-storage or fuel-to-liquids technology is developed to reduce CO_2 emissions from coal consumption, people living near mining complexes would still suffer the effects of blasting on their homes and in their communities; residents would still breathe inordinate amounts of coal dust and drink contaminated water. Furthermore, the Appalachian mountain chain would continue to be razed, additional streams buried, and large-scale deforestation continue unabated. For these reasons, activists such as Lorelei Scarbro say, "We are 100 percent against using coal as an energy source. We'd like to see it phased out as an energy source."[50] While anti-MTR activists and other environmentalists welcome a shift away from fossil fuel consumption and production, Big Coal uses every weapon in its arsenal to maintain its position in this neoliberal era, despite the adverse effects on both the human and the nonhuman global environments.

Big Coal's recent successes in the climate change legislation can be attributed to the well-funded media blitz and lobbying efforts guided by the American Coalition for Clean Coal Electricity. Marianne Lavelle reveals that ACCCE has forty-eight member companies from mining, rail, manufacturing, and power-generating companies, and an annual budget of $45 million.[51] This budget is three times larger than Big Coal's old lobbying and public relations groups combined.[52] Considering the massive scale of their media and lobbying assault in early 2009, Lavelle calls ACCCE a "juggernaut" that shaped the terms of the climate change debate in Washington, "even while weathering a high-profile assault by critics who accuse it of peddling hot air."[53] The power of the industry is indeed difficult to counter, particularly for small environmental justice groups fighting to preserve coalfield communities. However, local groups in West Virginia have established a national presence, and through lobbying have made MTR a national environmental issue. Since 2006, activists have met in Washington every spring for Mountaintop Removal Week, where they lobby politicians to end MTR and support other bills such as the Clean Water Act. Also, the first march on Washington, "Appalachia Rising," occurred in September 2010, with participants from all over the country and beyond.

Lorelei Scarbro points out that with all of their travels to Washington, DC, and to community centers and colleges and universities while trying to raise awareness of coal's negative influence, the power of Big Coal remains a formidable obstacle. Scarbro says, "With all that we do, we are certainly outnumbered, outmanned, and outgunned because of their numbers and the money and the power."[54] CRMW members were also on Capitol Hill during the American Clean Energy and Security Act debates, and Scarbro saw the power of the Big Coal lobby firsthand: "While there were a few of us, a handful of us walking the halls of the Capitol trying to get signatures on the Coal River wind resolution, the coal industry was, of course, there every day. They were waiting in the wings to throw these people lavish lunches so politicians would pass the latest bill in support of the coal industry."[55] Despite the power of the industry, and the support it receives from government, anti-MTR activists continue to work for environmental justice in the coalfields and beyond. As they seek a transition from a fossil fuel–based economy to one reliant on alternative energy sources, they know this transition is beneficial not only for coalfield communities, but for the health and well-being of other communities throughout the world.

When considering her efforts to end mountaintop removal, Sarah Haltom makes these important connections between her community and planetary health: She suggests that everyone is an environmentalist because we all breathe air and drink water. Haltom considers herself an environmentalist, but says, "I also consider myself a concerned citizen of the US and the world. . . . Mountaintop removal has so many facets to it, straight down to the coal-fired power plants that affect the entire planet. . . . I'm a concerned citizen of the planet because the planet has some really big problems."[56] In fact, many of the activists question the technological promise of clean coal, suggesting that technological innovation and the resources to implement it should be applied to developing green energy and a green economy. Judy Bonds said the United States should be "leading the world in renewable clean energy rather than leading the world down the wrong path of a Neanderthal industry that's going to destroy the earth."[57]

Environmental justice scholars Sylvia Hood Washington, Paul C. Rosier, and Heather Goodall argue for the importance of considering the experiences of local communities and their global connectedness, claiming that "understanding and appreciating the knowledge embedded in the memories of communities that have been environmentally disenfranchised is critical to knowing more fully the social ecology of the world at large and the environmental costs of technological developments."[58] Coal River Mountain Watch member Patty Sebok positions coal and the fossil fuel paradigm, regardless of the promotion of technologies to make coal more green, as dangerously outdated, suggesting that "our government is too short-sighted, local and federal, to invest in renewable energies. . . . You need to move into the future and not stay in the dinosaur age. And they claim that we impede progress. Excuse me? No, I'm trying to go forward and you are impeding progress. . . . We need renewable energy, and we need it now."[59] Anti-MTR activists are calling for a fundamental change in energy production in the coalfields and beyond, a truly progressive vision that counters the neoliberal agenda in local, regional, national, and global arenas.

Such a paradigm shift is invariably met with resistance. John Bellamy Foster says that the need for a "radical reorganization of production in order to create a more sustainable and just world, is invariably downplayed by the ruling elements of society. . . . Industry too fosters such an attitude of complacency, while at the same time assiduously advertising itself as socially responsible and environmentally benign."[60] This is certainly evident in Big Coal's claim to make "black the new green." Lorelei Scarbro points to the urgent need for this energy transition and the current injustices in coalfield communities:

> We are surrounded by mountaintop removal. And of course MTR is a very big part of the climate crisis. . . . They use three million pounds of explosives to blow the tops off of mountains . . . ammonium nitrate and fuel oil. . . . And ammonium nitrate and fuel oil is what Tim McVeigh used to blow up the federal building in Oklahoma City. When Tim McVeigh used it to blow up the federal building it was called a crime, when they use it here they call it "progress."[61]

Scarbro says, "With the technology we have today, we certainly don't need coal as an energy source anymore. We need to start today. Yesterday. Last year, phasing out coal as an energy source, because coal as an energy source, from cradle to grave, is very, very, very deadly."[62] Whether we consider the impacts on the human and the nonhuman environments in coal extraction production zones like central Appalachia, or the effects of emissions from coal consumption zones throughout the world, coal is indeed deadly.

At coal's point of production, natural waterways such as streams and rivers are being contaminated with heavy metals, including lead, arsenic, beryllium, and selenium. Also, area slurry ponds that contain waste from processing coal for market distribution are leaching into water supplies in coalfield communities. Some area physicians note an increase in patient health problems over the last decade, with many suffering from early onset dementia, kidney stones, thyroid problems, gastrointestinal problems, cancer, and birth defects.[63] The burning of coal releases sulfur, nitrogen oxide, mercury, and carbon dioxide into the atmosphere.[64] Regardless of the toxic nature of coal production and consumption to the human and the nonhuman environments, the use of coal continues to increase, Big Coal consistently reaps large profits, and governmental policy remains chained to a fossil fuel paradigm in this neoliberal era.

J. Timmons Roberts suggests that the "restructuring of the world economy in the current phase of increasingly global production is leading to an increasingly global pattern of environmental injustice. . . . Whether the 'culprits' are emitters near or far away, poor nations and especially their poorest people increasingly are suffering environmental injustices in a globalized economy."[65] Despite the formidable obstacles currently faced by environmental justice groups, Roberts suggests that awareness of the political-economic machinations that create and sustain environmental injustice can open up new avenues for global coalition building. John Bellamy Foster argues, "We must recognize that today's ecological problems are related to a system of global inequality that demands ecological destruction as a necessary condition of its existence. New social and democratic solutions need to be developed, rooted in human community and sustainability, embodying principles of conservation that are essential to life."[66] Indeed, an awareness of the global political-economic forces that create and sustain adverse environments and social injustice assist environmental justice groups, many of them spearheaded by women of color and working-class white women, in making those crucial connections between the local and the global, or the particular and the universal.

Global Environmental Justice, Gender, and the Anti–Mountaintop Removal Mining Movement's Challenge to Neoliberalism

Continued coal usage exacerbates problems associated with climate change and adversely impacts the human and nonhuman environments at production and consumption points, but disenfranchised populations around the globe are collectively responding to social and environmental problems in their communities. As we have seen, activists in West Virginia are part of networks of environmental justice groups that work to bring attention to the destruction caused by MTR, as well as its connection to climate change. While they are situated in specific locales, increasingly, EJ activists, many of them women living in socially and environmentally vulnerable communities, make important connections with similarly situated populations in the United States and beyond. Some Appalachian studies scholars note that this outward-looking perspective is different from previous instantiations of social justice activism in Appalachia. Stephen L. Fisher suggests that, historically, collective resistance in the region was largely single-issue focused and limited to locally based communities:

> While localism offers a number of advantages, few significant problems can be solved at the local level. Local resources have been depleted and local economies gutted by national and global market forces and the actions of the federal government and multinational corporations. Those organizing in Appalachia must find ways to make clear the connections that exist between local work and national and international institutions if local citizens are to understand the importance of national and international forces as determinants of what happens locally and to see themselves as actors at the national level.[67]

The movement to end MTR is different from previous social justice initiatives in that it connects the particular and the universal. Groups work to shape environmental policy and educate the public on the social and environmental impacts of the use of coal, viewing themselves as local, regional, national, and international actors. On the local level, the Ohio Valley Environmental Coalition, the Coal River Mountain Watch, and the Keepers of the Mountain are the three major organizations working on coal issues in West Virginia communities. These local groups also partner with regional organizations such as Appalachian Voices and Kentuckians for the Commonwealth. Nationally, the Sierra Club has representatives based in the coalfields, and the National Resources Defense Council is assisting in legal battles over mountaintop removal. Furthermore, Earth First! was instrumental in beginning Mountain Justice Summer in Appalachia, an annual event shaped by the civil rights campaign Mississippi Freedom Summer. As mentioned earlier, the locally based groups are also part of the Citizens Coal Council, a national federation of grassroots groups who work to protect people and the environment from harmful coal industry practices. These connections are important networks for locally based actors working on environmental justice issues that have global implications. These groups are also affiliated with the international organization Rainforest Action Network, which is based in San Francisco. Thus local, regional, national, and international networks make the issue of MTR and other deleterious coal industry practices a global issue, not strictly bound to the point of production or a particular place.

In this neoliberal era, ideas about place should, indeed, be conceived broadly if we are to make transformative environmental, economic, and political changes. David Harvey reminds us that connecting the local, or particular, to the global, or universal, has political-economic potential for the human and nonhuman environments. Harvey argues that "the contemporary emphasis on the local, while it enhances certain kinds of sensitivities, totally erases others and thereby truncates rather than emancipates the field of political engagement and action. While we all have some 'place' (or 'places') in the order of things, we can never be purely 'local' beings, no matter how hard we try."[68] Harvey suggests that a strict focus on the local without seeing webs of connectivity is ultimately politically disempowering. Environmental justice theory and activism firmly situated in particular places while making global connections is perhaps the most productive way of understanding and confronting environmental injustices wrought by neoliberal forces. Judy Bonds consistently expressed an awareness about the global implications of MTR on people and the environment in Appalachia and beyond:

> I can go on and on about West Virginia and mountaintop removal, but I can see the big picture. And the big picture is renewable energy. The big picture is America's reliance upon fossil fuels, and the growing reliance of China. . . . I can see what it's doing to the earth. . . . The mining and the extraction of coal is filthy . . . but the problem is, on the other end, the burning of it is poisoning our unborn children. It's doing damage to the earth that cannot be undone unless we do something really soon about it.[69]

Bonds's emphasis on the "big picture" of renewable energy demonstrates how anti-MTR activists are situated in local coalfield communities (production sites), but also see the importance of making broader national and global links between the extraction and the consumption of coal. Linking the particular and the universal is concomitant with geographer Doreen B. Massey's position that forging such connections is essential to a progressive political vision that avoids reactionary impulses. Massey argues that, historically, movements that solely emphasized the local were frequently defensive and too insular in their thinking to be successful. To avoid this counterproductive position, Massey encourages activists and theorists to envision places as

> articulated moments in networks of social relations and understandings, but where a large proportion of those relations, experiences and

understandings are constructed on a far larger scale than what we happen to define for that moment as the place itself, whether that be a street, or a region or a continent. And this in turn allows a sense of place which is extroverted, which includes a consciousness of its links with the wider world, which integrates in a positive way the global and the local.[70]

Massey argues that this perspective enables theory and activism situated in a particular place to have a universal outlook that is not defensive or isolated, but rather outward- looking and progressive. Her position is in concert with that of Chandra Talpade Mohanty, who declares, "We must be location-specific, but not location-bound."[71] Because it is impossible to be local citizens outside of the larger regional, national, and international web in this neoliberal era, environmental justice activists and theorists are increasingly developing this broader perspective. Thus, it is important to note EJ's transition from a US-based theory and praxis perspective to one with a more global outlook. In doing so we can ascertain the ways in which this shift is also gendered, with women all over the world leading the charge to fight for locally situated but globally conceived environmental justice.

Because environmental justice began in the United States, some scholars note an international dominance of the US experience in EJ discourse, even though EJ exists in other parts of the world, although with different articulations. For example, race is centralized in EJ theory in the United States because of its historical connections to civil rights and colonialism, with struggles for environmental justice by indigenous populations. In parts of Europe, however, EJ discourse is more focused on social class differences among populations, and the ways in which class intersects with environmental issues.[72] Ryan Holifield notes the inherent differences in environmental justice thought and practice globally:

> It is evident that issues of environmental justice, rather than adhering to a particular US-specific definition, manifest differently in different spatial and social contexts. In these new spaces environmental justice discourses have revealed a diversity of forms of environmental good and bad interacting with various forms of social difference (no longer only a matter of race and class) working across and between multiple scales.[73]

Indeed, as discussed below, gender and nationality are also social difference categories in need of more attention by EJ scholars. Agyeman, Bullard, and Evans argue that even though the "'environmental justice paradigm,' . . . including the environmental justice vocabulary and the range of organizations which exist in the US," are not necessarily a part of the EJ discourse in other parts of the world, there are obviously environmental issues in many disenfranchised communities—a reality that has the potential to foster global connections between organizations.[74] These authors also suggest, "There are political struggles around the world which are clearly evident in terms of both traditional siting issues, and also in areas such as housing, work or opposition to new developments. In this sense, the discourse of environmental justice may be seen as a unifying process, bringing together diverse situations and sharing understandings and experiences."[75] In this neoliberal era where vulnerable communities around the world are confronted with the worst social and environmental problems, the most recent environmental studies scholarship reflects a shift away from a US focus to a more global awareness in light of the global presence of environmental justice groups and campaigns.

Ryan Holifield argues that since the 1990s, many groups have emerged throughout the world, and the focus of EJ scholarship is adjusting to address these transformations: "While the corpus of US-based scholarship continues to grow, it is increasingly augmented by studies that examine the relationships among power, inequalities, and environments around the globe—relationships that activists and academics are increasingly identifying in terms of environmental justice and injustice."[76] This shift from a local to a global focus is indeed a positive trend for EJ activists because of the networking potential among groups, and the increased awareness gained from understanding issues facing similar communities around the globe. A global perspective among EJ groups, regardless of the particular place in which they are situated, can provide politically transformative knowledge of the neoliberal forces that shape jeopardized environments and adverse social and economic conditions for vulnerable communities, enabling them to effectively target and fight these forces. It is also a crucial transformation for EJ theorists in that academic production can be effectively used to assess current trends and assist transformative social and environmental changes in the world.

While we have noted the politically transformative potential of local and global connections in environmental justice, it is also important to highlight the too often neglected social difference of gender in environmental justice thought and praxis. As noted in chapter 2, much of the existing EJ scholarship focuses on the human social differences of race and/or class and their relationships to adverse social and environmental conditions in particular communities. Gender is less frequently considered, even though the majority of US environmental justice groups, and others throughout the world, are founded and led by women of color and poor white women. As such, it is imperative for scholars to assess the role of gender in environmental justice, and the ways in which it connects to other social differences such as race, class, ethnicity, nationality, and so forth. As many feminist environmentalists have noted, women, with their persistent connection to the domestic sphere, are frequently the first to detect environmental problems that impact their homes and communities. Filomina Chioma Steady argues that not considering gender in our frameworks contributes to social and environmental problems rather than rectifying them:

> Maintaining gender inequality is another predictor of environmental injustice, since women's multiple roles, including caregiving and home-nursing responsibilities, as well as the management of natural resources, can disproportionately ascribe to them the burdens and risks of environmental degradation and its social and human costs. Women's multiple burdens also include the responsibilities for environmental damage control, which has been described as the "third shift."[77]

Other feminists, such as Susan Buckingham-Hatfield, concur that women are uniquely connected to the natural environment because of their roles in social reproduction, but also biologically and economically as well. However, Buckingham-Hatfield urges us to note the differences between women in the global North and women in the global South:

> The relationship between gender and environment is less obvious in the West where most people are more distant from the source of their food supply, the energy and the water they use. However, because of their biology, it is women who conceive, carry, give birth to and suckle children and this exposes them to a number of environmental hazards. In addition, their social role as the main unpaid domestic worker in each household brings them closer to an awareness of environmental hazard.[78]

Buckingham-Hatfield also notes that worldwide, women tend to be poorer than men in most communities, an indispensable point for environmental justice scholars, who have long made the claim that environmental problems disproportionately and more adversely impact the poorest populations in the world. If environmental justice scholarship is committed to exposing how the poor are most impacted by social and environmental problems, gender analyses must be sufficiently addressed in EJ scholarship. Buckingham urges us to recognize that women are not a homogeneous group worldwide, but there are important commonalities economically, biologically, and in their social reproduction roles.[79]

Some scholars argue that because of their connections to the environment, as pointed out by Steady and Buckingham-Hatfield, women are not inherently closer to nature than men, but are in a unique position to understand both environmental and social problems because of their positions within the social world and the environment at large. Heather Eaton and Lois Ann Lorentzen claim that "since environmental problems affect women most directly, isn't it possible that women possess a greater knowledge and expertise that could prove useful in finding solutions to pressing environmental problems?"[80] Eaton and Lorentzen argue that women are "epistemologically privileged," and in a "good position to aid in creating new, practical and intellectual ecological paradigms."[81] This is an important point because environmental problems, whether the extraction of coal in West Virginia, drilling for oil in the Niger Delta, or locating waste incinerators in urban communities, are the result of decision-making processes by government and business, and women form a tiny percentage of decision makers in these arenas.[82] Women around the globe who join or organize environmental justice groups to improve social, economic, and environmental conditions in their communities (while making global connections) have their own kind of expertise, which could prove invaluable in fostering an alternative energy paradigm to replace the reliance on fossil fuels.

Considering women's small numbers in government and business, and their large presence in environmental justice movements throughout the world, it is important to highlight their connections to social and environmental justice, and the potential they have for constructing new "ecological paradigms."[83] Activists in local coalfield communities argue for a shift away from fossil fuel production and consumption and toward the creation of sustainable communities supported by alternative energy forms. Sarah

Haltom criticizes the slowness of government in supporting the development and use of renewables such as wind, solar, and geothermal energy sources. She says, "The government and the fossil fuel industry want people to believe that it is not possible to have *all* renewable and sustainable energy because it will ultimately mean less money to them. It is that simple really. It is all about money and power."[84] Such a paradigm shift has the potential to improve socioeconomic and environmental conditions not only in Appalachian communities, but also in similarly situated populations in other parts of the world. Maria Gunnoe maintains that mountaintop removal mining is connected to larger environments primarily through "global warming." She also reminds us,

> Coal's not going to last forever, and we keep creating this economy that is based on a constant flow of energy that we can waste. It's like throwing money at the window. The US is more wasteful with their resources . . . than any other country in the world, and conservation is the farthest thing on our minds, and we absolutely have to make the transition over to renewable energy and take advantage of the clean opportunities to offer our children, because right now it looks pretty bleak.[85]

The solutions offered by anti-MTR activists reveal a "locally situated" but not "locally bound" perspective, as is evident in their campaigns and their network participation.

Arguably, it is climate change and the work of activists that prompt this shift in EJ scholarship from a US- to a globally conceived environmental justice. Giovanna Di Chiro notes the changes environmental justice practice has undergone in this global, neoliberal era, and calls attention to the political potential of this transformation. She notes that many EJ groups are forming a "global sense of place," expanding notions of "community identification and forging local/global modes of political mobilization."[86] Di Chiro argues that many activists have developed "translocal, transnational, and 'global' political formations that acknowledge the interconnectedness of ecological, political, and economic systems."[87] She says this perspective is vital in promoting an inclusive environmental justice "that ensures that the externalities of industrial 'progress' do not end up in the 'backyards' of marginalized communities in the USA, or anywhere else in the world."[88] Considering the anti-MTR movement, there are numerous ways in which these particular and universal connections are forged.

In November 2009, West Virginia anti-MTR groups participated in the international Mass Action on Climate Change. The Coal River Mountain Watch publication *The Messenger* covered the mobilization for climate change, saying, "We welcome the active involvement of organizations that are united with us in our opposition to market-based, false solutions to climate change, and in support of real, effective and just solutions to climate change."[89] Their support of this international call to stand against climate change and the political and economic forces that contribute to climate change includes an inherent critique of neoliberalism and its impact on the human and nonhuman environments. Furthermore, the Ohio Valley Environmental Coalition's publication *Winds of Change* contains a "Global Warming/Climate Instability in the Mountain State" section that examines the links between the extraction of coal in West Virginia, its impact on people and the environment there, and the problems associated with climate change worldwide.

In October 2009 one OVEC member, Mel Tyree, critiqued the market-based cap and trade proposals geared toward curtailing industrial emissions, questioning its efficacy in addressing climate change. In this section of the OVEC newsletter, Tyree claims that "if cap and trade is enacted by the US and continues to be the primary mechanism to reduce greenhouse gas emissions by the rest of the world, our planet will be doomed to irreversible, catastrophic climate change."[90] OVEC advocates a carbon tax at the point of production instead of the current system where corporations trade emissions credits, enabling them to pollute more than the established government "cap" allows. This position echoes scientist Vandana Shiva's stance on cap and trade as market-based solutions that essentially privatize the earth's atmosphere. Shiva claims that these "market solutions in the form of emissions trading run counter to the bedrock environmental principle that the polluter should pay. Through emissions trading, private polluters are getting more rights and more control over the atmosphere, which rightfully belongs to all life on the planet. Emissions trading 'solutions' pay the polluter."[91]

Furthermore, Shiva argues that creating a pollution market is "ethically perverse," for the trade is between polluters, and "economic actors that *never* polluted were never allocated credits and therefore are never able to sell them. There is nothing to encourage truly sustainable development."[92] These market-based solutions are in keeping with neoliberal economic principles, and end up contributing to adverse environmental conditions and negatively impacting "those who have contributed the least to the degradation of the atmosphere."[93] West Virginia groups fighting mountaintop removal in the coalfields consistently link their efforts regionally, nationally, and internationally, realizing that what happens in their particular communities has universal implications. They recognize that razing a mountain chain to extract coal not only harms those situated near these sites, but citizens throughout the coal-burning, fossil fuel–based world.

Another important link made by Appalachian activists standing up to Big Coal is to protest the financing of socially and environmentally devastating industrial practices such as mountaintop removal coal mining. Local groups promote divestment and have targeted Bank of America, JP Morgan, and Citibank for financing MTR operations, hoping that the problems faced by coalfield communities will not be experienced by similarly situated communities in other parts of the world. For example, in 2007 the Coal River Mountain Watch participated in a global campaign organized by the Rainforest Action Network against Citibank and Bank of America. Chanting, "Global warming, who do we thank? Coal investments from Citbank," activists met near an MTR site in West Virginia on the day of the action because there are no Citibank franchises in their communities. Groups in other parts of the world organized outside Citibank offices. Pauline Canterbury, a Sylvester Dustbuster, carried a sign that read "Bank of America: Covering Our Communities in Coal Dust."

The Coal River Mountain Watch released a statement on the rationale for their participation in this campaign against Citibank and Bank of America: "Because both of them have lent billions of dollars to the coal industry. They fund coal at every step of its journey, from cradle to grave. They are behind mountaintop removal here in Appalachia, the destruction of the Dineh people's land in Arizona, and a whole lot of proposed new coal-fired plants."[94] This tactic of targeting banks that fund MTR has prompted major MTR funder JP Morgan to review the social and environmental risks associated with mountaintop removal coal mining in Appalachia. JP Morgan has financed twenty deals worth $8.5 trillion for coal companies that engage in MTR.[95] While activists consider this change a step forward, they recognize it as a tepid move that does not fully withdraw funding for MTR in Appalachia.[96]

As anti-MTR activists make connections between adverse social and environmental conditions in their communities and global environmental issues, they consistently highlight the need for a transition from fossil fuel–based energy production to the development of alternative energy sources. Patty Sebok says, "We need renewable energy, and we need it now! And not just here, the whole nation. . . . The pollution does not stop here. . . . What goes into our streams goes all the way to the Gulf of Mexico."[97] Indeed, Appalachian studies scholar Richard Hasler argues that the Appalachian Mountains are a "contested commons at local, national, and international levels."[98] Instead of looking at the world, its resources, and people as sources of privatization potential under global capitalism, many activists envision the world and its resources as a "commons," where the goods and bads of any society are equally and more justly allocated. In this sense they are organized social actors that refute the neoliberal agenda and offer alternative visions. Vandana Shiva defines the "commons":

> A commons embodies social relations based on interdependence and cooperation. There are clear rules and principles; there are systems of decision-making. Decisions about what crops to sow, how many cattle will graze, which trees will be cut, which streams will irrigate which field at what time, are made jointly and democratically by the members of the community. A democratic governance is what made, and makes, a commons a commons.[99]

Women environmental justice activists, whether fighting Big Coal in Appalachia or Big Oil in places like Costa Rica, Nigeria, and Ecuador, provide an alternative vision that understands and critiques the current system, offering solutions and alternatives that some feminist social theorists say "support 'commoning' understood as a feminist ecosocialist alternative to capitalist-driven ecocide."[100] The anti-MTR movement, by fighting MTR in their communities and making global connections to their political, economic, and environmental issues, advocates instead what Vandana Shiva calls "living economies," which are "people-centered, decentralized, sustainable, and livelihood-generating. They are based on co-ownership and coproduction, on sharing and participation. Living economies are not mere concepts: they exist and continue to emerge in our times. Living economies are being shaped by ordinary people in their everyday lives."[101] For Shiva, living economies unite the human and nonhuman environments. Many women in West Virginia promote living economies through sustainable development of the area's renewable natural resources and the global transition from the fossil fuel-based paradigm of energy production to alternative energy development. In doing so they work to stop MTR in West Virginia, end Big Coal's choke hold on their communities, and curtail the impact of climate change on the planet.

Conclusion

Communities in central Appalachia are ground zero for climate change because they house coal production sites that have substantial health impacts on the natural environment and the people who populate these mountain communities. The coal extracted in this region fuels the national economy and is shipped to many other countries throughout the world. Big Coal's contribution to climate change cannot be denied, and environmental justice analyses must consider both the production and the consumption of coal in addressing problems associated with climate change and the communities most adversely impacted. Activists in the anti-MTR movement, many of them working-class white women and Cherokee women, stress the importance of considering the production of coal and Big Coal's political and economic power as a fundamental way to account for what is happening in Appalachia and to the global environment in this era of neoliberalism. Merely focusing on clean coal technologies and cap and trade or other market-based approaches to regulating CO_2 emissions will not decrease the production of coal in Appalachia or improve the health of the human and nonhuman environments in these communities. We must put our energies into green alternatives to the production and consumption of fossil fuels, ensuring that a transition to a green economy includes populations and environments that have been most exploited under the fossil fuel–based paradigm of energy production. Environmental justice scholarship that has a global perspective is perhaps the best way to assess the injustice of the fossil fuel paradigm and work for equitable solutions that will benefit the global environment and those most harmed by these industrial practices.

NOTES

Epigraph (page vi)

Denise Giardina, "The Legacy of Coal," *Highland Voice* (March 1999): 3.

Introduction

1. Rob Perks, "Appalachian Heartbreak: Time to End Mountaintop Removal Coal Mining," National Resources Defense Council, http://www.nrdc.org/land/appalachian/default.asp.
2. Ibid.
3. Janice Nease, interview by author, June 17, 2006.
4. Ohio Valley Environmental Coalition, http://www.ohvec.org/issues/index.html.
5. Judy Bonds, interview by author, June 10, 2006.
6. Sarah Haltom, interview by author, August 5, 2010.
7. Perks, "Appalachian Heartbreak."
8. Ibid.
9. Ibid.
10. Ibid.
11. M. A. Palmer et al., "Mountaintop Mining Consequences," *Science* 327 (2010): 148; and Shirley Stewart Burns, *Bringing Down the Mountains: The Impact of Mountaintop Removal on Southern West Virginia Communities* (Morgantown: West Virginia University Press, 2007), 8.
12. Palmer et al., "Mountaintop Mining Consequences," 148.
13. Ibid.
14. Melissa M. Ahern et al., "The Association Between Mountaintop Mining and Birth Defects Among Live Births in Central Appalachia, 1996–2003," *Environmental Research* (2011): 1.
15. Penny Loeb, *Moving Mountains: How One Woman and Her Community Won Justice from Big Coal* (Lexington: University of Kentucky Press, 2007), 54.

16. Loeb, *Moving Mountains*, 142; and Perks, "Appalachian Heartbreak."

17. Burns, *Bringing Down the Mountains*, 86.

18. Perks, "Appalachian Heartbreak."

19. Ibid.

20. Loeb, *Moving Mountains*, 142.

21. Ibid., 99.

22. Ibid., 230.

23. Ibid., 239.

24. Michael Shnayerson, *Coal River* (New York: Farrar, Straus and Giroux, 2008), 305, 277.

25. "Court Rejects Mining Ruling," *Washington Post*, February 14, 2009, http://www.washingtonpost.com/wp-dyn/content/article/2009/02/13/AR2009021301827_pf.html.

26. Perks, "Appalachian Heartbreak."

27. "EPA Issues Comprehensive Guidance to Protect Appalachian Communities from Harmful Environmental Impacts of Mountaintop Mining," April 1, 2010, http://www.yosemite.epa.gov/opa/admpress.nsf/e77fdd4f5afd88a385 (site discontinued).

28. Ibid.

29. Ken Ward Jr., "EPA Gives Tentative OK to Logan Mine Permit," *Charleston Gazette*, June 29, 2010, http://www.sundaygazettemail.com/News/Business/201006291309.

30. John M. Broder, "Agency Revokes Permit for Major Coal Mining Project," *New York Times*, January 13, 2011, http://www.nytimes.com/2011/01/14/science/earth/14coal.html.

31. Maria Gunnoe, interview by author, April 2, 2010.

32. SustainableBusiness.com, "EPA OKs New Mountaintop Removal Coal Mine," July 6, 2010, http://www.sustainablebusiness.com/index.cfm/go/news.display/.

33. Judy Bonds, interview by author, August 7, 2009.

34. Haltom interview.

35. Gunnoe interview.

36. Ibid.

37. See, for example, Robert D. Bullard, *Dumping in Dixie: Race, Class, and Environmental Quality* (Boulder, CO: Westview Press, 1990), 9–17; and Bullard, ed., *The Quest for Environmental Justice: Human Rights and the Politics of Pollution* (San Francisco: Sierra Club Books, 2005), 29–30; Luke W. Cole and Sheila R. Foster, *From the Ground Up: Environmental Racism and the Rise of the Environmental Justice Movement* (New York: New York University Press, 2001), 16–17; David E. Camacho ed., *Environmental Injustices, Political Struggles: Race, Class, and the Environment* (Durham, NC : Duke University Press, 1998), 12; Mark Dowie, *Losing Ground: American Environmentalism at the Close of the Twentieth Century* (Cambridge, MA: MIT Press, 1995), 1–3, 30–32; and Eileen McGurty, *Transforming Environmentalism: Warren County, PCBs, and the Origins of Environmental Justice* (New Brunswick, NJ: Rutgers University Press, 2007), 10–18.

38. Carolyn Merchant, *The Columbia Guide to American Environmental History* (New York: Columbia University Press, 2002), 212; Filomina Chioma Steady, ed., *Environmental Justice in the New Millennium: Global Perspectives on Race, Ethnicity, and Human Rights* (New York: Palgrave Macmillan, 2009), 2.

39. Rachel Stein, ed., *New Perspectives on Environmental Justice: Gender, Sexuality and Activism* (New Brunswick, NJ: Rutgers University Press, 2004), 2.

40. Merchant, *The Columbia Guide to American Environmental History*, 212.

41. Steady, *Environmental Justice in the New Millennium*, 2.

42. Dianne Rocheleau, Barbara Thomas-Slayter, and Esther Wangari, *Feminist Political Ecology: Global Issues and Local Experiences* (New York: Routledge, 1996), 9.

43. Stein, *New Perspectives on Environmental Justice*, 2.

44. Nancy C. Unger, "Gendered Approaches to Environmental Justice: An Historical Sampling," in *Echoes from the Poisoned Well: Global Memories of Environmental Injustice*, edited by Sylvia Hood Washington, Paul C. Rosier, and Heather Goodall (Lanham, MD: Lexington Books, 2006), 17.

Chapter 1: Living in a Sacrifice Zone

Epigraph: Judy Bonds, interview by author, June 10, 2006.

1. Goldman Environmental Prize, http://www.goldmanprize.org/recipients/year.

2. Bonds interview.

3. Ibid.

4. Michael Shnayerson, *Coal River* (New York: Farrar, Straus and Giroux, 2008), 56.

5. Bonds interview.

6. Ibid.

7. Ibid.

8. Silas House and Jason Howard, *Something's Rising: Appalachians Fighting Mountaintop Removal* (Lexington: University of Kentucky Press, 2009), 133.

9. Ibid.

10. Bonds interview.

11. Ibid.

12. Ibid.

13. House and Howard, *Something's Rising*, 138.

14. Bonds interview.

15. Ibid.

16. Postcards from the West Virginia–based environmental group the Ohio Valley Environmental Coalition contain a picture of an active MTR site with the text: "Greetings from West Virginia: America's Energy Sacrifice Zone." In 2006, half of US energy consumption came from coal, according to Jeff Goodell, *Big Coal: The Dirty Secret Behind America's Energy Future* (New York: Houghton Mifflin, 2006), xiii.

17. U.S. Census Bureau, 2007 State and Country Quick Facts, http://wwwquickfacts.census.gov/qfd/states/54000.html.

18. In 2008, in the nine-county coalfield region of West Virginia, 13,156 coal miners were employed, according to the West Virginia Coal Association's *Coal Facts 2008*. This number is down from 150,000 miners employed in state mines in the 1950s, according to Shirley Stewart Burns in *Bringing Down the Mountains: The Impact of Mountaintop*

Removal on Southern West Virginia Communities (Morgantown: West Virginia University Press, 2007), 27.

19. Kelvin M. Pollard, *Appalachia at the Millennium: An Overview of Results from Census 2000* (Washington, DC: Appalachian Regional Studies Commission, 2003), 22.

20. Alemayehu Bishaw and Jessica Semega, *Income, Earnings, and Poverty Data from the 2007 American Community Survey* (Washington, DC: US Census Bureau, 2008), 21.

21. Suite101.com, http://www.suite101.com/article.cfm/poverty_in_West_Virginia.

22. Goodell, *Big Coal*, 28.

23. Pollard, *Appalachia at the Millennium*.

24. Drucilla K. Barker and Susan F. Feiner, *Liberating Economics: Feminist Perspectives on Families, Work, and Globalization* (Ann Arbor: University of Michigan Press, 2004), 3.

25. Pollard, *Appalachia at the Millennium*, 2.

26. Ibid.

27. Ibid., 4–5.

28. Ibid.

29. Ibid., 4.

30. Ibid.

31. Ibid., 18–19.

32. Deborah M. Figart, "Wage Gap," in *The Elgar Companion to Feminist Economics*, ed. Janice Peterson and Margaret Lewis (Northampton. MA: Edward Elgar, 1999), 748.

33. Frances S. Hensley, "Women in the Industrial Work Force in West Virginia, 1880–1945," *West Virginia History* 49 (1990), http://www.wvculture.org/hiStory/journal_wvh/wvh49-9.html.

34. Ibid.

35. Pollard, *Appalachia at the Millennium*, 16.

36. Ibid.

37. Ibid., 24–25.

38. Ibid.

39. Deborah M. Figart, Ellen Mutari, and Marilyn Power, *Living Wages, Equal Wages: Gender and Labor Market Policies in the United States* (New York: Routledge, 2002), 58.

40. Ibid.

41. Ibid.

42. Ibid., 59.

43. Institute for Women's Policy Research, *The Status of Women in West Virginia Highlights*, http://www.iwpr.org.

44. Ibid.

45. Ibid.

46. Ibid.

47. Ibid.

48. Ibid.

49. Ibid.

50. Ibid.

51. The 2009 National Women's Law Center report, *Falling Short in Every State: The Wage Gap and Harsh Economic Realities for Women Persist*, reveals that West Virginia has

the third-highest wage gap between men and women in the country, with white women earning 67 cents for every white male dollar, while African American women earn 62 cents, falling well below the national average of 78 cents. This report also states that poverty indexes for West Virginia women stand at 17 percent, compared to 13 percent for men. In addition, the 2008 *American Community Survey* claims that earnings for West Virginia women are the second lowest in the country at $26,719, compared to the average of $34,278. In terms of education, the *U.S. Census Bureau Educational Attainment in the US: 2007* report says that West Virginia had the lowest number of residents with high school diplomas at 81.2 percent, while only 17.3 percent of state residents had college degrees, the lowest ranking in the country.

52. Institute for Women's Policy Research, *The Status of Women in West Virginia Highlights*.

53. Goodell, *Big Coal*, 32.

54. Ibid.

55. Ibid.

56. Bonds interview.

57. Burns, *Bringing Down the Mountains*, 11.

58. Ibid.

59. Chris Weiss, "Organizing Women for Local Economic Development," in *Communities in Economic Crisis: Appalachia and the South*, ed. John Gaventa, Barbara Ellen Smith, and Alex Willingham (Philadelphia, PA: Temple University Press, 1990), 68.

60. The core-periphery model was developed by Immanuel Wallerstein in *The Modern World-System: Capitalist Agriculture and the Origins of the European World-Economy in the Sixteenth Century* (New York: Academic Press, 1976). For its application in an Appalachian context, see Wilma A. Dunaway, *The First American Frontier: Transition to Capitalism in Southern Appalachia, 1700–1860* (Chapel Hill: University of North Carolina Press, 1996).

61. James R. O'Connor, *Natural Causes: Essays in Ecological Marxism* (New York: Guilford Press, 1998), 307.

62. Maria Gunnoe, "My Life Is on the Line," in *Coal Country: Rising Up Against Mountaintop Removal Mining*, ed. Shirley Stewart Burns, Mari-Lynn Evans, and Silas House (San Francisco: Sierra Club Books, 2009), 218–19.

63. Ken Ward Jr., "Woman Makes Environmental Movement Move," Ohio Valley Environmental Coalition, http://www.ohvec.org/links/news/archive/2005/fair_use/03_09.html.

64. Michael Parenti, *Against Empire* (San Francisco: City Lights Books, 1995), 17.

65. Pauline Canterbury, interview by author, June 17, 2006.

66. See Wilma A. Dunaway, *Women, Work, and Family in the Antebellum Mountain South* (Cambridge: Cambridge University Press, 2008).

67. Ann Crittenden, *The Price of Motherhood: Why the Most Important Job in the World Is Still the Least Valued* (New York: Henry Holt, 2001), 49.

68. Ibid.

69. Judith Stacey, "The Family Is Dead, Long Live Our Families," in *The Socialist Feminist Project: A Contemporary Reader in Theory and Politics*, ed. Nancy Holmstrom (New York: Monthly Review Press, 2002), 91.

70. John Alexander Williams, *Appalachia: A History* (Chapel Hill: University of North Carolina Press, 2002), 259.

71. Ibid.

72. Mary Beth Pudup, "Women's Work in the West Virginia Economy," *West Virginia History* 49 (1990), http://www.wvculture.org/history/journal_wvh/wvh49-2.html.

73. Janet W. Greene, "Strategies for Survival: Women's Work in the Southern West Virginia Coal Camps," *West Virginia History* 49 (1990), http://www.wvculture.org/history/journal_wvh/wvh49-4.html.

74. Sally Ward Maggard, "From Farm to Coal Camp to Back Office and McDonald's: Living in the Midst of Appalachia's Latest Transformation," *Journal of the Appalachian Studies Association* 6 (1994): 16–17.

75. Barker and Feiner, *Liberating Economics*, 31.

76. Stacey, "The Family Is Dead,", 97.

77. Friends of Coal, "Voices of Reason on Mountaintop Mining," http://www.friendsofcoal.org/uncatorgorized/voices-of-reason-on-mountaintop-mining.html.

78. Friends of Coal, http://www.friendsofcoal.org/news/ladies-auxiliary/168-accomplishments.html (site discontinued).

79. Ibid.

80. Ibid.

81. Friends of Coal, http://www.friendsofcoal.org/news/21-spirit-of-beckley-goes-to-warren-hylton.html (site discontinued).

82. Friends of Coal, http://www.friendsofcoal.org/news/169-coal-in-classroom-wrapping-up-for-now.html (site discontinued).

83. Jackie Ayres, "Coal in the Classroom: Battle Lines Drawn in Education Process," *Raleigh Register-Herald*, December 16, 2009, http://www.register-herald.com/local/x546333929/Coal-in-the-classroom.

84. Friends of Coal, http://www.friendsofcoal.org/news/ladies-auxiliary/168-accomplishments.html.

85. Massey Energy Company, http://www.masseyenergyco.com (site discontinued).

86. Yahoo Finance, "Massey Energy Company," http://finance.yahoo.com/q/ks?s=mee.

87. Massey Energy Company, http://masseyenergyco.com.

88. Ibid.

89. Ibid.

90. Ibid.

91. Ibid.

92. Marsh Fork Elementary School is located next to a coal silo containing waste from nearby coal preparation plants. Also, coal processing waste is contained in huge earthen dams situated in the hills directly above the school. The school water is contaminated, and many children have experienced significant health problems. The Coal River Mountain Watch developed a campaign called Pennies for Promise aimed at obtaining an alternative school for area children.

93. Appalachian Institute for Renewable Energy, http://www.aire-nc.org/2009/06/.

94. Wikio, "West Virginia Coal Thugs Disrupt July 4th Picnic," http:www.wikio. com/video/1365837.

95. Carolyn E. Sachs, *Gendered Fields: Rural Women, Agriculture, and Environment* (Boulder, CO: Westview Press, 1996), 159.

96. Celene Krauss, "Challenging Power: Toxic Waste Protests and the Politicization of White, Working-Class Women," in *Community Activism and Feminist Politics: Organizing Across Race, Class, and Gender*, ed. Nancy A. Naples (New York: Routledge, 1998), 148.

97. Ibid.

98. Bonds interview.

99. Patty Sebok, interview by author, June 10, 2006.

100. Janice Nease, interview by author, June 17, 2006.

101. Ann R. Tickamyer and Debra A. Henderson, "Rural Women: New Roles for the New Century?" in *Challenges for Rural America in the Twenty-First Century*, ed. David L. Brown and Louis E. Swanson (University Park: Pennsylvania State University Press, 2003), 116.

102. Sebok interview.

103. Bonds interview.

104. Sarah Haltom, interview by author, June 10, 2006.

105. House and Howard, *Something's Rising*, 48.

Chapter 2: Gender and Anti–Mountaintop Removal Activism

Epigraph: Lorelei Scarbro, interview by author, August 4, 2009.

1. Scarbro interview. All information concerning Lorelei Scarbro and quotations in this section are from the August 4, 2009, interview.

2. Joni Seager, "'Hysterical Housewives' and Other Mad Women: Grassroots Environmental Organizing in the United States," in *Feminist Political Ecology: Global Issues and Local Experiences*, ed. Dianne Rocheleau, Barbara Thomas-Slayter, and Esther Wangari (New York: Routledge, 1996), 277.

3. The history of environmental justice in the United States is well-documented. EJ is a movement born out of an adversarial stance to the practices and policies of broader, more nationally conceived environmentalism. Environmentalism has historically conceived of the environment as nature apart from human existence, focusing on the preservation and conservation of wilderness areas, and plants and animals that have been negatively impacted by human behavior. Environmental justice praxis and theory connects the presence of humans to the natural world, defining the environment as where humans live, work, and play. As such, it highlights human social differences based on race, gender, class, nation, and so forth and their connections to the natural world. A number of sources define environmental justice and describe how it differs from mainstream environmentalism. See, for example, Robert D. Bullard, *Dumping in Dixie: Race, Class, and Environmental Quality* (Boulder, CO: Westview Press, 2000); Bunyan Bryant, "Issues and Potential Policies and Solutions for Environmental Justice: An Overview," in *Environmental Justice: Issues, Policies, and Solutions*, ed.

Bunyan Bryant (Ann Arbor: University of Michigan Press, 1995), 1–8; Luke W. Cole and Sheila R. Foster, *From the Ground Up: Environmental Racism and the Rise of the Environmental Justice Movement* (New York: New York University Press, 2001); Daniel R. Faber, introduction to *The Struggle for Ecological Democracy: Environmental Justice Movements in the U.S.*, ed. Daniel R. Faber (New York: Guilford Press, 1998), 1–27; Ronald Sandler and Phaedra C. Pezzullo, eds., *Environmental Justice and Environmentalism: The Social Justice Challenge to the Environmental Movement* (Cambridge, MA: MIT Press, 2007); David Naguib Pellow and Robert J. Brulle, eds., *Power, Justice, and the Environment: A Critical Appraisal of the Environmental Justice Movement* (Cambridge, MA: MIT Press, 2005).

4. Ted Nordhaus and Michael Shellenberger, *Break Through: From the Death of Environmentalism to the Politics of Possibility* (New York: Houghton Mifflin, 2007), 7.

5. Ibid., 4–5.

6. Ibid., 18.

7. Rachel Stein, introduction to *New Perspectives on Environmental Justice: Gender, Sexuality and Activism*, ed. Rachel Stein (New Brunswick, NJ: Rutgers University Press, 2004), 2.

8. Van Jones, *The Green Collar Economy: How One Solution Can Fix Our Two Biggest Problems* (New York: HarperOne, 2008), 71.

9. David Naguib Pellow and Robert J. Brulle, "Power, Justice, and the Environment: Toward Critical Environmental Justice Studies," in Pellow and Brulle, *Power, Justice, and the Environment*, 13.

10. Ibid., 8.

11. Eileen McGurty, *Transforming Environmentalism: Warren County, PCBs, and the Origins of Environmental Justice* (New Brunswick, NJ: Rutgers University Press, 2007), 19–20.

12. Nordhaus and Shellenberger, *Break Through*, 67, 71.

13. Faber, "The Struggle for Ecological Democracy," 4.

14. Nordhaus and Shellenberger, *Break Through*, 68.

15. Ibid.

16. Ibid.

17. Christopher Sellers, "Environmental Justice as a Way of Seeing," *Environmental Justice* 1, no. 4 (2008): 178.

18. Julie Sze and Jonathan K. London, "Environmental Justice at the Crossroads," *Sociology Compass* 2, no. 4 (2008): 1347–48.

19. Ibid., 1332.

20. Cole and Foster, *From the Ground Up*, 20, 26.

21. Robert D. Bullard "Environmental Justice in the Twenty-First Century," in *The Quest for Environmental Justice: Human Rights and the Politics of Pollution*, ed. Robert D. Bullard (San Francisco: Sierra Club Books, 2005), 20.

22. Ibid.

23 Ibid.

24. McGurty, *Transforming Environmentalism*, 19–20.

25. Bunyan Bryant and Elaine Hockman, "A Brief Comparison of the Civil Rights Movement and the Environmental Justice Movement," in Pellow and Brulle, *Power, Justice and the Environment*, 28, 29.

26. Cole and Foster, *From the Ground Up*, 20.

27. Ibid.

28. Ibid., 20–27.

29. Pellow and Robert Brulle, "Power, Justice, and the Environment," 13.

30. Ibid.

31. Sze and London, "Environmental Justice at the Crossroads," 1332.

32. Ibid., 1336.

33. Pellow and Brulle, "Power, Justice, and the Environment," 5.

34. John Bellamy Foster, *Ecology Against Capitalism* (New York: Monthly Review Press, 2002), 10.

35. Daniel R. Faber, "A More 'Productive' Environmental Justice Politics: Movement Alliances in Massachusetts for Clean Production and Regional Equity," in Sandler and Pezzullo, *Environmental Justice and Environmentalism*, 141.

36. The only book collection focused expressly on the connections between gender and environmental justice is Stein, *New Perspectives on Environmental Justice*. A few environmental justice book collections containing one essay on gender and environmental justice include: Faber, *The Struggle for Ecological Democracy*; David E. Camacho, ed., *Environmental Injustices, Political Struggles: Race, Class, and the Environment* (Durham, NC: Duke University Press, 1998); and Bullard, *The Quest for Environmental Justice*.

37. Stein, *New Perspectives on Environmental Justice*, 2.

38. Nancy C. Unger, "The Role of Gender in Environmental Justice," *Environmental Justice* 1, no. 3 (2008): 115.

39. Rich Newman, "Making Environmental Politics: Women and Love Canal Activism," *Women's Studies Quarterly* 29, nos. 1–2 (2001): 68.

40. Valerie Ann Kaalund, "Witness to Truth: Black Women Heeding the Call for Environmental Justice," in Stein, *New Perspectives on Environmental Justice*, 79.

41. Robert D. Bullard and Damu Smith, "Women Warriors of Color on the Front Line," in Bullard, *The Quest for Environmental Justice*, 62, 65.

42. Stein, *New Perspectives on Environmental Justice*, 2.

43. Giovanna Di Chiro, "Environmental Justice from the Grassroots: Reflections on History, Gender, and Expertise," in Faber, *The Struggle for Ecological Democracy*, 118–19.

44. In an interview on June 17, 2006, Janice Nease informed me that she was one of the charter members of the Coal River Mountain Watch. She is also credited with forming this organization, along with Randy Sprouse and Freda Williams, in Silas House and Jason Howard, *Something's Rising: Appalachians Fighting Mountaintop Removal* (Lexington: University of Kentucky Press, 2009), 138. Randy Sprouse and Freda Williams are credited with forming the Coal River Mountain Watch in Michael Shnayerson, *Coal River* (New York: Farrar, Straus and Giroux, 2008), 48.

45. Nease interview.

46. Ibid.

47. Judy Bonds, interview by author, June 17, 2006.

48. Ibid.

49. Patty Sebok, interview by author, June 10, 2006.

50. Ibid.

51. Sarah Haltom, interview by author, June 10, 2006.

52. Cole and Foster, *From the Ground Up*, 14.

53. Newman, "Making Environmental Politics," 67–68.

54. Susan Buckingham and Rakibe Kulcur, "Gendered Geographies of Environmental Injustice," *Antipode* 41, no. 4 (2009): 660–61.

55. Ibid., 664.

56. Ibid.

57. Ibid., 667.

58. Ibid., 665–66.

59. Linda L. Layne, "In Search of Community: Tales of Pregnancy Loss in Three Toxically Assaulted U.S. Communities," *Women's Studies Quarterly* 29, nos. 1–2 (2001): 25.

60. Buckingham and Kulcur, "Gendered Geographies," 665.

61. Rayna Rapp, "Family and Class in Contemporary America: Notes toward an Understanding of Ideology," in *Rethinking the Family: Some Feminist Questions*, ed. Barrie Thorne and Marilyn Yalom (Boston, MA: Northeastern University Press, 1992), 50–51.

62. Ibid., 54.

63. Stein, *New Perspectives on Environmental Justice*, 2.

64. Carolyn Becker, interview by author, August 4, 2009.

65. Ibid.

66. Arun Agrawal and Clark C. Gibson, "The Role of Community in Natural Resource Conservation," in *Communities and the Environment: Ethnicity, Gender, and the State in Community-Based Conservation*, ed. Arun Agrawal and Clark C. Gibson (New Brunswick, NJ: Rutgers University Press, 2001), 1.

67. Pauline Canterbury and Mary Miller, "We're Called the Dustbusters," in *Coal Country: Rising Up Against Mountaintop Removal Mining*, ed. Shirley Stewart Burns, Mari-Lynn Evans, and Silas House (San Francisco: Sierra Club Books, 2009), 232.

68. Pauline Canterbury, interview by author, June 10, 2006.

69. Ibid.

70. Ibid.

71. Pauline Canterbury, "The Dustbuster Sisters of Sylvester," http://www.ilovemountains.org/memorial/c295/39.

72. Canterbury interview.

73. Melissa M. Ahern and Michael Hendryx, "Health Disparities and Environmental Competence: A Case Study of Appalachian Coal Mining," *Environmental Justice* 1, no. 2 (2008): 82.

74. Canterbury, "The Dustbuster Sisters of Sylvester."

75. Canterbury interview.

76. Vivian Stockman, "Sylvester 'Dustbusters' Beat up on Massey Energy," http://www.ohvec.org/newsletters/woc_2003_02/article_08.html.

77. Ibid.

78. Canterbury interview.

79. Newman, "Making Environmental Politics," 66.

80. Di Chiro, "Environmental Justice from the Grassroots," 121.

81. Kaalund, "Witness to Truth," 79.

82. Robert Gottlieb, *Forcing the Spring: The Transformation of the American Environmental Movement* (Washington, DC: Island Press, 1993), 209.

83. Joni Seager, "Hysterical Housewives," 276–77.

84. Ibid., 276.

85. Shnayerson, *Coal River*, 222.

86. See Pennies of Promise, http://www.penniesofpromise.org.

87. Ibid.

88. Ibid.

89. Ibid.

90. Joe Manchin, "Statement from the Governor Regarding Marsh Fork Elementary School," March 16, 2007, http://www.wvgov.org/sec.aspx?id=32&articleid=1492.

91. Kari Lydersen, "A School in Coal's Shadow," *Progressive*, January 2007, http:www//progressive.org/lydersen0107.html.

92. Shnayerson, *Coal River*, 222.

93. Ibid.

94. Scott Simonton, "Initial Expert Report, Fugitive and Respirable Coal Dust, Marsh Fork Elementary School, Raleigh County, WV," http://sludgesafety.org/sites/default/files/biblio/userfiles/coal_dust_reort.pdf.

95. Sarah Plummer, "Dirt to Move at New Marsh Fork School Site," *Raleigh Register-Herald*, June 29, 2011, http://www.register-herald.com/local/x349138006/Dirt-to-move-at-new-Marsh-Fork-school-site .

96. Lisa Lambert, "Grandpa Marches on DC for Clean Air and Safe Schools," http://www.sludgesafety.org/news/2006/09_13a.html.

97. A sampling of the paternalistic references used in media reports to describe Ed Wiley are contained in: Lisa Lambert, "Grandpa Marches on DC": Vivian Stockman, "Grandfather Wants Safe School for Elementary Kids," http://www.ohvec.org/galleries/people_in_action/2006/08_02/index.html; and Mike Roselle, "The Elementary School vs. the Strip Mine: Ed Wiley's Long March," http://www.sludgesafety.org/news/2006/09_21.html.

98. Maril Hazlett, "Voices from the *Spring: Silent Spring* and the Ecological Turn in American Health," in *Seeing Nature Through Gender*, ed. Virginia J. Scharff (Lawrence: University of Kansas Press, 2003), 115.

99. "Ed Wiley Could Kick Chuck Norris' Ass (For the Kids)," http://www.dc.indymedia.org/newswire/display/135377/index.php.

100. Robert Verchick, "Feminist Theory and Environmental Justice," in Stein, *New Perspectives on Environmental Justice*, 63, 64.

101. Nease interview; Judy Bonds, interview by author, June 10, 2006; Sebok interview.

102. Di Chiro, "Environmental Justice from the Grassroots," 118.

Chapter 3: Remembering the Past, Working for the Future

First epigraph: Janice Nease, interview by author, June 21, 2006; in an interview on June 17, 2006, Janice Nease informed me that she was one of the charter members of the Coal River Mountain Watch. She is also credited with forming this organization, along with Randy Sprouse and Freda Williams, in Silas House and Jason Howard, *Something's Rising: Appalachians Fighting Mountaintop Removal* (Lexington: University of Kentucky Press, 2009), 138. Randy Sprouse and Freda Williams are credited with forming the Coal River Mountain Watch in Michael Shnayerson, *Coal River* (New York: Farrar, Straus and Giroux, 2008), 48. Second epigraph: Patty Sebok, interview by author, June 21, 2006.

1. Nease interview.
2. Ibid.
3. Ibid.
4. Rudy Abramson and Jean Haskell, eds., *Encyclopedia of Appalachia* (Knoxville: University of Tennessee Press), 562.
5. Nease interview.
6. Sebok interview.
7. Ibid.
8. Ibid.
9. Ibid.
10. *Coal Country*, DVD, directed by Phylis Gellar (Evening Star Productions, 2009).
11. John Alexander Williams, *Appalachia: A History* (Chapel Hill: University of North Carolina Press, 2002), 86.
12. Nease interview.
13. Thomas Plaut, "Extending the Internal Periphery Model: The Impact of Culture and Consequent Strategy," in *Colonialism in Modern America: The Appalachian Case*, ed. Helen Matthews Lewis, Linda Johnson, and Donald Askins (Boone, NC: Appalachian Consortium Press, 1978), 358.
14. Ann Pancake, *Strange as This Weather Has Been* (San Francisco: Shoemaker and Hoard, 2007), 314.
15. John Gaventa, *Power and Powerlessness: Quiescence and Rebellion in an Appalachian Valley* (Urbana: University of Illinois Press, 1980), 1.
16. Ibid., 21–22.
17. Nease interview.
18. House and Howard, *Something's Rising*, 11–12.
19. Karaleah S. Reichart, "Narrating Conflict: Women and Coal in Southern West Virginia," *Journal of Appalachian Studies* 7 (2001): 6.
20. Virginia Renaldo Seitz, "Class, Gender, and Resistance in the Appalachian Coalfields," in *Community Activism and Feminist Politics: Organizing Across Race, Class, and Gender*, ed. Nancy A. Naples (New York: Routledge, 1998), 218.
21. Sally Ward Maggard, "Gender Contested: Women's Participation in the Brookside Coal Strike," in *Women and Social Protest*, ed. Guida West and Rhoda Lois Blumberg (New York: Oxford University Press, 1990), 75, 77.
22. Ibid., 75.

23. Barbara Kopple, *Harlan County USA* (New York: Cabin Creek Films, 1976).

24. Maggard, "Gender Contested," 75.

25. Ibid., 81.

26. Ibid.

27. Karen Beckwith, "Collective Identities of Class and Gender: Working-Class Women in the Pittston Coal Strike," *Political Psychology* 19, no. 1 (1998): 153.

28. Ibid., 152.

29. Ibid., 154.

30. Ibid., 159.

31. Benjamin Kline, *First Along the River: A Brief History of the U.S. Environmental Movement* (Lanham, MD: Rowman and Littlefield, 2007), 101.

32. Ibid., 116.

33. Ronald D. Eller, *Uneven Ground: Appalachia Since 1945* (Lexington: University of Kentucky Press, 2008). 36.

34. Judy Bonds, interview by author, June 17, 2006.

35. Eller, *Uneven Ground*, 36.

36. Ibid., 144.

37. Ibid., 145.

38. Mary Beth Bingman, "Stopping the Bulldozers: What Difference Did It Make?" in *Fighting Back in Appalachia: Traditions of Resistance and Change*, ed. Stephen L. Fisher (Philadelphia: Temple University Press, 1993), 21.

39. Chad Montrie, *To Save the Land and People: A History of Opposition to Surface Coal Mining in Appalachia* (Chapel Hill: University of North Carolina Press, 2003), 105, 146.

40. Eller, *Uneven Ground*, 147.

41. Ibid.

42. Ibid.

43. Bingman, "Stopping the Bulldozers," 29, 27.

44. Freda Williams, interview by author, December 27, 2002.

45. Montrie, *To Save the Land and People*, 4.

46. Kline, *First Along the River*, 77, 80.

47. Ibid., 84, 89.

48. Ibid., 76, 77, 81.

49. Ibid., 81.

50. Ibid., 80.

51. Nease interview.

52. Shirley Stewart Burns, *Bringing Down the Mountains: The Impact of Mountaintop Removal on Southern West Virginia Communities* (Morgantown: West Virginia University Press, 2007), 13; West Virginia Office of Miners' Health, Safety and Training, http://www.wvminesafety.org/Month96htm; http://www.wvminesafety.org/month2009.htm.

53. Nease interview.

54. Kline, *First Along the River*, 155.

55. Coal River Mountain Watch, http://www.crmw.org.

56. Ibid.

57. Ohio Valley Environmental Coalition, http://www.ohvec.org.

58. Maria Gunnoe, "My Life Is on the Line," in *Coal Country: Rising Up Against Mountaintop Removal Mining*, ed. Shirley Stewart Burns, Mari-Lynn Evans, and Silas House (San Francisco: Sierra Club Books, 2009), 219–20.

59. Carolyn Merchant, *Reinventing Eden: The Fate of Nature in Western Culture* (New York: Routledge, 2004), 223.

60. Ibid., 224.

61. West Virginia Department of Forestry, http://www.wvforestry.com/ginseng.cfm?Menucall=ginseng.

62. Anthony P. Cavender, *Folk Medicine in Southern Appalachia* (Chapel Hill: University of North Carolina Press, 2003), 63.

63. West Virginia Department of Forestry, http://www.wvforestry.com/ginseng.cfm?Menucall=ginseng.

64. Sebok interview.

65. "Black Cohosh," Office of Dietary Supplements, National Institute of Health, http://www.ods.od.nih.gov/factsheets/blackcohosh/.

66. Sharon A. Sharp, "Folk Medicine Practices: Women as Keepers and Carriers of Knowledge," *Women's International Forum* 9, no. 3 (1986): 243.

67. Anthony P. Cavender, "Folk Medical Uses of Plant Foods in Southern Appalachia, United States," *Journal of Ethnopharmacology* 108 (2006): 75, 76.

68. Cavender, *Folk Medicine in Southern Appalachia*, 64.

69. Merchant, *Reinventing Eden*, 228.

70. Sebok interview.

71. Al Fritsch and Paul Gallimore, *Healing Appalachia: Sustainable Living through Appropriate Technology* (Lexington: University of Kentucky Press, 2007), 51.

72. Ibid., 49.

73. Paul Gipe, *Wind Power for Home and Business: Renewable Energy for the 1990s and Beyond* (Post Mills, VT: Chelsea Green Publishing, 1993), 271.

74. Ibid., 55.

75. Todd Woody, "Judge Halts Wind Farm Over Bats," *New York Times*, December 10, 2009.

76. Fritsch and Gallimore, *Healing Appalachia*, 51–52.

77. Ibid., 52.

78. American Wind Energy Association, http://www.awea.org.

79. Lorelei Scarbro, interview by author August 4, 2009.

80. Sebok interview.

81. "Wind or Mountaintop Removal?: Study Shows West Virginia Mountain Could Be Permanent Power Source for 150,00 Homes," *Earth Times*, http://www.Earthtimes.org/articles/show.wind-or-mountaintop-removal-study,510055.

82. Ibid.

83. Ibid.

84. Merchant, *Reinventing Eden*, 226.

85. Van Jones, *The Green Collar Economy: How One Solution Can Fix Our Two Biggest Environmental Problems* (New York: HarperCollins, 2008), 62.

86. Thomas Heyd, "Nature, Culture, and Natural Heritage: Toward a Culture of Nature," *Environmental Ethics* 27, no. 4 (2005): 340.

87. Ibid.

88. Emma Belle Miles, *The Spirit of the Mountains* (Knoxville: University of Tennessee Press, 1975), 17, 18–19.

89. Maggie Anderson, "The Mountains Dark and Close Around Me," in *BloodRoot: Reflections on Place by Appalachian Women Writers*, ed. Joyce Dyer (Lexington: University of Kentucky Press), 33.

90. Doris Diosa Davenport, "All This, and Honeysuckles Too," in Dyer, *BloodRoot*, 92.

91. Sebok interview.

92. Nease interview.

93. Deborah Feyerick, "The Battle Over Coal River Mountain," October 7, 2008, http://www.cnn.com/2008/US/10/07/coal.river/.

94. Denise Giardina, quoted in House and Howard, *Something's Rising*, 57.

95. Renku Sen, *Stir It Up: Lessons in Community Organizing and Advocacy* (San Francisco: John Wiley, 2003), 148.

96. West Virginia Coal Association, *Coal Facts 2006* (Charleston: West Virginia Coal Association), 2.

97. Ibid.

98. West Virginia Coal Association, http://www.wvcoalassociation.org.

99. "More Than Coal," http://www.youtube.com/watch?v=jcqzC70FDI8.

100. Ibid.

101. "Clean Green Coal," http://www.youtube.com/watch?v=3-WtKQAloSA.

102. Bonds interview.

103. Sen, *Stir It Up*, 149.

104. Ibid.

Chapter 4: Saving the Endangered Hillbilly

Epigraph: Maria Gunnoe, interview by author, April 23, 2010.

1. Ibid.

2. Ibid.

3. Ibid.

4. See Goldman Environmental Prize, http://www.goldmanprize.org/2009/northamerica.

5. Gunnoe interview.

6. Goldman Environmental Prize.

7. Gunnoe interview.

8. Ibid.

9. Ibid.

10. Sam Roberts, "New Demographic Racial Gap Emerges," *New York Times*, May 17, 2007.

11. "Quick Facts," U.S. Census Bureau, http://www.quickfacts.census-gov/qfd./states/54000.html.

12. Dwight B. Billings, introduction to *Back Talk from Appalachia: Confronting Stereotypes*, ed. Dwight B. Billings, Gurney Norman, and Katherine Ledford (Lexington: University of Kentucky Press, 1999), 3–5.

13. David M. Brown, "Film's Casting Call Wants That 'Inbred Look,'" *Pittsburgh Tribune*, February 26, 2008.

14. Ibid.

15. Ibid.

16. Jake Stump, "West Virginians Blast Back After Cheney Remark," *Charleston Daily Mail*, June 3, 2008.

17. Sally Ward Maggard, "Coalfield Women Making History," in Billings, Norman, and Ledford, *Back Talk from Appalachia*, 229.

18. Ibid.

19. Ibid.

20. Ibid.

21. Ibid.

22. Elizabeth S. D. Engelhardt, "Creating Appalachian Women's Studies: Dancing Away from Granny and Elly May," in *Beyond Hill and Hollow: Original Readings in Appalachian Women's Studies*, ed. Elizabeth S. D. Engelhardt (Athens: Ohio University Press, 2005), 3.

23. Ibid., 9.

24. David C. Hsiung, "Stereotypes," in *High Mountains Rising: Appalachia in Time and Place*, ed. Richard A. Straw and H. Tyler Blethen (Urbana: University of Illinois Press, 2004), 102.

25. Ronald D. Eller, foreword to Billings, Norman, and Ledford, *Back Talk from Appalachia*, viii.

26. Ibid.

27. Jill M. Fraley, "Appalachian Stereotypes and Mountain Top Removal," *Peace Review* 19, no. 3 (2007): 365.

28. Henry D. Shapiro, *Appalachia On Our Mind: The Southern Mountains and Mountaineers in the American Consciousness, 1870–1920* (Chapel Hill: University of North Carolina Press, 1978), ix.

29. Ibid.

30. Ibid.

31. Allen Batteau, *The Invention of Appalachia* (Tucson: University of Arizona Press, 1990), 1.

32. Ibid.

33. For examples of nineteenth-century local color writing in Appalachia, see Will Wallace Harney, "A Strange Land and a Peculiar People," *Lippincott's Magazine* 12 (1873): 429–38; Mary Noailles Murfree, *In the Tennessee Mountains* (New York: Houghton, Mifflin, 1885); and Ellen Churchill Semple, "The Anglo-Saxons of the Kentucky Mountains," in *Appalachian Images in Folk and Popular Culture* (Ann Arbor: University of Michigan Press, 1989), 145–74.

34. Anthony Harkins, *Hillbilly: A Cultural History of an American Icon* (Oxford: Oxford University Press, 2004), 33–34.

35. Ibid., 32–33.

36. Ibid., 34–35.

37. Ronald L. Lewis, "Beyond Isolation and Homogeneity: Diversity and the History of Appalachia," in Billings, Norman, and Ledford, *Back Talk from Appalachia*, 22.

38. Ibid.

39. Billings, *Back Talk from Appalachia*, 3.

40. Wilma A. Dunaway, *The First American Frontier: Transition to Capitalism in Southern Appalachia, 1700–1860* (Chapel Hill: University of North Carolina Press, 1996).

41. Joe William Trotter Jr., *Coal, Class, and Color: Black in Southern West Virginia, 1915–1932* (Urbana: University of Illinois Press, 1990).

42. William H. Turner and Edward J. Cabbell, eds, *Blacks in Appalachia* (Lexington: University of Kentucky Press, 2009); John C. Inscoe, *Appalachians and Race: The Mountain South from Slavery to Segregation* (Lexington: University of Kentucky Press, 2005).

43. Silas House, "A Conscious Heart," *Journal of Appalachian Studies* 14, nos. 1–2 (2008): 18–19.

44. Denise Giardina, "Appalachian Mirror," *New York Times*, October 31, 1992.

45. Janice Nease, "Remembering the Past, Working for the Future: Coal River Mountain Watch Director Janice Nease Talks About the Real Appalachia," *Appalachian Voices*, http://www.appvoices.org/index.php?/site/voice_stories/remembering_the_past_working_for_the_future/issue/180.

46. Peter Phillip and Project Censored, *Censored 2006: The Top 25 Censored Stories* (New York: Seven Stories Press, 2005), 77.

47. Bret McCabe, "Tragic Mountains," *Baltimore City Paper*, March 29, 2006.

48. Fraley, "Appalachian Stereotypes and Mountaintop Removal," 370.

49. Judy Bonds, interview by author, December 10, 2003.

50. Ibid.

51. Judy Bonds, interview by author, August 7, 2009.

52. Gunnoe interview.

53. Harkins, *Hillbilly*, 6, 4.

54. Engelhardt, "Creating Appalachian Women's Studies," 4–5.

55. Susan Sarnoff, "Central Appalachia—Still the *Other* America," *Journal of Poverty* 17, nos. 1–22 (2003): 133.

56. *Online Etymology Dictionary*, s.v. "hillbilly," http://www.etymonline.com/index.php?search=hillbilly&searchmode=none.

57. Ibid.

58. Dictionary.com, s. v. "hillbilly," http://www.dictionary.reference.com/browse/hillbilly.

59. John Hartigan Jr., "Who Are These White People?: 'Rednecks,' 'Hillbillies,' and 'White Trash' as Marked Racial Subjects," in *White Out: The Continuing Significance of Racism*, ed Ashley W. Doane and Eduardo Bonilla-Silva (New York: Routledge, 2003), 104.

60. Ibid., 101, 102.

61. Harkins, *Hillbilly*, 13, 4.

62. Ibid., 16.

63. Ibid., 7.

64. Walter Precourt, "The Image of Appalachian Poverty," in *Appalachia: Social Context Past and Present*, ed. Bruce Ergood and Bruce E. Kuhre, 3rd ed. (Dubuque, IA: Kendall/Hunt, 1991), 179, 181.

65. Ruth Frankenberg, *White Women, Race Matters: The Social Construction of Whiteness* (Minneapolis: University of Minnesota Press, 1993), 6.

66. Ibid., 1.

67. Woody Doane, "Rethinking Whiteness Studies," in Doane and Bonilla-Silva *White Out*, 7.

68. Ibid.

69. Frankenberg, *White Women*, 6.

70. Ibid.

71. Birgit Brander Rasmussen, Eric Klinenberg, Irene J. Nexica, and Matt Wray, introduction to *The Making and Unmaking of Whiteness*, ed. Birgit Brander Rasmussen, Eric Klinenberg, Irene J. Nexica, and Matt Wray (Durham, NC: Duke University Press, 2001), 1.

72. Doane, "Rethinking Whiteness Studies," 8.

73. Mab Segrest, "The Souls of White Folks," in Rasmussen, Klinenberg, Nexica, and Wray, *The Making and Unmaking of Whiteness*, 45.

74. Ibid.

75. Harkins, *Hillbilly*, 7.

76. Ibid.

77. Ibid., 8.

78. Gregory Mantsios, "Class in America—2006," in *Race, Class, and Gender in the United States*, comp. Paula S. Rothenberg 7th ed. (New York: Worth Publishers, 2007), 182.

79. Ibid., 183–84.

80. Michael Zweig, *The Working Class Majority: America's Best Kept Secret* (Ithaca, NY: Cornell University Press, 2000), 3.

81. Ibid., 84.

82. John Hartigan Jr., *Odd Tribes: Toward a Cultural Analysis of White People* (Durham, NC: Duke University Press, 2005), 148.

83. Ibid.

84. Matt Wray, *Not Quite White: White Trash and the Boundaries of Whiteness* (Durham, NC: Duke University Press, 2006), 23.

85. See, for example: Mary Mellor, *Feminism and Ecology* (New York: New York University Press, 1997), 69; Val Plumwood, *Feminism and the Mastery of Nature* (New York: Routledge, 1993), 43; Charlene Spretnak, "Radical Nonduality in Ecofeminist Philosophy," in *Ecofeminism: Women, Culture, Nature*, ed. Karen J. Warren (Bloomington: Indiana University Press, 1997), 425; Karen J. Warren, *Ecofeminist Philosophy: A Western Perspective on What It Is and Why It Matters* (Oxford: Rowman and Littlefield, 2000), 23–24; Lois Ann Lorentzen, "Indigenous Feet: Ecofeminism, Globalization, and the Case of Chiapas," in *Ecofeminism and Globalization: Exploring Culture, Context, and Religion,*

ed. Heather Eaton and Lois Ann Lorentzen (Lanham, MD: Rowman and Littlefield, 2003), 59.

86. Ynestra King, "Feminism and Ecology," in *Toxic Struggles: The Theory and Practice of Environmental Justice*, ed. Richard Hofrichter (Salt Lake City: University of Utah Press, 2002), 76.

87. Warren, *Ecofeminist Philosophy*, 1.

88. Plumwood, *Feminism and the Mastery of Nature*, 43.

89. Greta Gaard, "Toward a Queer Ecofeminism," in *New Perspectives on Environmental Justice: Gender, Sexuality, and Activism*, ed. Rachel Stein (New Brunswick, NJ: Rutgers University Press, 2004), 26.

90. Harkins, *Hillbilly*, 5.

91. Ibid., 33, 148.

92. Herbert Reid and Betsy Taylor, *Recovering the Commons: Democracy, Place, and Global Justice* (Urbana: University of Illinois Press, 2010), 45.

93. Ibid.

94. Patty Sebok, interview by author, June 16, 2006.

95. Bonds interview, December 10, 2003.

96. Ann Pancake, quoted in Bret McCabe, "Tragic Mountains," *Baltimore City Paper*, March 29, 2006.

97. Pauline Canterbury, interview by author, June 16, 2006.

98. Bonds interview, August 7, 2009.

99. Ibid.

100. Lorelei Scarbro, interview by author, August 7, 2009.

101. Nease, "Remembering the Past."

102. Carolyn Merchant, *The Columbia Guide to American Environmental History* (New York: Columbia University Press, 2002), 210–11.

103. William Cronon, "The Trouble with Wilderness, or, Getting Back to the Wrong Nature," in *American Environmental History*, ed. Louis S. Warren (New York: Blackwell, 2003), 226.

104. Sylvia Hood Washington, Paul C. Rosier, and Heather Goodall, *Echoes from the Poisoned Well: Global Memories of Environmental Justice* (Lanham, MD: Rowman and Littlefield, 2006), xxi.

105. Kevin DeLuca, "A Wilderness Environmentalism Manifesto: Contesting the Infinite Self-Absorption of Humans," in *Environmental Justice and Environmentalism: The Social Justice Challenge to the Environmental Movement*, ed. Ronald Sandler and Phaedra C. Pezzullo (Cambridge, MA: MIT Press, 2007), 27.

106. Ibid.

107. Bonds interview, December 10, 2003.

108. Michael Janofsky, "As Hills Fill Hollows, Some West Virginia Residents are Fighting King Coal," *New York Times*, May 7, 1998.

109. DeLuca, "A Wilderness Environmentalism Manifesto," 27.

110. David E. Camacho, "The Environmental Justice Movement: A Political Framework," in *Environmental Injustices, Political Struggles: Race, Class, and the Environment*, ed. David E. Camacho (Durham, NC: Duke University Press, 1998), 12.

111. Ibid.

112. Bonds interview, August 7, 2009.

113. Ibid.

114. Ibid.

115. Ibid.

116. Washington, Rosier, and Goodall, *Echoes from the Poisoned Well*, xxi–xxii.

117. Bill Price, interview by author, May 18, 2007.

118. "Beyond Coal," Sierra Club, http://www.sierraclub.org.

119. "No More Mountaintop Removal," National Resources Defense Fund, http://www.nrdc.org.

120. The Sierra Club, http://www.sierraclub.org; and the National Resources Defense Council Fund, http://www.nrdc.org.

121. Mountain Justice Summer, http://www.mountainjusticesummer.org.

122. Earth First!, http://earthfirst.org.

123. "American Tragedy," Rainforest Action Network, http://www.ranorg.

124. Ibid.

Chapter 5: Situating the Particular and the Universal

Epigraph: Sarah Haltom, interview by author, June 16, 2006.

1. Haltom interview, June 16, 2006. Comments by Haltom in the following few paragraphs are from this interview.

2. Climate Ground Zero, http://www.climategroundzero.org.

3. David Harvey, *Justice, Nature and the Geography of Difference* (Cambridge, MA: Blackwell, 1996), 5.

4. Gwyn Kirk, "Standing on Solid Ground: A Materialist Ecological Feminism," in *Materialist Feminism: A Reader in Class, Difference, and Women's Lives*, ed. Rosemary Hennessey and Chrys Ingraham (New York: Routledge, 1997), 346.

5. Daniel R. Faber and Deborah McCarthy, "Neo-liberalism, Globalization and the Struggle for Ecological Democracy: Linking Sustainability and Environmental Justice," in *Just Sustainabilities: Development in an Unequal World*, ed. Julian Agyeman, Robert D. Bullard, and Bob Evans (Cambridge, MA: MIT Press, 2003), 38.

6. Ibid., 41.

7. Ibid., 42.

8. Ibid., 43.

9. Ibid.

10. Vandana Shiva, *Earth Democracy: Justice, Sustainability, and Peace* (Cambridge, MA: South End Press, 2005), 14.

11. Melanie Warner, "Is America Ready to Quit Coal?" *New York Times*, February 14, 2009.

12. Keith Goetzman, "Fighting Coal Is a Dirty Job," *UTNE Reader*, November 24, 2009, http://www.utne.com/print-article.aspx?id=2147485829.

13. Warner, "Is America Ready to Quit Coal?"; and Scott Bittle and Jean Johnson, *Who Turned Out the Lights?: Your Guided Tour to the Energy Crisis* (New York: HarperCollins, 2009), 63.

14. "Existing U.S. Coal Plants," Source Watch, http://www.sourcewatch.org/index. php?title=Existing_U.S._Coal_Plants#U.S._Coal-Fired_Power_Production_in_the_ Global_Context.

15. Scott Martelle, "Bad Energy," *Sierra* (March/April 2009): 32.

16. "Existing U.S. Coal Plants."

17. American Coalition for Clean Coal Electricity, http://www.cleancoalusa.org.

18. Ibid.

19. Ibid.

20. Citizens Coal Council, http://www.citizenscoalcouncil.org.

21. Ibid.

22. Janice Nease, interview by author, June 21, 2006.

23. Ross Gelbspan, *Boiling Point: How Politicians, Big Oil and Coal, Journalists and Activists Have Fueled the Climate Crisis—and What We Can Do to Avert Disaster* (New York: Basic Books, 2004), 5.

24. Ibid.

25. Jeff Goodell, *Big Coal: The Dirty Secret Behind America's Energy Future* (New York: Houghton Mifflin, 2006), 180–81.

26. Ibid., 78.

27. Ibid.

28. American Coalition for Clean Coal Electricity.

29. Peabody Energy, http://www.peabodyenergy.com/Vodep/2010.

30. John Bellamy Foster, *Ecology Against Capitalism* (New York: Monthly Review, 2002), 9.

31. Terry Townsend, "Capitalism's Anti-ecology Treadmill," in *The Global Fight for Climate Justice: Anticapitalist Responses to Global Warming and Environmental Destruction*, ed. Ian Angus (London: Resistance Books, 2009), 115.

32. Paul Bedard, "Group Says Clean Coal Means More Jobs," *U.S. News & World Report*, May 6, 2010, http://www.usnews.com/news/washington-whispers/articles/2010/05/06/ group-says-clean-coal-means-more-jobs.

33. "Trouble in Store," *Economist*, March 7, 2009.

34. Ariel Berman, "The Dirt on Clean Coal," *Nation*, April 13, 2009, 20.

35. "Trouble in Store," 74–75.

36. Jeff Goodell, "As the World Burns," *Rolling Stone*, January 21, 2010, 30–62, http://web. ebsohost.com/ehost/delivery?vid=&hid=9&sid=1.

37. Bradford Plummer, "Mine, Mine, Mine," *New Republic*, June 4, 2007, 14.

38. Ibid.

39. Ibid.

40. Foster, *Ecology Against Capitalism*, 20.

41. Berman, "The Dirt on Clean Coal," 17.

42. Marianne Lavelle, "The 'Clean Coal' Lobbying Blitz," April 20, 2009, http://www. publicintegrity.org/investigations/climate_change/articles/entry/1280.

43. "Trouble in Store," 74–75.

44. Berman, "The Dirt on Clean Coal," 17.

45. Goodell, "As the World Burns," 30–62.

46. Ibid.

47. David Naguib Pellow, *Resisting Global Toxics: Transnational Movements for Environmental Justice* (Cambridge, MA: MIT Press, 2007), 231.

48. Maria Gunnoe, interview by author, April 2, 2010.

49. Foster, *Ecology Against Capitalism*, 19.

50. Lorelei Scarbro, interview by author, August 7, 2009.

51. Lavelle, "The 'Clean Coal' Lobbying Blitz."

52. Ibid.

53. Ibid.

54. Scarbro interview.

55. Ibid.

56. Haltom interview.

57. Judy Bonds, interview by author, August 7, 2009.

58. Sylvia Hood Washington, Paul C. Rosier, and Heather Goodall, *Echoes from the Poisoned Well: Global Memories of Environmental Justice* (Lanham, MD: Rowman and Littlefield, 2006), xxii.

59. Patty Sebok, interview by author, June 21, 2006.

60. Foster, *Ecology Against Capitalism*, 24.

61. Scarbro interview.

62. Ibid.

63. Goodell, *Big Coal*, 40–41.

64. Bittle and Johnson, *Who Turned Out the Lights?*, 114–15.

65. J. Timmons Roberts, "Globalizing Environmental Justice," in *Environmental Justice and Environmentalism: The Social Justice Challenge to the Environmental Movement*, ed. Ronald Sandler and Phaedra C. Pezzullo (Cambridge, MA: MIT Press, 2007), 287.

66. John Bellamy Foster, "A New War on the Planet?" in *The Global Fight for Climate Justice: Anticapitalist Responses to Global Warming and Environmental Destruction*, ed. Ian Angus (London: Resistance Books, 2009), 87.

67. Stephen L. Fisher, "The Grass Roots Speak Back," in *Back Talk from Appalachia: Confronting Stereotypes*, ed. Dwight B. Billings, Gurney Norman, and Katherine Ledford (Lexington: University of Kentucky Press, 1999), 207.

68. Harvey, *Justice, Nature and the Geography of Difference*, 353.

69. Judy Bonds, interview by author, June 10, 2006.

70. Doreen B. Massey, *Space, Place, and Gender* (Minneapolis: University of Minneapolis Press, 1994), 154–55.

71. Chandra Talpade Mohanty, "Towards a Radical Transnational Feminist Praxis" (lecture, Hamilton College, April 22, 2010).

72. Julian Agyeman, Robert D. Bullard, and Bob Evans, "Joined-up Thinking: Bringing Together Sustainability, Environmental Justice and Equity," in Agyeman Bullard, and Evans, *Just Sustainabilities*, 8.

73. Ryan Holifield, Michael Porter, and Gordon Walker, "Introduction: Spaces of Environmental Justice—Frameworks for Critical Engagement," in *Spaces of Environmental Justice* (Oxford: Wiley-Blackwell, 2010), 7.

74. Agyeman, Bullard, and Evans, "Joined-up Thinking," 9.

75. Ibid.

76. Holifield, Porter, and Walker, "Introduction: Spaces of Environmental Justice-Frameworks," 6.

77. Filomina Chioma Steady, introduction to *Environmental Justice in the New Millennium: Global Perspectives on Race, Ethnicity, and Human Rights*, ed. Filomina Chioma Steady (New York: Palgrave Macmillan, 2009), 4.

78. Susan Buckingham-Hatfield, *Gender and Environment* (New York: Routledge, 2000), 1.

79. Ibid., 1–2.

80. Heather Eaton and Lois Ann Lorentzen, introduction to *Ecofeminism and Globalization: Exploring Culture, Context, and Religion* (Lanham, MD: Rowman and Littlefield, 2003), 3.

81. Ibid.

82. Ibid.

83. Ibid.

84. Sarah Haltom, interview by author, August 5, 2010.

85. Gunnoe interview.

86. Giovanna Di Chiro, "Performing a 'Global Sense of Place': Women's Actions for Environmental Justice," in *A Companion to Feminist Geography*, ed. Lise Nelson and Joni Seager (Oxford: Blackwell, 2005), 496.

87. Ibid., 499.

88. Ibid., 498.

89. Coal River Mountain Watch, *The Messenger* (Fall 2009): 5.

90. Mel Tyree, "Carbon Tax: Our ACES in the Hole for Real Change," *Winds of Change* (October 2009): 23.

91. Vandana Shiva, *Soil Not Oil: Environmental Justice in an Age of Climate Crisis* (Cambridge, MA: South End Press, 2008), 18.

92. Ibid., 20.

93. Ibid.

94. Coal River Mountain Watch, *The Messenger* (Winter 2007): 5.

95. Andy Krall, "JP Breaks Silence on MTR," *Mother Jones*, May 18, 2010, http://www.motherjones.com/mojo/2010/05/jpmorgan-breaks-silence-mtr.

96. Ibid.

97. Sebok interview.

98. Richard Hasler, "The Tragedy of Privatization: Moving Mountains in Appalachia, a Southern African Critique," *Journal of Appalachian Studies* 11, nos. 1–2 (2005): 97.

99. Shiva, *Earth Democracy*, 21.

100. Terisa E. Turner and Leigh Brownhill, "Towards a Global Economy of Commoning: A 'Gift to Humanity': Third World Women's Global Action to Keep the Oil in the Ground," in *Globalization and Third World Women: Exploitation, Coping and Resistance*, ed. Ligaya Lindio-McGovern and Isidor Wallimann (Burlington, VT: Ashgate, 2009), 122.

101. Shiva, *Earth Democracy*, 63.

SELECTED BIBLIOGRAPHY

Abramson, Rudy, and Jean Haskell, eds. *Encyclopedia of Appalachia*. Knoxville: University of Tennessee Press, 2006.

Agrawal, Arun, and Clark C. Gibson. "The Role of Community in Natural Resource Conservation." In *Communities and the Environment: Ethnicity, Gender, and the State in Community-Based Conservation*, edited by Arun Agrawal and Clark C. Gibson, 1–32. New Brunswick, NJ: Rutgers University Press, 2001.

Agyeman, Julian, Robert D. Bullard, and Bob Evans. "Joined-up Thinking: Bringing Together Sustainability, Environmental Justice and Equity." In *Just Sustainabilities: Development in an Unequal World*, edited by Julian Agyeman, Robert D. Bullard, and Bob Evans, 1–16. Cambridge, MA: MIT Press, 2003.

Ahern, Melissa M., and Michael Hendryx. "Health Disparities and Environmental Competence: A Case Study of Appalachian Coal Mining." *Environmental Justice* 1, no. 2 (2008): 81–86.

American Coalition for Clean Coal Electricity. http://www.cleancoalusa.org.

American Wind Energy Association. http://www.awea.org.

Anderson, Maggie. "The Mountains Dark and Close Around Me." In *BloodRoot: Reflections on Place by Appalachian Women Writers*, edited by Joyce Dyer, 32–39. Lexington: University of Kentucky Press, 1998.

Appalachian Institute for Renewable Energy. http://www.aire-nc.org.

Appalachian Voices. http://www.appvoices.org.

Barker, Drucilla K., and Susan F. Feiner. *Liberating Economics: Feminist Perspectives on Families, Work, and Globalization*. Ann Arbor: University of Michigan Press, 2004.

Batteau, Allen. *The Invention of Appalachia*. Tucson: University of Arizona Press, 1990.

Beckwith, Karen. "Collective Identities of Class and Gender: Working-Class Women in the Pittston Coal Strike." *Political Psychology* 19, no. 1 (1998): 147–67.

Billings, Dwight B. Introduction to *Back Talk from Appalachia: Confronting Stereotypes*, edited by Dwight B. Billings, Gurney Norman, and Katherine Ledford, 3–20. Lexington: University of Kentucky Press, 1999.

Bingman, Mary Beth. "Stopping the Bulldozers: What Difference Did It Make?" In *Fighting Back in Appalachia: Traditions of Resistance and Change*, edited by Stephen L. Fisher, 17–30. Philadelphia: Temple University Press, 1993.

Bittle, Scott, and Jean Johnson. *Who Turned Out the Lights?: Your Guided Tour to the Energy Crisis*. New York: HarperCollins, 2009.

Bryant, Bunyan, and Elaine Hockman. "A Brief Comparison of the Civil Rights Movement and the Environmental Justice Movement." In Pellow and Naguib, *Power, Justice, and the Environment*, 23–36.

Buckingham, Susan, and Rakibe Kulcur. "Gendered Geographies of Environmental Injustice." *Antipode* 41, no. 4 (2009): 659–83.

Buckingham-Hatfield, Susan. *Gender and Environment*. New York: Routledge, 2000.

Bullard, Robert D. "Environmental Justice in the Twenty-first Century." In *The Quest for Environmental Justice: Human Rights and the Politics of Pollution*, edited by Robert D. Bullard, 19–42. San Francisco: Sierra Club Books, 2005.

Bullard, Robert D., and Damu Smith. "Women Warriors of Color on the Front Line." In Bullard, *The Quest for Environmental Justice*, 62–84.

Burns, Shirley Stewart. *Bringing Down the Mountains: The Impact of Mountaintop Removal on Southern West Virginia Communities*. Morgantown: West Virginia University Press, 2007.

Camacho, David E. "The Environmental Justice Movement: A Political Framework." In *Environmental Injustices, Political Struggles: Race, Class, and the Environment*, edited by David E. Camacho, 11–30. Durham, NC: Duke University Press, 1998.

Cavender, Anthony P. *Folk Medicine in Southern Appalachia*. Chapel Hill: University of North Carolina Press, 2003.

Citizen's Coal Council. http://www.citizenscoalcouncil.org.

Climate Ground Zero. http://www.climategroundzero.org.

Coal Country. DVD. Directed by Phylis Geller. Evening Star Productions, 2009.

Coal River Mountain Watch. http://wwwcrmw.net.

Cole, Luke W., and Sheila R. Foster. *From the Ground Up: Environmental Racism and the Rise of the Environmental Justice Movement*. New York: New York University Press, 2001.

Crittenden, Ann. *The Price of Motherhood: Why the most Important Job in the World Is Still the Least Valued*. New York: Henry Holt, 2001.

Cronon, William. "The Trouble with Wilderness, or, Getting Back to the Wrong Nature." In *American Environmental History*, edited by Louis S. Warren, 212–36. New York: Blackwell, 2003.

Davenport, Doris Diosa. "All This, and Honeysuckles Too." In Dyer, *BloodRoot*, 88–97.

DeLuca, Kevin. "A Wilderness Environmentalism Manifesto: Contesting the Infinite Self-Absorption of Humans." In Sandler and Pezzullo, *Environmental Justice and Environmentalism*, 27–55.

Di Chiro, Giovanna. "Environmental Justice from the Grassroots: Reflections on History, Gender, and Expertise." In *The Struggle for Ecological Democracy: Environmental Justice Movements in the United States*, edited by Daniel Faber, 104–36. New York: Guilford Press, 1998.

———. "Performing a 'Global Sense of Place': Women's Actions for Environmental Justice." In *A Companion to Feminist Geography*, edited by Lise Nelson and Joni Seager, 496–515. Oxford: Blackwell, 2005.

Doane, Ashley W., and Eduardo Bonilla-Silva. *White Out: The Continuing Significance of Racism.* New York: Routledge, 2003.

Doane, Woody. "Rethinking Whiteness Studies." In Doane and Bonilla-Silva, *White Out,* 3–21.

Dunaway, Wilma A. *The First American Frontier: Transition to Capitalism in Southern Appalachia, 1700–1860.* Chapel Hill: University of North Carolina Press, 1996.

———. *Women, Work, and Family in the Antebellum Mountain South.* Cambridge: Cambridge University Press, 2008.

Dyer, Joyce, ed. *Bloodroot: Reflections on Place by Appalachian Women Writers.* Lexington: University of Kentucky Press, 1998.

Earth First. http://earthfirst.org.

Eaton, Heather, and Lois Ann Lorentzen. Introduction to *Ecofeminism and Globalization: Exploring Culture, Context, and Religion,* edited by Heather Eaton and Lois Ann Lorentzen, 1–7. Lanham, MD: Rowman and Littlefield, 2003.

Eller, Ronald D. Foreword to Billings, Norman, and Ledford, *Back Talk from Appalachia,* viii–xi.

———. *Uneven Ground: Appalachia Since 1945.* Lexington: University of Kentucky Press, 2008.

Engelhardt, Elizabeth S. D. "Creating Appalachian Women's Studies: Dancing Away from Granny and Elly May." In *Beyond Hill and Hollow: Original Readings in Appalachian Women's Studies,* edited by Elizabeth S. D. Engelhardt, 1–19. Athens: Ohio University Press, 2005.

Faber, Daniel R. "A More 'Productive' Environmental Justice Politics: Movement Alliances in Massachusetts for Clean Production and Regional Equity." In Sandler and Pezzullo, *Environmental Justice and Environmentalism,* 135–64.

Faber, Daniel R., and Deborah McCarthy. "Neo-liberalism, Globalization and the Struggle for Ecological Democracy: Linking Sustainability and Environmental Justice." In Agyeman, Bullard, and Evans, *Just Sustainabilities,* 35–63.

Figart, Deborah M. "Wage Gap." In *The Elgar Companion to Feminist Economics,* edited by Janice Peterson and Margaret Lewis, 748–50. Northampton, MA: Edward Elgar, 1999.

Figart, Deborah M., Ellen Mutari, and Marilyn Power. *Living Wages, Equal Wages: Gender and Labor Market Policies in the United States.* New York: Routledge, 2002.

Fisher, Stephen L. "The Grass Roots Speak Back." In Billings, Norman, and Ledford, *Back Talk from Appalachia,* 203–14.

Foster, John Bellamy. *Ecology Against Capitalism.* New York: Monthly Review Press, 2002.

Fraley, Jill M. "Appalachian Stereotypes and Mountain Top Removal." *Peace Review* 19, no. 3 (2007): 365–70.

Frankenberg, Ruth. *White Women, Race Matters: The Social Construction of Whiteness.* Minneapolis: University of Minnesota Press, 1993.

Friends of Coal. http://www.friendsofcoal.org.

Fritsch, Al, and Paul Gallimore. *Healing Appalachia: Sustainable Living through Appropriate Technology.* Lexington: University of Kentucky Press, 2007.

Gaard, Greta. "Toward a Queer Ecofeminism." In Stein, *New Perspectives on Environmental Justice*, 21–44.

Gaventa, John. *Power and Powerlessness: Quiescence and Rebellion in an Appalachian Valley.* Urbana: University of Illinois Press, 1980.

Gelbspan, Ross. *Boiling Point: How Politicians, Big Oil and Coal, Journalists, and Activists Have Fueled the Climate Crisis—and What We Can Do to Avert Disaster.* New York: Basic Books, 2004.

Gipe, Paul. *Wind Power for Home and Business: Renewable Energy for the 1990s and Beyond.* Post Mills, VT: Chelsea Green Publishing, 1993.

Goldman Environmental Prize. http://www.goldmanprize.org.

Goodell, Jeff. *Big Coal: The Dirty Secret Behind America's Energy Future.* New York: Houghton Mifflin, 2006.

Gottlieb, Robert. *Forcing the Spring: The Transformation of the American Environmental Movement.* Washington, DC: Island Press, 1993.

Greene, Janet W. "Strategies for Survival: Women's Work in the Southern West Virginia Coal Camps." *West Virginia History* 49 (1990): 37–54. http://www.wvculture.org/history/journal_wvh/wvh49-4.html

Harkins, Anthony. *Hillbilly: A Cultural History of an American Icon.* Oxford: Oxford University Press, 2004.

Hartigan, John, Jr. *Odd Tribes: Toward a Cultural Analysis of White People.* Durham, NC: Duke University Press, 2005.

———. "Who Are These White People?: 'Rednecks,' 'Hillbillies,' and 'White Trash' as Marked Racial Subjects." In Doane and Bonilla-Silva, *White Out*, 95–113.

Harvey, David. *Justice, Nature, and the Geography of Difference.* Cambridge, MA: Blackwell, 1996.

Hasler, Richard. "The Tragedy of Privatization: Moving Mountains in Appalachia, a Southern African Critique." *Journal of Appalachian Studies* 11, nos. 1–2 (2005): 95–103.

Hazlett, Maril. "Voices from the *Spring*: *Silent Spring* and the Ecological Turn in American Health." In *Seeing Nature Through Gender*, edited by Virginia J. Scharff, 103–28. Lawrence: University of Kansas Press, 2003.

Hensley, Frances S. "Women in the Industrial Work Force in West Virginia, 1880–1945." *West Virginia History* 49 (1990): 115–24. http://www.wvculture.org/hiStory/journal_wvh/wvh49-9.html.

Heyd, Thomas. "Nature, Culture, and Natural Heritage: Toward a Culture of Nature." *Environmental Ethics* 27, no. 4 (2005): 339–55.

Holifield, Ryan, Michael Porter, and Gordon Walker. "Introduction: Spaces of Environmental Justice—Frameworks for Critical Engagement." In *Spaces of Environmental Justice*, edited by Ryan Holifield, Michael Porter, and Gordon Walker, 1–22. Oxford: Wiley-Blackwell, 2010.

House, Silas. "A Conscious Heart," *Journal of Appalachian Studies* 14, nos. 1–2 (2008): 7–19.

House, Silas, and Jason Howard. *Something's Rising: Appalachians Fighting Mountaintop Removal.* Lexington: University of Kentucky Press, 2009.

Hsiung, David C. "Stereotypes." In *High Mountains Rising: Appalachia in Time and Place*, edited by Richard A. Straw and H. Tyler Blethen, 101–13. Urbana: University of Illinois Press, 2004.

I Love Mountains. http://www.ilovemountains.org.

Jones, Van. *The Green Collar Economy: How One Solution Can Fix Our Two Biggest Problems.* New York: HarperOne, 2008.

Kaalund, Valerie Ann. "Witness to Truth: Black Women Heeding the Call for Environmental Justice." In Stein, *New Perspectives on Environmental Justice*, 78–92.

King, Ynestra. "Feminism and Ecology." In *Toxic Struggles: The Theory and Practice of Environmental Justice*, edited by Richard Hofrichter, 76–86. Salt Lake City: University of Utah Press, 2002.

Kirk, Gwyn. "Standing on Solid Ground: A Materialist Ecological Feminism." In *Materialist Feminism: A Reader in Class, Difference, and Women's Lives*, edited by Rosemary Hennessy and Chrys Ingraham, 345–63. New York: Routledge, 1997.

Kline, Benjamin. *First Along the River: A Brief History of the U.S. Environmental Movement.* New York: Rowman and Litlefield, 2007.

Kopple, Barbara. *Harlan County USA.* New York: Cabin Creek Films, 1976.

Krauss, Celene. "Challenging Power: Toxic Waste Protests and the Politicization of White, Working-Class Women." In *Community Activism and Feminist Politics: Organizing Across Race, Class, and Gender*, edited by Nancy A. Naples, 129–50. New York: Routledge, 1998.

Layne, Linda L. "In Search of Community: Tales of Pregnancy Loss in Three Toxically Assaulted U.S. Communities." *Women's Studies Quarterly* 29, nos. 1–2 (2001): 25–50.

Lester, James P., David W. Allen, and Kelly M. Hill. *Environmental Injustice in the United States: Myths and Realities.* Boulder, CO: Westview Press, 2001.

Lewis, Ronald L. "Beyond Isolation and Homogeneity: Diversity and the History of Appalachia." In Billings, Norman, and Ledford, *Back Talk from Appalachia*, 21–43.

Loeb, Penny. *Moving Mountains: How One Woman and Her Community Won Justice from Big Coal.* Lexington: University of Kentucky Press, 2007.

Maggard, Sally Ward. "Coalfield Women Making History." In Billings, Norman, and Ledford, *Back Talk from Appalachia*, 228–50.

———. "From Farm to Coal Camp to Back Office and McDonald's: Living in the Midst of Appalachia's Latest Transformation." *Journal of the Appalachian Studies Association* 6 (1994): 14–38.

———. "Gender Contested: Women's Participation in the Brookside Coal Strike." In *Women and Social Protest*, edited by Guida West and Rhoda Lois Blumberg, 75–98. New York: Oxford University Press, 1990.

Mantsios, Gregory. "Class in America—2006." In *Race, Class, and Gender in the United States*, compiled by Paula S. Rothenberg, 182–98. 7th ed. New York: Worth Publishers, 2007.

Massey, Doreen B. *Space, Place, and Gender.* Minneapolis: University of Minnesota Press, 1994.

Massey Energy Company. http://www.masseyenergyco.com.

McGurty, Eileen. *Transforming Environmentalism: Warren County, PCBs, and the Origins of Environmental Justice.* New Brunswick, NJ: Rutgers University Press, 2007.

Merchant, Carolyn. *The Columbia Guide to American Environmental History*. New York: Columbia University Press, 2002.

———. *Reinventing Eden: The Fate of Nature in Western Culture*. New York: Routledge, 2004.

Miles, Emma Belle. *The Spirit of the Mountains*. Knoxville: University of Tennessee Press, 1975.

Montrie, Chad. *To Save the Land and People: A History of Opposition to Surface Coal Mining in Appalachia*. Chapel Hill: University of North Carolina Press, 2003.

Mountain Justice Summer. http://www.mountainjusticesummer.org.

Naples, Nancy A., ed. *Community Activism and Feminist Politics: Organizing Across Race, Class, and Gender*. New York: Routledge, 1998.

National Resources Defense Council. http://www.nrdc.org.

Newman, Rich. "Making Environmental Politics: Women and Love Canal Activism." *Women's Studies Quarterly* 29, nos. 1–2 (2001): 65–84.

Nordhaus, Ted, and Michael Shellenberger. *Break Through: From the Death of Environmentalism to the Politics of Possibility*. New York: Houghton Mifflin, 2007.

O'Connor, James R. *Natural Causes: Essays in Ecological Marxism*. New York: Guilford Press, 1998.

Ohio Valley Environmental Coalition. http://www.ohvec.org.

Palmer, M. A., et al. "Mountaintop Mining Consequences." *Science* 327 (2010): 148–49.

Pancake, Ann. *Strange as This Weather Has Been*. San Francisco: Shoemaker and Hoard, 2007.

Parenti, Michael. *Against Empire*. San Francisco: City Lights Books, 1995.

Pellow, David Naguib. *Resisting Global Toxics: Transnational Movements for Environmental Justice*. Cambridge, MA: MIT Press, 2007.

Pellow, David Naguib, and Robert J. Brulle. "Power, Justice, and the Environment: Toward Critical Environmental Justice Studies." In *Power, Justice, and the Environment: A Critical Appraisal of the Environmental Justice Movement*, edited by David Naguib Pellow and Robert J. Brulle, 1–19. Cambridge, MA: MIT Press, 2005.

Pennies of Promise. http://www.penniesofpromise.org.

Phillip, Peter, and Project Censored. *Censored 2006: The Top 25 Censored Stories*. New York: Seven Stories Press, 2005.

Plaut, Thomas. "Extending the Internal Periphery Model: The Impact of Culture and Consequent Strategy." In *Colonialism in Modern America: The Appalachian Case*, edited by Helen Matthews Lewis, Linda Johnson, and Donald Askins, 351–64. Boone, NC: Appalachian Consortium Press, 1978.

Plumwood, Val. *Feminism and the Mastery of Nature*. New York: Routledge, 1993.

Precourt, Walter. "The Image of Appalachian Poverty." In *Appalachia: Social Context Past and Present*, edited by Bruce Ergood and Bruce E. Kuhre, 173–85. 3rd ed. Dubuque, IA: Kendall/Hunt, 1991.

Pudup, Mary Beth. "Women's Work in the West Virginia Economy." *West Virginia History* 49 (1990): 7–20. http://www.wvculture.org/history/journal_wvh/wvh49-2.html.

Rainforest Action Network. http://ran.org.

Rapp, Rayna. "Family and Class in Contemporary America: Notes toward an Understanding of Ideology." In *Rethinking the Family: Some Feminist Questions*, edited by Barrie

Thorne and Marilyn Yalom, 49–70. Boston, MA: Northeastern University Press, 1992.

Rasmussen, Birgit Brander, Eric Klinenberg, Irene J. Nexica, and Matt Wray. Introduction to *The Making and Unmaking of Whiteness*, edited by Birgit Brander Rasmussen, Eric Klinenberg, Irene J. Nexica, and Matt Wray, 1–24. Durham, NC: Duke University Press, 2001.

Roberts, J. Timmons. "Globalizing Environmental Justice." In Sandler and Pezzullo, *Environmental Justice and Environmentalism*, 285–307.

Rocheleau, Dianne, Barbara Thomas-Slayter, and Esther Wangari. "Gender and Environment: A Feminist Political Ecology Perspective." In *Feminist Political Ecology: Global Issues and Local Experiences*, edited by Dianne Rocheleau, Barbara Thomas-Slayter, and Esther Wangari, 3–23. New York: Routledge, 1996.

Sachs, Carolyn E. *Gendered Fields: Rural Women, Agriculture, and Environment.* Boulder, CO: Westview Press, 1996.

Sandler, Ronald, and Phaedra C. Pezzullo, eds. *Environmental Justice and Environmentalism: The Social Justice Challenge to the Environmental Movement.* Cambridge, MA: MIT Press, 2007.

Sarnoff, Susan. "Central Appalachia—Still the *Other* America." *Journal of Poverty* 7, nos. 1–2 (2003): 123–39.

Seager, Joni. "'Hysterical Housewives' and Other Mad Women: Grassroots Environmental Organizing in the United States." In Rocheleau, Thomas-Slayter, and Wangari, *Feminist Political Ecology*, 271–83.

Segrest, Mab. "The Souls of White Folks." In Rasmussen, Klinenberg, Nexica, and Wray, *The Making and Unmaking of Whiteness*, 43–71.

Seitz, Virginia Rinaldo. "Class, Gender, and Resistance in the Appalachian Coalfields." In Naples, *Community Activism and Feminist Politics*, 213–36.

Sellers, Christopher. "Environmental Justice as a Way of Seeing." *Environmental Justice* 1, no. 4 (2008): 177–78.

Sen, Renku. *Stir It Up: Lessons in Community Organizing and Advocacy.* San Francisco: John Wiley, 2003.

Shapiro, Henry D. *Appalachia on Our Mind: The Southern Mountains and Mountaineers in the American Consciousness, 1870–1920.* Chapel Hill: University of North Carolina Press, 1978.

Sharp, Sharon A. "Folk Medicine Practices: Women as Keepers and Carriers of Knowledge." *Women's International Forum* 9, no. 3 (1986): 243–49.

Shiva, Vandana. *Earth Democracy: Justice, Sustainability, and Peace.* Cambridge, MA: South End Press, 2005.

———. *Soil Not Oil: Environmental Justice in an Age of Climate Crisis.* Cambridge, MA: South End Press, 2008.

Shnayerson, Michael. *Coal River.* New York: Farrar, Straus and Giroux, 2008.

Sierra Club. http://www.sierraclub.org.

Stacey, Judith. "The Family Is Dead, Long Live Our Families." In *The Socialist Feminist Project: A Contemporary Reader in Theory and Politics*, edited by Nancy Holmstrom, 90–101. New York: Monthly Review Press, 2002.

Steady, Filomina Chioma. Introduction to *Environmental Justice in the New Millennium: Global Perspectives on Race, Ethnicity, and Human Rights*, edited by Filomina Chioma Steady, 1–16. New York: Palgrave Macmillan, 2009.

Stein, Rachel. Introduction to *New Perspectives on Environmental Justice: Gender, Sexuality and Activism*, edited by Rachel Stein,1–17. New Brunswick, NJ: Rutgers University Press, 2004.

Sze, Julie, and Jonathan K. London. "Environmental Justice at the Crossroads." *Sociology Compass* 2, no. 4 (2008): 1331–54.

Tickameyer, Ann R., and Debra A. Henderson. "Rural Women: New Roles for the New Century?" In *Challenges for Rural America in the Twenty-First Century*, edited by David L. Brown and Louis E. Swanson,109–17. University Park: Pennsylvania State University Press, 2003.

Townsend, Terry. "Capitalism's Anti-ecology Treadmill." In *The Global Fight for Climate Justice: Anticapitalist Responses to Global Warming and Environmental Destruction*, edited by Ian Angus, 110–20. London: Resistance Books, 2009.

Turner, Terisa E., and Leigh Brownhill. "Towards a Global Economy of Commoning: A 'Gift to Humanity': Third World Women's Global Action to Keep the Oil in the Ground." In *Globalization and Third World Women: Exploitation, Coping and Resistance*, edited by Ligaya Lindio-McGovern and Isidor Wallimann, 121–38. Burlington, VT: Ashgate, 2009.

Unger, Nancy C. "Gendered Approaches to Environmental Justice: An Historical Sampling." In Washington, Rosier, and Goodall, *Echoes from the Poisoned Well*, 17–27.

———. "The Role of Gender in Environmental Justice." *Environmental Justice* 1, no. 3 (2008): 115–20.

Verchick, Robert R. M. "Feminist Theory and Environmental Justice." In Stein, *New Perspectives on Environmental Justice*, 63–77.

Warren, Karen J. *Ecofeminist Philosophy: A Western Perspective on What It Is and Why It Matters*. Lanham, MD: Rowman and Littlefield, 2000.

Washington, Sylvia Hood, Paul C. Rosier, and Heather Goodall. *Echoes from the Poisoned Well: Global Memories of Environmental Injustice*. Lanham, MD: Rowman and Littlefield, 2006.

Weiss, Chris. "Organizing Women for Local Economic Development." In *Communities in Economic Crisis: Appalachia and the South*, edited by John Gaventa, Barbara Ellen Smith, and Alex Willingham, 61–70. Philadelphia, PA: Temple University Press, 1990.

West Virginia Coal Association. *Coal Facts 2006*. Charleston: West Virginia Coal Association, 2006. http://www.wvcoalassociation.org.

Williams, John Alexander. *Appalachia: A History*. Chapel Hill: University of North Carolina Press, 2002.

Wray, Matt. *Not Quite White: White Trash and the Boundaries of Whiteness*. Durham, NC: Duke University Press, 2006.

Zweig, Michael. *The Working Class Majority: America's Best Kept Secret*. Ithaca, NY: Cornell University Press, 2000.

Index

Index